4th edition

Planning and Managing Public Relations Campaigns

A strategic approach

PR in Practice

Anne Gregory

KoganPage

First published as *Planning and Managing a Public Relations Campaign* in Great Britain
   and the United States in 1996 by Kogan Page Limited
Second edition published as *Planning and Managing Public Relations Campaigns*
   by Kogan Page, 2000
Third edition 2010
Fourth edition 2015

2nd Floor, 45 Gee Street
London
EC1V 3RS
United Kingdom

1518 Walnut Street, Suite 1100
Philadelphia PA 19102
USA

4737/23 Ansari Road
Daryaganj
New Delhi 110002
India

ISBN   978 0 7494 6873 6
E-ISBN 978 0 7494 6874 3

British Library Cataloguing-in-Publication Data

A CIP record for this book is available from the British Library.

Library of Congress Control Number:

2015031290

Typeset by Graphicraft Limited, Hong Kong
Printed and bound by CPI Group (UK) Ltd, Croydon, CR0 4YY

A strategic approach

Planning and Managing Public Relations Campaigns

PR in Practice Series

Published in association with the Chartered Institute of Public Relations

Series Editor: Professor Anne Gregory

Kogan Page has joined forces with the Chartered Institute of Public Relations to publish this unique series which is designed specifically to meet the needs of the increasing numbers of people seeking to enter the public relations profession and the large band of existing PR professionals. Taking a practical, action-oriented approach, the books in the series concentrate on the day-to-day issues of public relations practice and management rather than academic history. They provide ideal primers for all those on CIPR, CAM and CIM courses or those taking NVQs in PR. For PR practitioners, they provide useful refreshers and ensure that their knowledge and skills are kept up to date.

Other titles in the series:

Creativity in Public Relations by Andy Green
Effective Internal Communication by Lyn Smith with Pamela Mounter
Effective Media Relations by Michael Bland, Alison Theaker and David Wragg
Effective Personal Communications Skills for Public Relations by Andy Green
Effective Writing Skills for Public Relations by John Foster
Ethics in Public Relations by Patricia J Parsons
Evaluating Public Relations by Tom Watson and Paul Noble
Managing Activism by Denise Deegan
Online Public Relations by David Phillips and Philip Young
Public Affairs in Practice by Stuart Thomson and Steve John
Public Relations in Practice edited by Anne Gregory
Public Relations Strategy by Sandra Oliver
Public Relations: A practical guide to the basics by Philip Henslowe
Risk Issues and Crisis Management in Public Relations by Michael Regester and Judy Larkin
Running a Public Relations Department by Mike Beard

The above titles are available from all good bookshops and from the CIPR website www.cipr.co.uk/books. To obtain further information, please go to: www.koganpage.com

CONTENTS

Acknowledgements viii
About the author ix

01 Planning and managing: the context 1

What is the point of planning? 4
The role of public relations in organizations 6
The role of the public relations professional within
    organizations 8
The position of public relations within organizations 12
Organizing for action 19
Who does what in public relations? 21

02 Public relations in context 25

Context is vitally important 25
Stakeholders and publics 26
Sectoral considerations 29
Organizational development – business stage 30
Organizational characteristics 33
Issues 34
Public opinion 35
Timescales 36
Resources 37

03 Starting the planning process 38

Responsibilities of practitioners 38
Public relations policy 39
Why planning is important 43
Basic questions in planning 45
The 12 stages of planning 47
Linking programme planning to the bigger picture 50

04 Research and analysis 53

Embedding research in the planning process 53
The first planning step 55
Analysing the environment 57
Analysing the organization 62
Analysing the stakeholder 64

Who should undertake the research?   66
Research techniques   67
Investment in research pays – two cases in point   73

05   Communication theory and setting aims and objectives   90

Knowing where you're going   90
Attitude is all important   90
The communication chain   92
How 'receivers' use information   100
Setting realistic aims and objectives   102
Golden rules of objective setting   106
Constraints on aims and objectives   107
Different levels of aims and objectives   108

06   Knowing the publics and messages   111

Who shall we talk to and what shall we say?   111
What is public opinion?   112
Types of publics   114
Using other segmentation techniques   117
So what about the media?   120
The implications for targeting publics   120
How to prioritize publics   121
What shall we say?   123
Constructing the content   124
Crafting messages   128
How the message should be presented   129

07   Strategy and tactics   131

Getting the strategy right   131
What is strategy?   131
From strategy to tactics   133
What tactics should be employed?   134
Different campaigns need different tactics   139
Sustaining long-term programmes   154
Contingency and risk planning   160

08   Timescales and resources   164

Timescales   164
Task planning techniques   165
Longer-term plans   169
Resources   176

09   Knowing what has been achieved: evaluation and review   183

Measuring success   183
The benefits of evaluation   184
Why practitioners don't evaluate   185
Principles of evaluation   187
Evaluation terminology   188
Levels of evaluation   190
A campaign evaluation model and some other measures   193
Reviewing the situation   202
And finally   205

Index   206

Free online support material can be downloaded from the
Kogan Page website. Please go to:
www.koganpage.com/PlanningAndManagingPublicRelationsCampaigns

ACKNOWLEDGEMENTS

In drawing up a list of those organizations and individuals who should be thanked for helping with the writing of this book, it is difficult to know where to start.

There are all those organizations that I have worked for and with over many years who provide me with constant opportunities to learn about the exciting and dynamic profession of public relations. They have built my knowledge and understanding both of the best of practice and the worst. Sometimes the hardest and best learning has come through my own mistakes and through the generosity of others who have been prepared to share theirs.

I need to thank my students and those working professionals for whom I prepare materials on planning and managing campaigns and programmes and who constantly challenge and stimulate my thinking.

Thank you to all those who have provided me with case studies and great ideas including Marks & Spencer, Lansons Communications and unbiased.co.uk, the Cabinet Office, Argyle Communication and GlaxoSmithKline, Creative Territories and McArthur River Mine, WRAP, Philip Sheldrake… Without your generous help this book would have never got off the ground.

To the team at Kogan Page and the CIPR many thanks for your encouragement and support.

Dedication

For my mother, who died last year. You never really did understand what I do; sometimes I don't understand it either. What I do know is that you loved me and for that I will always be thankful.

ABOUT THE AUTHOR

Dr Anne Gregory is Professor of Corporate Communication at the Business School of the University of Huddersfield, which she joined in September 2014.

Before entering academic life, Anne spent many years in public relations and communication management at senior levels both in-house and in consultancy, ending her practitioner career as a Board member of a large UK consultancy.

In her academic career Anne has been responsible for a number of major research and consultancy projects, including obtaining the largest European research grant in communications at her previous university. Her consultancy clients have included the UK Cabinet Office, the National Health Service, Tesco Corporate and SAAB. She teaches on a range of executive education programmes in the UK and overseas and is also a non-executive director of Airedale NHS Foundation Trust.

Anne was President of the Chartered Institute of Public Relations (CIPR) in 2004, leading it to Chartered status. She was Chair of the Global Alliance of Public Relations and Communication Management from June 2013 to June 2015 and is the recipient of the Sir Stephen Tallents Medal for her outstanding contribution to public relations. In 2015 she was made an Honorary Fellow of the CIPR in recognition of her contribution to the profession.

Anne is an academic and strategic adviser of international standing. She is published widely in books and leading journals, is editor of the *Journal of Communication Management* and is a speaker in demand. She initiated the CIPR/Kogan Page series of books *PR in Practice* and is its consultant editor.

01
Planning and managing: the context

The world of public relations has changed radically in the last few years. Indeed, as a barometer of society itself, it has had to. The challenges we face as a society, such as globalization, climate change, the need to re-base our notions of business post the 2008/09 financial crisis and to re-evaluate the way values are developed and lived, are unparalleled.

Added to that are the seismic changes that new, communications-based technologies bring to the way we connect and the nature of the interactions we have. These changes are generating fundamental shifts in power away from traditional sources of authority. Those individuals and groups who can understand what is going on and are able to work with the new communication tools at our disposal are emerging as a new elite.

It is not the remit of this book to explore the details and ramifications of all these deep and wide changes that are happening, but the impact on the practice of public relations overall is profound and therefore cannot be ignored. A report by the Arthur W Page Society in 2007 called *The Authentic Enterprise*[1], predicted the impact of some of these issues and concluded that we had reached a point of 'strategic inflection' which required organizations to embrace a new way of operating which had communication at its heart and with the key being authenticity. It went on to enumerate four new practices and skills for which the more senior public relations practitioner must assume a leadership role:

- defining and instilling company values;
- building and managing multi-stakeholder relationships;
- enabling the enterprise with 'new media' skills and tools;
- building and managing trust in all its dimensions.

Since the publication of this report there has been considerable progress in translating these predictions into reality. Values have become central to how organizations articulate what they stand for, and how they live them

FIGURE 1.1 Organizational Character as described by the Global Alliance

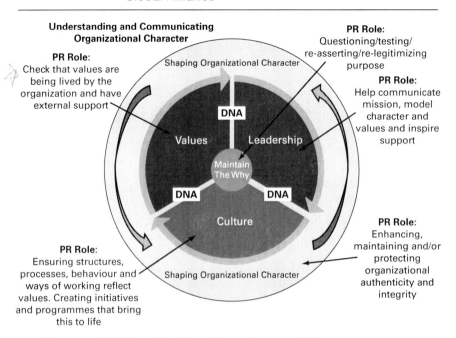

helps them to justify their place in the world. The difference between how values are articulated and lived specifies the authenticity gap. Values have become central to what has become known as corporate character[2,3], that combination of purpose, values and culture that define an organization's DNA. The Global Alliance has illustrated this as shown in Figure 1.1.

The world of social media has brought home with force the requirement to build stakeholder relationships, but 'managing' them is more problematic. Dialogue and engagement, partnership and influencing in subtle, ethical ways by gaining respect through behaviour rather than words is what is needed now.

Enabling the enterprise with new media skills and tools is certainly a requirement now, although there is still a lag in some organizations between the capability and willingness of their employees to take up these tools personally, and the enterprise being enabled. A key implication for public relations is that the gate-keeping role that it held in the past is diminishing. Everyone is a communicator now and the opportunity for the profession is to work with colleagues so that they can engage with others in appropriate and meaningful ways.

As for building and managing trust, again the Arthur W Page Society has evidence[4] that some leading companies have redefined the way they engage with stakeholders. They use data to inform their thinking and employees as their principal means of connecting. They understand that engagement has to move away from the instrumental and transactional towards being long-lasting and collaborative. What has become apparent is that employees are crucial to an organization building and maintaining their brand and reputation in ways that were never recognized in the past.

What is also apparent is that organizations will have to be even more adept at responding to a variety of societal issues, they will have to engage with a range of stakeholders who to date have not been on their radar and who will hold them to account in new ways and they will need to engage in different ways. They will have to demonstrate that they are living their espoused values and the mandate, or 'licence to operate', given them by this complex web of multi-stakeholders which will be fragile and dynamic and in need of attention and reinforcement constantly. Their organizations will be judged not only by their corporate words and actions, but by the myriad of individual transactions that they and their employees engage in – hence the increased emphasis on internal communication and coaching.

It is important to be clear about the profound changes in how organizations now have to operate when planning and managing public relations campaigns. The simple belief was never true that if you told people to do something often enough and loud enough they would eventually do what you wanted them to. It is even less true today. There are so many other sources and alternative views that any organization, without the power of legislation to back them, must regard itself as only one influence among many. The trick is to be as influential as possible.

Philip Sheldrake in his book *The Business of Influence*[5] puts it well when he notes that there six influence flows:

- The organization's influence with stakeholders
- Stakeholders' influence with each other regarding the organization
- Stakeholders' influence with the organization
- Competitors' influence with stakeholders
- Stakeholders' influence with each other regarding competitors
- Stakeholders' influence with competitors

In the list above my view is that the word 'competitor' should be taken not only as referring to commercial competitors, but to all those with competing views.

Sheldrake's point is that organizations need to be influential in all these flows of influence if they are to gain traction with stakeholders. That traction is gained because there is sympathy and support for the purpose, values and behaviours of the organization. Crucial to this is that the organization has to be open to being influenced. Listening, responding and changing where appropriate and being seen to do these things is vitally important. This kind of thinking leads Sheldrake to conclude that,

> 'We can begin to think of an organization as not being defined by its payroll but rather as a collaborative network of individuals coalescing around a nexus of shared values and common purpose.'

What is the point of planning?

It is quite legitimate to ask, therefore, what is the point of planning and managing public relations programmes at all given the level of fluidity and complexity that public relations practitioners face and the fact that things require to be done quickly to be responsive to the constant change and flux that constitutes contemporary organizational life. It is true, modern practitioners have to be fleet of foot and be able to cope with ambiguity. Undoubtedly there are individual communicators who thrive in chaos, who 'sense' their way through situations and are very good at it. Most people are not like that. Neuroscience tells us that human beings seek a level of order and as far as possible, want to be able to operate in a work environment that has some control and predictability about it. Having a sense of direction and of what is important is part of well-being at work and indeed being able to mark off progress and milestones is an intrinsic element of job satisfaction.

Furthermore, organizations are purposeful entities. They exist for a reason, whether that is to fulfil a primarily social or business purpose. They too are mainly based on rational and tested business models that comprise recognized working principles and established methods of planning. Their ways of working vary enormously between those organizations that employ quite mechanistic processes and bureaucratic planning approaches, to those who are more entrepreneurial and intuitive in their planning, but who are nonetheless strict in identifying and evaluating business opportunities and ensuring that new ventures are in line with what the brand stands for. A good example of this is how Google decided to end the development of Google Glass in 2015 despite all the public expectations around it.

Public relations as a functional department needs to follow the same disciplines that other functional departments such as legal, finance, HR and operations do if its activities are to properly support and shape the organization. A key feature of the strategic role of public relations (which will be explored in this book) is that it is founded on a clear understanding of the contribution that the function can make and an underpinning philosophy and way of operating that are research-informed. Tactical public relations on the other hand is characterized by being reactive and focuses on the delivery of communication services as directed by others.

It is important to state, however, that strategic planning does not mean that everything can be controlled: that is never possible, but it does take the planner through a process that helps them define the contribution they can make, how they can go about their tasks and how they are to measure

if they have been successful. They must be mindful that a
agility and pragmatic adjustment is required along the
unforeseen events may require a radical departure from t
plans. Planning and managing strategic programmes is botl.
creative. It is a process that stimulates the intellect, engages
and puts the building blocks in place for creating efficient a.
interventions for the planner's organization.

A starting point

A starting point when conducting strategic public relations planning is to
examine some of the definitions. According to the UK Chartered Institute of
Public Relations (CIPR), which is Europe's largest professional body in the
field:

> Public relations is the discipline which looks after reputation, with the aim of
> earning understanding and support and influencing opinion and behaviour.
> It is the planned and sustained effort to establish and maintain goodwill and
> mutual understanding between an organization and its publics.

At the heart of this definition is the notion that public relations has to be
planned. It is a deliberate, carefully thought-through process. It also requires
ongoing (sustained) activity: it is not haphazard. The activity is concerned
with initiating (establishing) and maintaining a process of mutual understanding. In other words it involves a dialogue where an organization and
its various publics, including those in the wider influencer network, listen to
each other and seek to understand each other in order to make judgements
about them. Those judgements may be to support them, oppose them,
change behaviour or ignore them. This will often result in some change or
action by the parties involved. Note, the change can be both ways.

The first part of this definition covers the idea of reputation. A good
reputation is not something that is earned overnight. It has to be carefully
and considerately cultivated. It is something that is earned over a period of
time as understanding and support develop for an organization. The development of reputation has to be meticulously undertaken with integrity and
honesty and because reputation is a notion that exists in the perceiver's
mind (like image) this is a complex process. It is also something that is very
fragile and can be lost quickly if words or actions are found to be out of step
with reality, or if rumour gets out of hand. There is no better example of that
than Nike, who despite their statements on ethical business are constantly
being reminded of previous accusations of exploiting child labour.

On the other hand the careful handling by fresh fruit drinks producer
Innocent of their reputations means that they have enjoyed public esteem
for many years. The reality of their spoken, public claims is borne out by
their actual products and services.

A virtuous circle is created where a good reputation raises expectations
about the kind of products or services a company supplies and the quality
of the products or services enhances reputation.

Public relations has a major contribution to make

All this means that public relations has a significant contribution to make. It can contribute directly to organizational success. If its task is guarding and managing reputation and relationships this must have a demonstrable effect, and not just result in a 'feelgood' factor. Spending money on establishing a dialogue with key publics and building a reputation does result in tangible benefits to the organization. Publics are influenced in their favour.

If a company has a good reputation the evidence is that people are more likely to:

- try its new products;
- buy its shares;
- believe its advertising;
- want to work for it;
- do business with it when all other things are equal;
- support it in difficult times;
- give it a higher financial value.

Public relations helps build the intangible asset base of an organization. Research by US intellectual capital experts Ocean Tomo[6] shows that intangibles, which include reputation, account for 80 per cent of the value of commercial organizations. For private sector companies these benefits often become apparent when the organization is sold. The actual fixed asset value of a company will be declared, but on top of that a buyer will pay a premium for goodwill or the good name of the company – its reputations. Reputations are built by developing strong and valuable relationships with stakeholders who count. Establishing and maintaining a good reputation with key publics is a meticulous, time- and energy-consuming business, requiring all the skills and attributes of planners and managers of the highest calibre.

The role of public relations in organizations

To understand how public relations programmes and campaigns are planned and managed, it is first essential to understand the role of public relations in organizations.

It is not the aim of this book to go into the detail of how organizations are structured and managed, and how they function. There are many excellent textbooks on this. It is, however, incumbent on all public relations practitioners to understand these issues; otherwise they will not be able to fulfil their proper role within their organization and certainly will not be able to operate as senior managers.

Simply put, an organization consists of three elements:

- fixed assets such as its buildings, office furniture, car fleet and products;
- liquid assets or the money which lubricates the business;
- people.

Its fixed assets have a finite value and can be accounted for on a balance sheet. Similarly, the amount of liquid assets an organization has can be measured. It is obvious that the number of people that work for an organization can be counted as can their employment costs, but in many ways employees are an unquantifiable asset, and they form the intangible asset base of the organization. Their capabilities are basically unbounded. They are the ones who put life into an organization to create added value. They are the ones who create intellectual capital by using their creativity and come up with ideas, ingenuity to design new products and sell them. They provide the customer service. They make organizations work and make them what they are.

Furthermore, people interact with other people who are not necessarily a formal part of the organization. They create customer relationships, they have families and friends who may or who may not support their organization. They deal with suppliers, with local and central government, with the local community and so on. They are an increasingly important asset since they are the brand and the best brand ambassadors. At long last the importance of employees is being recognized as the most important stakeholders of the organization.

People are an infinitely expandable resource and they blur the edges of an organization's boundaries by drawing into the organization other people, who strictly speaking are external to its operation. Furthermore, some employees are key players in the influence networks discussed earlier. They are influential on Twitter and as bloggers. They are highly networked and important in their own right as well as employees. They have an almost infinite variety of potential connections at their disposal.

In times past, the public relations department was the formal conduit for internal and external communications. Of course there was always a flourishing grapevine of informal communication internally and externally, but the limitations of technology, or the requirement to meet one to one, meant that this was largely bounded in time and reach. Now there is no such barrier. Everyone has the potential to be a powerful channel of communication and can create their own content with ease. Thus organizational boundaries become ever more porous... information can emanate from any source. In addition, organizations are much more penetrable: people from outside can look in very easily and connect with a range of individuals to build up their own picture of the organization. If that picture is different from the one presented in formal channels, there is a potential issue for the organization. This level of interconnectedness produces a very permeable organization, linked to a host of formal and informal stakeholders through a host of formal and informal channels. This reality has prompted many organizations to adopt 'radical transparency' as a way of operating, and this has led to some surprises. For example in 2014 mobile phone giant Vodafone revealed the extent of government agency surveillance of telephone conversations in the countries in which it operates.

The role of the public relations professional within organizations

An organization's strategy (which determines how its vision will be realized and its purpose lived) is determined after a great deal of analysis and decision-making. Analysis of how chief executives go about determining strategies reveals that it is often conversation based. Ideas are advanced and tested and revised, rejected or re-ordered. Out of this iterative process a route map to the realization of the vision and purpose is developed. Many people, both outside and inside the organization, will contribute to this process. Having developed a strategy, this will need to be communicated so that it can be supported and implemented. Public relations has an essential role to play in this process, both in helping to develop the strategy itself and in its communication.

Relationships provide intelligence

The job of the public relations professional is to communicate with and build relationships with the organization's publics. They are (or should be) acutely aware of the environment in which the organization operates. This is vital because publics exist within a context and it is not possible to understand people fully unless there is a clear appreciation of the social, technological, economic, political and cultural issues and factors that influence them and drive their lives. Being in touch with the public mood, having contextual intelligence is essential. Organizations that are not conscious of the public mood find themselves in difficulties, whereas those in touch with it can find that it provides a significant advantage. Thus the Walmart-owned supermarket chain Asda stopped using celebrity models for its George range of clothing because its Pulse of the Nation[7] research told it that the excesses of the celebrity lifestyle clashed with the experience of their customers, many of whom were facing the harsh realities of the recession. Instead they used 'ordinary' people, representative of their customer base. Pulse of the Nation provides a vital 'sense check' for Asda as it seeks to understand the daily concerns of its customers.

Public relations professionals, along with other colleagues, can supply that contextual intelligence to decison-making planners. Thus they can be seen to have a 'boundary-spanning' role. They operate at the edge of the organization, bridging the gap between it and its external publics. They have one foot in the organization and one foot outside. Being able to represent the views of external publics, and their likely reactions to decisions, is a vital perspective that public relations professionals can bring to strategic planning. Furthermore, public relations professionals are also usually the communication managers within organizations and can draw information together about an organization's internal publics. The issues and concerns of external publics may well be reflected internally, but there will also be additional issues and concerns that affect employees as members of the organization. Furthermore, these employees can provide that 'reality check' on strategy. Is it realistic? Is it something they can buy into and support publicly? What needs adjusting? Indeed developing strategy without employee involvement is just plain stupid – they are the principal brand ambassadors and know what will land well and what will be opposed by stakeholders and influencers.

Information about the specifics of contextual factors, for example economic and financial facts, and intelligence about public opinion generally, will also be provided by specialists scattered throughout the organization. The public relations function, because of its 'boundary-spanning role', can act as a central intelligence-gathering function for this information but most specifically about stakeholders and the issues that affect them. They can also, provided there are suitably trained individuals, supply an analysis and interpretation service too. These stakeholders include those who oppose the organization, activist groups and, further afield, those think tanks and other sources of intelligence that have a broad perspective on the issues in society that affect the public mood.

This strategic use of the public relations function implies that there is a recognition of its status by management. Public relations is more than a tactical tool used purely to 'communicate' information or add a gloss to a 'story'. It is an integral part of the strategic development process grounded on thorough-going research and skilled, objective analysis.

Some of the linkages that the public relations function have are invaluable sources of early information and can pinpoint emerging issues that may have profound impact on an organization. For example, monitoring of the blogosphere or of Twitter traffic can help to identify emerging 'hot' issues. Media content analysis can identify the importance of an issue or the direction that public opinion is likely to take on an issue. Public affairs contacts can flag up government thinking on prospective legislation and think tanks can give opinions on likely social or economic change.

Being able to make sense of the environment, public relations professionals not only provide intelligence to the strategic development process, but contribute to the general decision-making within organizations. Because they have antennae that are alert to the external and internal environment that the organization operates within, they can bring an invaluable, independent perspective to decision-making by managers who are often too close to a situation to act objectively, or who are unaware of some of the ramifications of those decisions as far as the wider world is concerned. It could well be that what on the face of it appears to be correct business decisions have to be questioned when they are set within a broader, stakeholder context. For example, it might make apparent business sense for an organization to obtain supplies from the cheapest, most reliable source. But what if that source is thousands of miles away and the environmental impact of transporting these supplies is considerable? Renewed concerns about climate change may bring a challenge from stakeholders.

There is therefore a twofold role for the public relations professional here. First, it is to keep senior management informed of what is happening in the social environment, which is peopled by its stakeholders, so that this is taken into account as decisions are made.

Second, it is to counsel management on the implications of its decisions, taking into account the likely reaction of key publics who directly affect the well-being or otherwise of a company. The public relations professional is the monitor of public opinion, and the conscience and ethical mentor of the organization. The communication process is two-way as Figure 1.2 shows.

FIGURE 1.2   The two-way information flow between an organization and its environment

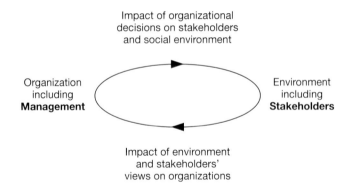

Communication skill

Once strategy is determined, it needs to be communicated. Ideally, during the process of strategic development, external and internal stakeholders will have been involved. The organization will have tested various propositions and have asked for the input of employees and other stakeholders. So, again, ideally there will be no surprises, and through the process of prior discussion and engagement stakeholders will already be amenable to the final version. Technology-driven tools make this type of consultation relatively easy and the benefits of building up a web of influence and positive relationships while strategy is being developed are obvious. The converse is deeply undesirable. Because strategic information and plans are so important, management are often tempted to communicate them in technical and/or pompous language and in an inappropriate form, for example a glossy brochure that permits no discussion or feedback. The information is seen as a 'done deal'. The communication professional must resist such actions and provide skilled advice on how to undertake the communication task in a way that maximizes stakeholder engagement.

The very process of insisting that communication is clear and relevant for the people who will consume it helps to put rigour into strategic thinking and decision-making. It helps to eliminate woolly, unrealistic aspirations and forces management to think through the practical implications of their planning. It is possible to cloak aspirations behind fine-sounding words, but distilling ideas down to clear and relevant language also provides a mechanism for checking how realistic the connection is between what's said and what then needs to be done to close the gap between words and achievable actions. The task of the public relations professional is to check whether the reality meets the claim, and if not, to point this out.

At a tactical level, the role of the public relations practitioner is to manage appropriate communication between an organization and its stakeholders and vice versa by ensuring that both the content and the channel are suitable and timely.

For example, shareholders will want to know about the future development plans of a company in some detail, including its overseas aspirations. How and when that information is relayed to them is very important. UK customers, on the other hand, may be less likely to be so concerned about this. They will want to know that a particular shop will be open next week, or that a favourite product will continue to be available. The fact that the company plans to open outlets in Hong Kong or Russia in 2020 will probably not concern them, unless of course they are shareholders too, or an activist group with a particular concern about trading in these markets.

The importance of communication

So why is communication important?

First of all it helps to further the strategic objectives of an organization because it is a vehicle used to enlist the support of all the various groups or key publics. It does this by helping to ensure the purpose, vision and values of the chief executive and organization are understood. The point of the communication is not just to pass on information about the vision, but to gain active pursuit of, or at least assent to, those objectives (depending on the public). The communication is designed to influence attitudes, opinions and behaviour.

Of course, if the organization listens as well as speaks and acts, its communication will have been influenced by research undertaken with those key publics as mentioned earlier, but it will also continue to be affected by them as it continues to listen. It is, therefore, more likely to be effective in its communication and action. This is not to say that organizational strategy is determined by public whim, but it means that it is alert to and sensitive to public opinion. It can then choose to align itself with public opinion or marshall arguments that are in line with its purpose and value if it finds itself opposing, or in a position to influence, public opinion.

Second, it positively fosters relationships with key publics. These publics are ultimately responsible for the destiny of the organization for good or ill. Good communication enhances the opportunities for incremental intelligence providing an 'early warning' system for the organization. In this way it can capitalize on opportunities that are presented to it by both identifying them early and facilitating the actions that are required to capture them (for example, if this is an opportunity to influence legislation). It also helps minimize the threats by spotting problems or potential conflicts early (for example, identifying increasing employee disquiet, or discontent with a proposed company action coming from an influential blogger).

The position of public relations within organizations

More detailed information on the role of public relations practitioners is given in Chapter 2. At this stage it is important to look at the position and status that public relations occupies within organizations, since that is linked to its role as a strategic or tactical function.

A good indication of how public relations is regarded is to establish where the function is placed. It is no surprise that the European Communication Monitor 2014[8] found that there was a link between the seniority of the public relations practitioner and the influence they have. If senior public relations managers are part of the 'dominant coalition' of company decision-makers, then public relations is likely to serve a key strategic role. Those individuals are likely to undertake the research and counselling activities already outlined. If not, public relations is likely to be largely tactical. It could well be seen just as a part of the marketing communications mix or regarded as mainly to do with presenting information about the organization in an acceptable (usually to the organization) way.

Another indication of how seriously the activity is taken is to gauge whether it is mainly reactive or proactive. There is always a level of reactive public relations in any organization. However good the planning, the unexpected is likely to occur, whether that be a pressure group making an unexpected attack (justified or ill-founded) or another organization making a takeover bid out of the blue. And a speedy reaction to what is online is essential. There are also opportunistic openings that should be grasped. For example, hot sunny weather provides timely opportunities for health product companies to remind people to protect their skin.

In organizations where public relations is taken seriously and proactively, it is normally found that the senior practitioner holds an influential position in the organization. Apart from being a good all-round business manager with the battery of appropriate skills and knowledge that all managers must have, he or she will provide a counselling role for fellow senior managers and directors and will have overall responsibility for the communication strategy of the organization. That might include determining the key overall marketing, advertising and promotional strategy. It will certainly involve working very closely with those disciplines.

Activity will be directed at building reputation positively and will have a strategic purpose. Issues like social responsibility and corporate governance will be taken seriously. Programmes will be based on careful formal and informal research, and a knowledge of who the key publics are, how these publics regard the organization and what they see as priorities. Communication with publics will be dialogue-based with the organization being responsive, indeed willing to collaborate with these publics. The programmes that are devised will be concerned with impact, and aim to influence attitudes, opinions and behaviours. They will not be obsessed with process such as how many news releases are produced, but the effectiveness of public relations activity will be closely monitored as will the quality of the relationships that are being built. Often these organizations will be industry leaders and set the pace in the market. They will usually be the ones available to the media and seen to be the voice of their industry. They are open, communicative organizations.

In organizations where public relations is seen as a lower order activity and where its practice is normally reactive, certain telltale traits will be evident. The practitioner will not hold a senior management role and will not be involved in decision-making. The task will be to respond to events and will often be defensive. The function will tend to communicate what has already happened, and the activity will be largely one-way, with the organization telling the world what it has done or is doing and not being influenced by what the world is saying to it. Any progress will be an evolution of what has happened in the past. The practitioner will not feel valued or in control and will not be a part of the 'dominant coalition'.

It is partly the public relations industry itself and individual practitioners who have perpetuated this reactive, technical role for public relations. Too often public relations has been regarded as primarily media relations and recruitment has been largely from the field of journalism where the priority is to 'get the story out'. Public relations is restricted to free publicity in the marketing communication mix. The schematic in Figure 1.3 shows the relationship between public relations and marketing, and indicates the shared areas of activity and those areas where public relations has a quite separate remit.

FIGURE 1.3 The inter-relationship of public relations and marketing

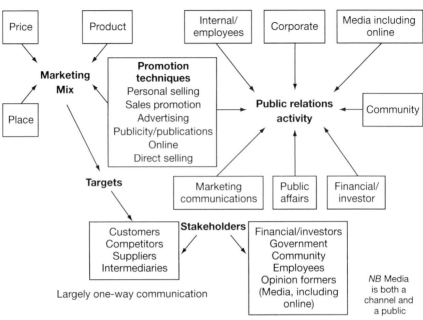

Research by Moss and colleagues[9] has found that the main reason why practitioners are not taken seriously as senior organizational players is because they do not know enough about how the sector and the business operates. How can they be at the decision-making table if they have no real grasp on what makes a business tick?

The European Communication Monitor 2014[10] also found that the biggest challenge facing the profession was linking communication to business strategy.

To mature fully as a discipline, public relations must take on the responsibilities of strategy, planning and management just as any other business function.

The contribution of public relations at different levels in the organization

It goes without saying that organizations operate at different levels and it is important to understand these in order to define the contribution that public relations can make at these various levels. There is often confusion about terms like strategy and how it is used; for example, corporate strategy, programme strategy and operational strategy. Being clear about the levels of strategy helps public relations practitioners to talk about their role in a way that is meaningful throughout the organization.

British academics Anne Gregory and Paul Willis in their book *Strategic Public Relations Leadership*[11] have identified that public relations can make a contributions at four levels of strategy within an organization. These can be viewed as different levels of accountability at which an organization has obligations to and opportunities with different types stakeholders and which involves different kinds of decision-making.

Societal

At the societal level, an organization seeks to gain and maintain legitimacy by having support from society as a whole. Its place, standing and reputation in society determines whether its 'licence to operate' is granted and supported by public opinion. Here the values on which the organization is based are tested and are either found to be sound or wanting. Its purpose and direction are also tested.

As mentioned earlier, public relations should play a central role in helping to clarify the organization's values and mission, as well as monitoring the way it goes about achieving those to determine whether they are acceptable to society. The organization's reputation is an indicator of current societal approval or, indeed, disapproval. Acting as the organization's boundary-spanners the public relations function brings vital intelligence into the organization so that its management can act accordingly. It also promotes the organization by the clear communication of its values and purpose and demonstrating consistency of performance against them.

Corporate level

At the corporate level, organizations focus on business goals and often decision-making is financially oriented. This is the level at which the resources of the organization are marshalled and the scope and nature of its operations determined so that it can achieve its mission. Even in times of organizational plenty, resources have to be used efficiently and effectively for it to maintain stakeholder approval. Apart from the more obvious resources that have to be in place such as financial, human, technological, estate and so on as Laurati[12] argues, the cognitive and behavioural resources of the organization also have to be secured to ensure success. There are three elements to this. First, the organization has to ask if it has the reputation it needs in order to achieve what it aspires to do. For example, a local company with a reputation for ignoring local community concerns will not be believed if it wants to position itself as an exemplar of social responsibility. It will have to build local reputational capital in community responsibility first, or it could well find itself exposed to ridicule and opposition.

Second, the organization will need to ensure it has the relationships that it needs to achieve its objectives. For example, a hospital may have a good reputation, but unless it has spent time building relationships with the organizations that fund and commission its services, it will not be able to gain the necessary support for the changes it feels it should make to the services it delivers.

Thirdly, unless the culture of the organization internally is aligned to what it wishes to promote externally, again it will not succeed. For example, if a company is presenting itself as responsive and the experience of those contacting the organization is that staff are slow and generally unhelpful, then it will lose all credibility. It will need to ensure staff are trained and 'bought-in' culturally to the customer-service ethos before it attempts to promote this value externally.

Arguing a case based on what reputational, relational and cultural resources are required for the organization to succeed positions the public relations function in quite a different place. This kind of approach is very different from asking for resources to mount an online campaign aimed at the local community, which will be a purely tactical discussion. It could well be that to build the reputational and relational capital required an online campaign aimed at the local community is required, but the starting point for the discussion is entirely different: it is corporate and strategic, not operational and tactical. Using the language and disciplines of business at corporate level is important. The HR director will argue for the human assets required to deliver the organizational vision and the business unit director will make a case for their operational area in similar terms. Public Relations should be no exception.

As well as presenting the case for public relations being a strategic asset, the public relations area makes another critical contribution at corporate level. It supports management in making enlightened decisions by ensuring that multiple-stakeholder perspectives are taken into account when resource decisions are made. So, for example, shareholders are a very important stakeholder group, but if their interests are put before all other stakeholders' legitimate claims, the organization will create issues for itself. The interests of all stakeholders must be properly weighted and the actions arising from decisions seen to be fair and in accordance with declared values. So, for example, if an organizational value is to protect the interests of the most disadvantaged, then the needs of that group must be properly accommodated even in difficult times. It is the job of the public relations function to ensure these less powerful interests are represented and that all stakeholder interests are balanced. Recognizing this imperative the beauty company L'Oreal declare, 'a company's behaviour is as important as its economic performance or the quality of its products'[13].

As mentioned earlier, it is also the task of the public relations professional to provide intelligence on how the organization's corporate decisions are likely to be perceived by stakeholders and, of course, to involve stakeholders in, and inform them of, corporate level decisions as appropriate. Stakeholder involvement can have a profound impact on the nature and scope of the business and its facilitation is a strategic contribution by public relations. Harley Davidson, for example, involve their Harley Owners' Group (HOG) in discussions about the nature of the business and in product development and this guides management decision-making.

Finally, as indicated earlier, it is neither desirable nor possible for the public relations function to be totally responsible for all the organization's relationship-building and communication activity. An essential role of the senior public relations professional at corporate level is to coach and mentor other senior managers in communicating the organization's objectives and decisions to their peers and stakeholder groups, and ensuring that they too are alert to the reputational and relational opportunities and threats inherent in doing so.

Value-chain level

At the value-chain level, the focus will be on those stakeholders directly involved in, and with the organization. It is their closeness to the organization that distinguishes them from broad societal level stakeholders, often called the 'general public', who may have no specific or strong link with it but who will, nevertheless hold the organization to account. Typical value-chain stakeholders will include customers, service users, delivery partners, suppliers, distributors, regulators, employees, etc... It is at this value-chain stakeholder level that societal and corporate intentions and decisions are operationalized. The public relations function has a part to play in engaging with these 'close' stakeholders, including those who may be regarded as troublesome, such as activist groups and certain on-line communities. Specific expertise in stakeholder identification, segmentation, insight, engagement and collaboration and/or management, can be offered by the public relations department alongside coaching and mentoring for those colleagues who interact with these stakeholders regularly. In addition, the public relations function can offer help in detecting, balancing and managing what could well be the conflicting demands of different stakeholder groups and navigating complex negotiations and relationships with them and between them.

As indicated earlier, being alert to the differences between internal culture and behaviours and external expectations of that culture and behaviour is especially important at this level. Individuals are representatives of the organization and the brand, and how they behave and communicate will affect the reputation of the whole organization. This is precisely why so much attention is now being paid to the internal stakeholder, with communication being central to successful cultural and organizational change. As beauty company L'Oreal says 'values express themselves in the daily actions of all our teams across the globe'[14] and the values that are expressed each day are the actual or lived values, so if they are out of line with the values that are expressed corporately, the organization will have a problem.

The role of the public relations function in being attuned to and representing all these 'close' stakeholder communities, internal and external, to senior managers in the organization, is critical to organizational success.

Functional level

At the functional level, it is the role of public relations to liaise with the other specialist functional areas in the organization such as legal, HR and operations, to determine how the public relations department as a whole can contribute its specific skills to the organization achieving its mission and objectives at an operational level. For public relations this will involve planning specific programmes and campaigns which support these objectives, offering specialist public relations advice and services to other functional areas of the organization in support of their objectives, and coaching and mentoring colleagues throughout the organization to be 'communicatively competent', or at least communicatively aware, so that they can either undertake certain public relations tasks themselves to an adequate standard, or be clear about when they need to enlist the help of the specialists. The types of specific activities the public relations function will be involved in commonly include (but this is not the complete list):

- Developing communication programmes and activities to support delivery of organizational priorities.
- Advising management and delivering campaigns of different types depending on the requirements of the stakeholder group involved, for example, social marketing programmes for behaviour change (eg childhood obesity), mass campaigns for information dissemination (eg new on-line services to support more traditional retail services), personalized/one-to-one engagement (eg with regulators or key delivery partners).
- Using recognized business disciplines to design effective communication plans which also embrace the full range of communication techniques.
- Moving seamlessly between reactive, pro-active and interactive roles depending on the relationship with the stakeholder involved.
- Evaluating programmes and communication activities for effectiveness.

Each plan will be different depending on its purpose, who is involved, their communication channel-use habits, the timing of the campaign etc. However, the disciplines behind the planning process are the same as this book explains.

The point of going through the strategic levels at which public relations can make a contribution is to:

- Generate a better understanding of organizational strategy and how this might be conceptualized for PR practitioners.
- Clarify the types of input that public relations can make to the organization as a whole, including its input to organizational decision-making.

- Demonstrate that public relations contributes more to an organization than just programmes and campaigns – it can make a strategic input at all levels.
- Show that programmes and campaigns have to be seen within a broader context and ensure all programmes are aligned to societal, corporate and/or stakeholder objectives.
- Enable the practitioner to articulate and move between the various roles that they must play within the organization.

Organizing for action

There is not room here to describe in detail how the public relations function should be organized. However, this is covered briefly here to provide an indication of the main things to be considered.

The way the public relations operation is usually structured is to split it along either task or functional lines. Single operators, however, have to do everything.

Some organizations have a task-oriented structure, that is, tasks requiring particular skills and knowledge are separated out and given to small groups or individuals to perform. Thus the structure may be as follows:

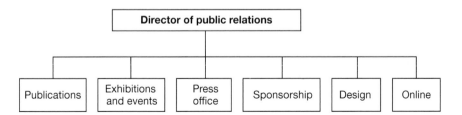

Other organizations split on functional lines. That is, the areas of activity are separated out and groups or individuals tackle all the tasks. A functional structure may look something like this:

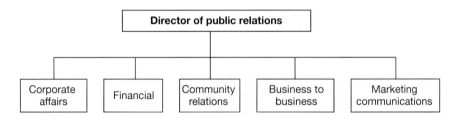

However, in some organizations neither of these structures are employed. The view is that the public relations team effectively operates as an internal consultancy, working on long- or short-term public relations projects that will require a range of tasks and functions to be undertaken. The department is therefore structured in teams depending on the requirements of the project. Any one individual may belong to a number of project teams. Working like this can cut across some of the silo thinking that comes about with task- or functional-based teams. It also means that individuals can work with colleagues with a variety of knowledge and skills, facilitating learning from each other and determining together the best way to approach the project. Teamworking in this way can bring a great deal of variety and job satisfaction, but it also requires good team leadership and management and greater flexibility in the public relations department.

A typical structure in this matrix arrangement, which can appear quite 'messy', might look like the diagram below.

Where public relations is conducted for a company that is split into separate operating companies, sometimes with different names, the situation is infinitely more variable. Some groups have very large corporate departments which undertake activity for the group as a whole and for all the operating companies. In other groups there is a very small corporate operation dealing with major corporate activities such as financial and government affairs, and maybe corporate sponsorship. The rest of the activity is then devolved to the operating companies. Normally the operating pattern that applies in the business as a whole also applies to public relations activity, that is, if business is very much driven from the centre then public relations is likely to be located in the centre also. On the other hand, if the approach is to let the operating companies function as virtually autonomous units, then it is also likely that public relations will be devolved to them.

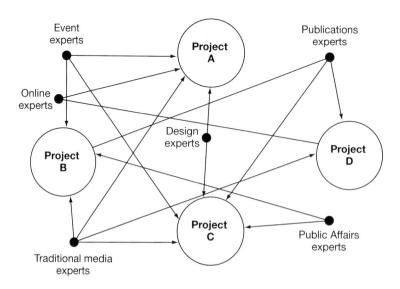

Who does what in public relations?

Seminal work on public relations roles spearheaded by Glen Broom[15] and David Dozier[16] identified two dominant public relations roles:

- *The communication technician.* Who is not involved in making organizational decisions but who carries out public relations programmes such as writing press releases, editing house magazines and designing web pages. This person is probably not too involved in undertaking research or evaluating programmes; he or she is concerned primarily with implementation.

- *The communication manager.* Who plans and manages public relations programmes, counsels management, makes communication policy decisions and so on.

Within this second category, there are three main types of manager role.

- *The expert prescriber.* Who researches and defines public relations problems, develops programmes and implements them, maybe with the assistance of others.

- *The communication facilitator.* Who acts as a go-between, keeping two-way communication between an organization and its publics. He or she is a liaison person, interpreter and mediator.

- *The problem-solving process facilitator.* Who helps others in the organization solve their public relations problems. This person acts as a sort of counsellor/adviser on the planning and implementation of programmes. (This is a role often fulfilled by specialist consultancies.)

David Dozier also identifies two middle-level roles that sit between the manager and the technician role.

- *Media relations role.* This is a two-way function where the individual keeps the media informed, and informs the organization of the needs and concerns of the media. This is not just the production and dissemination of messages from the organization to the media, but a highly skilled role requiring detailed knowledge and a profound understanding of the media. It is often fulfilled by someone who has made the crossover from journalism to public relations. It also goes some way to explaining why, if a former journalist is employed to undertake public relations, the function remains focused on media relations. For media also include online media.

- *Communication and liaison role.* A higher-level public relations role representing the organization at events and meetings, and positively creating opportunities for management to communicate with internal and external publics.

The broad technician and manager roles vary from organization to organization. At the lower level, in large organizations split on task lines, a technician may only write copy for online platforms. In other organizations he or she may do several other writing jobs too, such as preparing speeches and writing copy for the annual report and accounts, especially if the department is functional in orientation or if it is small.

At the middle level, practitioners may be responsible for a whole campaign or undertake employee relations only. They may be involved in both. Some may specialize in research or planning and have little to do with implementation, or they may be an account executive in a consultancy who is responsible for a range of planning and implementation tasks.

At higher levels, public relations managers plan the activity of the whole department and counsel senior management on policy, as well as supervise middle- and lower-level practitioners.

In practice most public relations activities require a mixture of technician and manager roles, and even at the most senior levels very few are entirely removed from the implementation role.

Dozier and Broom[17] also identified a 'senior advisor' role at the managerial level: someone who acted as a high-level counsellor, constantly advising the Chief Executive Officer, or Chair of the Board. They have a broad-ranging remit, but are effectively charged with spotting issues or difficulties for the individual they work with and advising them on how to respond.

More recently, Moss, Newman and De Santo[18] reported the findings of empirical work they had undertaken in both the UK and the United States that isolated five elements in the senior public relations role. Four are very much linked to the managerial role: monitor and evaluator (for the whole organization's performance as measured by reputation and relationships, see earlier in this chapter); key policy and strategy advisor; trouble shooter/problem solver; and issues management expert. They also discovered that even the most senior managers take on some technical work, usually high risk or complex work, such as, for example, dealing with senior people in the financial world on corporate earnings.

Gregory and Willis[19] have developed a role descriptor for practitioners as they operate at the four levels of strategy outlined earlier in this chapter.

Orienter – Societal level

The public relations role is as protector of the organization, ensuring that the licence to operate and its societal mandate is maintained by keeping the system orientated in a direction that maintains stakeholder support. Articulating and living values is critical and communication has an essential role to play by informing, involving and engaging with societal level stakeholders to maintain the organization's legitimacy.

Navigator – Corporate level

The role here is to bring stakeholder perspectives into decision-making, ensuring that relational and reputational capital and cultural alignment is factored in as a key resource and integral to the organization navigating a way through conflicting stakeholder demands is a key role.

Catalyst – Value chain level

Embedding a value-chain, stakeholder perspective in the design, creation and delivery of products and services requires the public relations function to provide vision-critical intelligence, engagement capability and evaluation to ensure the delivery of organizational objectives. Here the function is a catalyst ensuring values are lived and changing the realities of systems, processes and structures to reflect those values rather than attempting to change perceptions.

Implementer – Functional level

In this technical role the communication function designs and delivers (or commissions) appropriate communication activities and programmes which will deliver societal, corporate, stakeholder and service-user objectives.

In the European Communication Monitor 2014 mentioned earlier, only one in five communication functions were regarded as 'excellent', defined as being both influential internally and gaining results. All the evidence points to there still being some way to go in establishing senior public relations practitioners as being automatically involved in strategy making.

The growing complexity of the issues that public relations practitioners are being asked to handle is leading to increasing specialization in some areas. At the simplest level this is demonstrated by the fact that many consultancies now bill themselves as boutique specialists in, for example, fashion or celebrity or online public relations and the larger, one-stop agencies have for a long time had quite discrete specialist functions within them, such as public affairs or consumer divisions. Indeed, the evidence is that many now are splitting along technician and senior counsellor lines, with the technical aspects of public relations becoming increasingly commoditized and automated as much as possible, thereby keeping prices down. At the other end of the scale, however, there is a growing requirement for in-house practitioners and consultancies to promote high level advice to the Board and most senior executives of organizations. However, there is also another trend to note: many consultancies and agencies are integrating all their communication functions (marketing, public relations, investor relations etc) and platforms so that they can deliver a consistent and coordinated narrative across a diversity of channels. In this situation juniors and seniors work together with the usually younger digital natives taking the lead in those areas.

So what can be concluded from all this is that public relations is at a most exciting juncture in its development. The profession is changing as society and the needs of organizations change in response. What is certainly true is that the opportunities have never been greater. The challenge to the profession is to demonstrate its capabilities to take on a leadership role as communication becomes increasingly important in organization life.

Notes

1 A W Page Society (2007) *The Authentic Enterprise*. Available at http://www. awpagesociety.com/wp-content/uploads/2011/09/2007AuthenticEnterprise.pdf

2 Global Alliance (2012) *The Melbourne Mandate*. Available at http://melbournemandate.globalalliancepr.org/wp-content/uploads/2012/11/Melbourne-Mandate-Text-final.pdf

3 A W Page Society (2012) *Building Belief: A new model for activating corporate character*. Available at http://www.awpagesociety.com/wp-content/uploads/2012/11/Building-Belief-New-Model-for-Corp-Comms.pdf

4 A W Page Society (2014) *Authentic advocacy: how five leading companies are redefining stakeholder engagement*. Available at http://www.awpagesociety.com/wp-content/uploads/2014/09/2014_AWPS-Authentic-Advocacy.pdf

5 Sheldrake, P (2011) *The business of influence*. Chichester: Wiley

6 Ocean Tomo (2015) Annual study of intangible asset value. Available at http://www.oceantomo.com/2015/03/04/15-intangible-asset-market-value-study

7 Asda's Pulse of the Nation survey is available at https://pulse.asda.com/Portal/default.aspx

8 Zerfass, A, Tench, R, Vercic, D, Verhoeven, P and Moneno, A (2014) European Communication Monitor 2014. Brussels: EACD/EUPRERA, Helios Media

9 Moss, D (2011) *A managerial perspective of public relations: locating the function and analysing the environmental and organisational context*. In D Moss & B DeSanto (eds) *Public Relations: a managerial perspective*, Los Angeles: Sage

10 Op Cit

11 Gregory, A and Willis, P (2013) *Strategic Public Relations Leadership*, Abingdon: Routledge

12 Laurati, F (2008) Institutionalizing public relations. Plenary Panel, European Public Relations Research and Education Association. Milan, October

13 See L'Oreal statement on ethics at http://www.loreal.com/group/governance/acting-ethically.aspx

14 See L'Oreal statement on Values at http://www.loreal.com/group/governance/acting-ethically.aspx

15 Broom, G M and Smith, G D (1979) Testing the practitioner's impact on Clients, *Public Relations Review*, **5** (3), 47–59

16 Dozier, D M and Broom, G M (1995) Evolution of the manager role in public relations practice, *Journal of Public Relations Research*, **7** (1), 3–26

17 Op Cit

18 Moss, D, Newman, A and De Santo, B (2005) What do communication managers do? Defining and redefining the core elements of management in public relations/communication context, *Journalism and Moss Communication Quarterly*, **32**, pp 873–90

19 Op Cit

02
Public relations in context

Context is vitally important

To plan and manage programmes (long term, planned activities aimed at addressing difficult and/or complex issues and opportunities that require an ongoing approach) and campaigns (shorter term, planned activities aimed at addressing a specific and time-limited issue or opportunity) effectively it is vitally important to look at the context in which public relations activity takes place, since this differs from organization to organization. It helps to look at the factors affecting organizations in a systematic way, and addressing the areas outlined in Figure 2.1 provides a blueprint for doing this.

FIGURE 2.1 Factors to be considered when researching the background for public relations activity

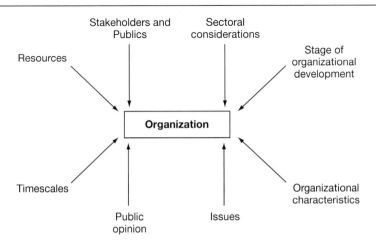

This contextual research is not about specific public relations problems or opportunities necessarily (more of this in Chapter 3), but it is vital background information required in order to plan and manage effectively. As mentioned earlier, programmes and campaigns have to be seen with this wider context because issues and opportunities and the plans aimed at addressing them do not exist in isolation. These days everything is connected and the organization is looked at and judged as a whole, not as a set of discrete activities.

Stakeholders and publics

Chapter 6 has a much more detailed discussion on stakeholders and publics, but from the outset it is important that the public relations practitioner is, as far as possible, aware of the whole range of stakeholders that must be communicated with. Of course it is not always possible to predict all those who may take a stake in any particular issue, but the very act of considering stakeholders systematically will prompt lines of thinking that will reveal potential as well as actual stakeholders. This will be a major factor in deciding the public relations task. Each stakeholder will have a different communication requirement, although the information given to each must not conflict.

Before going further, it is important to obtain clarity about terms. In public relations there are a group of terms that are often used interchangeably, but they have slightly different meanings.

The word 'stakeholder' rather than 'publics', is growing in popularity. The word was first brought to the fore by Freeman[1] in the debates on corporate governance in the United States in the 1980s. The view was that companies had a primary responsibility to shareholders, but Freeman insisted that there are others with a legitimate stake in the company. He defined stakeholders as 'those who are affected by, or who can affect' an organization.

For some organizations, their range of stakeholders can be quite small. For example, a niche manufacturer of mobile phone parts will have a relatively contained group of stakeholders since they operate in a confined business-to-business environment and the end user of the telephone may not even know the company's name, or even that they exist: unless the part is faulty.

An organization such as the US Army, on the other hand, will have many stakeholders, not only in the United States, but also around the world. Indeed, it could be argued that ultimately just about everyone could have a stake in the US Army, because its presence is widespread and potentially it could be involved in operations in any part of the world. In addition, there are millions of people around the world who take a virtual stake in the US Army, discussing its activities online and sometimes using social networking sites and so on to organize virtual or physical protests, or to support action.

However, to talk of everyone being a stakeholder is a difficult and impractical notion to handle. Most organizations wish to identify those who they should prioritize because resources are limited. More on this in Chapter 6.

Publics are stakeholders, but they are stakeholders with a particular relationship with the organization. Grunig and Hunt[2] describe publics as those for whom an organization has created a problem or an issue. More commonly now, publics are described as stakeholders who become active either for or against the organization. The author's view is that publics combine both these factors: issues or opportunities, and activity.

Typically, stakeholders are categorized into broad groups that describe the nature of the stake. For example, shareholders, customers and employees are typical stakeholders. Publics on the other hand can be drawn from across all these groups and they coalesce around an issue. For example, a company may wish to close down a factory; this creates an issue for a range of stakeholders – employees, local shopkeepers, local community, suppliers, etc. They could all group together to oppose the closure: they are active and they are a recognizable and coherent group drawn together because of the issue.

Conversely, there are often important stakeholders who remain inactive. For example, there may be a number of individuals who have invested significant sums of money in a company. As long as there is a reasonable return on their investment they remain passive, even disinterested in the activities of the company. If, however, returns decline, they and other stakeholders may become active around this issue and therefore become a public.

The word 'audience' is sometimes used in public relations. Audiences are usually broad, undifferentiated groups, reflecting the fact that the word originates from the world of the mass media. Hence, TV and radio have audiences, and these not only comprise large numbers, but also include isolated individuals who are not organized into recognized groups.

Finally, 'target groups' is a term sometimes used in public relations. These are the groups at which the campaign or programme is aimed: it is their attitudes and behaviours that the originator of the communication wishes to affect in some way. They are not to be confused with intermediary individuals or groups who may receive communication (receivers), but then pass it on to the target group. So, for example, schoolteachers may be used to communicate information about summer holiday activities in the local park: the schoolteachers are the receivers of the information, but the schoolchildren are the target group.

The object of the exercise in communication is to enlist the support of stakeholders and publics. Sometimes that support will need to be active and immediate, for example, an organization wanting customers to buy their products or voters to vote for a political party in tomorrow's general election. Sometimes the support is less active and not bound by specific timescales. For example, a company might organize a community relations campaign, simply because they feel it right to put something back into a community that provides most of its workforce. There might be no specific business objectives at the time of implementing the programme apart from the general objective of enhancing the reputation of the company and building positive relationships generally. However, the feeling of goodwill that the campaign engenders may make recruitment easier or minimize the possibility of objections automatically being raised if they want to extend their factory in the future. Having undertaken a longer-term, goodwill-building programme they can, if they need to, switch more easily to a focused programme which seeks to enlist active support on particular issues.

With some publics a change in opinions and behaviour may be wanted, with others existing behaviour or opinions may need to be confirmed, and yet with others engendering an opinion or pattern of behaviour may be wanted where previously that public was entirely neutral.

Factors to bear in mind when considering stakeholders and publics include the following:

- *Range.* That is the breadth of stakeholders and publics concerned. For some organizations, for example, an association for professional antique dealers, the range of publics may be very narrow. For other organizations, for instance, a government's Department of Health, the range of stakeholders and publics is very large indeed.

- *Numbers and location.* Some organizations have a range of stakeholders and publics that fall into large uniform blocks, for example, the multiple retailers will have large groups of customers, suppliers and planning regulators as some of their stakeholders. Others, for example engineering projects, will have a whole range of publics, often small in number, attached to each project. Some organizations have publics covering a wide geographical or socio-economic spread; others have very focused groups to concentrate on. Some organizations have limited online presence with few interactions. Some will have a major presence and with most of their contact with external publics and stakeholders being conducted online.

- *Influence and power.* Some publics, for example active pressure groups, can gain a great deal of power, particularly if they catch the public mood. They may not be large in number or have any direct link to the organization, but they can be highly influential over the way an organization conducts its business. They are usually very skilled at putting together or linking with other networks with whom they can forge common ground, especially online. The current antipathy in the UK against genetically modified foods was generated by a highly effective campaign spearheaded by Friends of the Earth back in the 1990s, but whose legacy has been long-lasting. In a different way, shareholders wield a great deal of power. They have an obvious stake in an organization and, although they can be few in number, can determine its future overnight. One of the tasks of the public relations practitioner is to determine the relative influence and power of all the publics concerned, and weight the public relations programme accordingly. This is not to say that the most powerful and influential publics always need to have the most attention, but obviously their concerns and communication needs are important.

- *Connection with organization.* Some publics are intimately connected with an organization, for example its employees. Others have a more remote connection, for example those making an occasional visit to the website. Some publics will have an amicable relationship with the organization, others will find themselves in opposition to it. Again, the public relations practitioner needs to have a clear perception of the nature of these relationships and to gauge their changing nature. Some relationships could be in danger of becoming distant or of deteriorating. Others may ameliorate over time and indeed turn from negative to positive, for example, if a pressure group's legitimate concerns are addressed. Some groups are always active, some very rarely. Furthermore, some publics may have very active sub-groups within them, whereas other sections of the same public may be apparently quiescent, but with the potential to become active. Shareholders and online communities are classic examples of this. Thus the needs not only of the whole group, but parts of it also need to be considered.

Sectoral considerations

The nature of the sector in which the organization operates will profoundly influence the way public relations is conducted. Public relations for a market-leading manufacturer of fast-moving consumer goods is quite different from public relations for a university.

Each sector has its own particular opportunities, threats and constraints. Just some of the sectors in the public or non-profit-making area are:

- education;
- government departments;
- health and medical care;
- voluntary organizations;
- charities;
- emergency services;
- the armed services;
- professional associations;
- NGOs (non-governmental organizations), for example the World Health Organization;
- local government.

Some of the organizations in these sectors are enormous and the public relations support required for a major government department or a large international charity such as Oxfam are as large or larger and as complex as anything that would be found in the private sector. In fact, because of the constraints placed on some of those organizations, for example the requirements of Freedom of Information legislation or the need to account for every single pound spent on promotional activity, the challenges can be seen to be greater than for those in private industry where it could be argued there is less direct external accountability.

The private sector, too, cannot be regarded as a uniform mass. It can be split up into many sectors including:

- extraction industries;
- commerce;
- agriculture;
- finance;
- manufacturing;
- services;
- retail;
- pharmaceutical;
- professional services (eg law, accountancy, management consultancy).

The growing number of online businesses can almost be regarded as a sector in its own right.

Working in the manufacturing environment where there may be great emphasis on marketing communication activities that demonstrate a physical product, will require sales promotion contexts such as exhibitions, virtual and physical demonstrations, conferences, glossy brochures, etc, where the product can be touched and sampled, virtually or actually. This can be quite different from working in the service sector where the balance may be towards descriptive techniques such as case studies, testimonials and online advocacy sites that give confidence in the people providing the service.

Organizational development – business stage

Public relations activities are often dictated by the stage of development at which an organization finds itself.

Development depends on the sort of sector an organization operates within. For example, in the fashion or in the hi-tech industries, development and decline can be very rapid indeed. Other industries, the motor trade or food retailing being cases in point, mature more slowly and can maintain their position for many years. Car maker SAAB is a good example of a mature, established company, but even it went bankrupt in 2011 and only restarted production in 2013 under new Chinese ownership.

Then there are variations within industries. Apple's iPhone grew rapidly in an industry dominated for many years by Nokia.

Factors affecting organizational development are:

- the nature of the industry;
- competitor activity;
- technological impacts;
- the power of suppliers;
- the power of consumers;
- management decisions on direction;
- resources, both financial and human.

Looking at the various stages of an organization's development reveals that there will be specific public relations requirements at different times:

- *Start-up.* Usually companies start small. The owners may know suppliers, customers and their employees, and often there will not be a separate public relations function. Public relations will be in the form of one-to-one contact with the various publics, with maybe some literature and an online presence with various levels of interactivity to attract business and publicise the company. The main emphasis will be on marketing communication, since growth will be a priority. The opportunity for public relations, especially in building online relationships, will be essential, but the work may be done by the owners and not necessarily recognized as a specialist function.

- *Growth.* With more employees and more customers, face-to-face contact may not be possible and management time will be taken up managing the business. At this stage an individual public relations practitioner or a consultancy may be employed. Public relations may still be viewed quite narrowly, largely as part of the marketing communication mix. Externally activity will focus on raising awareness of the company, its products and services. Internally there may be the beginnings of a formal communication programme including briefings, use of online, notice boards, social activities and so on.

    The priority will be on expansion, and capital costs could be quite high, especially if new premises have to be acquired. Resource constraints are likely to be a major factor influencing the role of public relations. Activities like a comprehensive community relations programme may be low on the agenda.

- *Maturity.* At this stage the organization is likely to be well established. The public relations function probably will be expanded and certainly the range of activities it is involved in is likely to be considerably broadened.

It could well be that a stockmarket flotation is being considered. Capital might be needed for expansion or acquisition. If this is the case an active financial public relations campaign will be pursued.

Employee relations will be more developed. The objective will be to have an efficient and well-motivated workforce who are working to agreed organizational objectives and who help to maintain a competitive edge by being the organization's principal brand representatives. They will also be active themselves in communication about the organization. There will also be the need to attract good-quality new staff to the organization.

Employee communications will be well developed, including techniques such as employee briefings, conferences, creative events and the full range of online communication. Public relations may be involved in supporting other departments such as the training function in producing interactive training programmes, and HR in staff recruitment. Indeed, it will be advising a variety of managers and their departments on communication matters as well as taking on the strategic role discussed in Chapter 1.

The public relations department may be assisted by one or more public relations consultancies and will be running a full corporate programme as well as continuing to support marketing efforts. The organization should, at this stage, have a cohesive identity and an established reputation. Furthermore, it should have a developed sense of corporate responsibility, as it impacts more and more on the environment in which it operates (both local and remote). It will probably be involved actively in a range of community relations projects, including sponsorships, help in kind and support of local initiatives.

The public relations department will be using the full range of communication channels at its disposal and be interacting with a potentially large number of publics and stakeholders with a complex range of connections with both the organization and each other.

- *Decline.* Many companies avoid decline by adjusting their orientation or by moving into new areas of activity. However, for whatever reason, takeover, financial or legislative change, or downright bad management, some organizations move into a period of temporary or permanent decline. Even here there is a vital role for public relations to play. Spotting the issues before they become terminal crises is a key role (see Chapter 4 for more on this). Handling crises with honesty and integrity if they do happen (for example a major product recall, as in the textbook case of Johnson & Johnson's handling of the Tylenol recall, or a major incident such as Richard Branson's handling of the Virgin train crash in Cumbria, UK) can help maintain reputation and minimize the risk of a crisis unravelling out of control.

Ultimately, if a business is non-viable, there is nothing public relations can do to rescue it. However, managing the expectations, and trying to influence the behaviour of those publics critical to the eventual fate of an organization in decline is very much within the remit of public relations. This is not a manipulative or unethical exercise, but it is managing the situation professionally, bearing in mind the legitimate interests of all those involved.

Organizational characteristics

There should be no skeletons unknown to the public relations practitioner who should know the organization inside out: history, its current status, its future plans, its past misdemeanours, everything there is to know. The following headings give a framework for systematically gaining knowledge:

- *Nature of sector.* Know the sector. What are the trends for the sector? Is it expanding, contracting and are there new, exciting markets? What is the operating environment? Is the economy in recession and are there any major issues facing the industry or the organization, such as new legislation or pressing environmental demands? What is the reputation of the sector? If the sector as a whole has a bad reputation, this is an additional issue.

- *Competitor activity.* How is the organization placed in relation to the competition? Is it possible to take market leadership in some or all areas? Are competitors new, aggressive young Turks likely to steal the market? Are there few or many competitors? Which ones are making headway and why? What are their strengths and weaknesses? Are some smarter than others in using all communication channels and techniques effectively?

- *Mission.* What is the mission of the organization? Is it to be the biggest, the best, the most innovative? Is it possible to be distinctive or will it be a 'Me too'? Is the mission realistic or a pious hope which needs to be challenged? Will the mission be supported by stakeholders? If not, why not?

- *Size and structure.* How large is the organization compared to others inside and outside the sector? How much 'clout' does it have? Does it have a single, simple structure or is it a complex conglomerate? Is it hierarchical or flat, restructured or re-engineered? Does it operate in one or several countries? (Different countries have different reputations: an engineering company operating from Germany will be regarded differently from one operating from Ghana, where there is no established engineering tradition.) What is the structure of the public relations operation given these factors? Is it an appropriate structure? Should consultancies be used or should everything be handled in-house?

- *Nature of the organization.* What activities does the organization perform? Is it single or multi-product or service? Does it operate in a single sector or several sectors? What is its geographic location and reach? Are specialist public relations skills and knowledge needed, for example is a lobbying division needed, or can all activities be served from a unified or devolved public relations department?

- *Tradition and history.* Is the company old and established or is it new with a position to establish? Is it well known for doing things in certain ways or is it an unknown quantity? Closely linked to this is the philosophy and culture of the organization. Is it open and participative or is it hierarchical and directive? What are its values? Are these clear, known and acted upon?

- *Reputational history.* How has the organization been perceived over the years? Is it market- or thought-leading, innovative, reliable, plodding and slow, or slightly shifty? Has the image been constant or has it been subject to rapid or developmental change? Who is influential in shaping that reputation and how?

- *Types of employees.* White collar? Blue collar? Graduate? Semi- or unskilled? A complete mixture?

All these organizational factors profoundly affect how the public relations function is structured, and how and what the activities are that need to be carried out.

Issues

It is obvious that the issues affecting the society or an industry in which an organization operates, as well as the specific issues that the organization faces, are likely to set an agenda for much of the public relations work. Issues generally fall into a number of categories, as follows:

- *Structural.* The major long-term trends in society, such as an ageing population, globalization, technological developments: things over which the individual organization will have very little control, but of which it needs to be aware.

- *External.* Largely contextual issues such as environmental concerns, community concerns, political imperatives.

- *Crises.* Normally short term and arising from unforeseen events, for example a factory disaster, war, product recall. However, sometimes crises have long-term effects on the organization's reputation. It will take many years and billions of pounds for BP to recover from the Gulf of Mexico oil spill.

- *Internal.* Long- or short-term issues that the company faces from within, for example succession policy, employee relations and organizational change.

- *Current affairs.* Those things that are of immediate public interest and which often are the subject of intense media coverage at the time, for example, gun and knife legislation, child abuse, nationalism, genetic engineering developments.

- *Potential.* Those issues that have not yet emerged. It might seem rather odd to list this, but it is very much the case that some issues do appear to arise from nowhere, except that the careful practitioner will have an intelligence system at his or her disposal that can give early warning of potential issues likely to become real. Content analysis of the media and of online sources can often give an indicator of what may be on the public agenda in the future, and is a vastly underutilized resource by organizations. Also, contact with think tanks, the scientific community, universities and futures groups can provide a rich picture of possible scenarios.

The identification and handling of issues is a core skill of senior public relations practitioners, and a prized contribution that can be made to the organization. As Gregory and Willis point out in their book *Strategic Public Relations Leadership*[3], senior managers value someone with the equivalent of a crystal ball, who can tell them the issues they face, before they hit the organization. This is a key function of risk management and it is not an accident that some Board-level practitioners are dubbed the Chief Risk Manager – risks to reputation and in relationships that is.

This area of public relations work is of increasing importance, especially since online communities can collect around an issue very quickly and pose a threat to the organization. As one CEO has said, 'I used to be threatened by a city analyst and I had many days notice of impending problems. I am now threatened by a spotty youth using an iPad in their bedroom, and I have no notice of either the issue or the time of attack.'[4] Hence, careful monitoring of online chatter and a connection to popular sites and services is vital. If only a few hours' notice is given for a significant issue, that is valuable time to engage with a response which deflates the issue, or buys some time for a more studied response, to prepare for a crisis, or alert others who may act as sources of authoritative information or act as advocates.

Public opinion

Public opinion, expressed through or led by the traditional media or online sources, is a very potent influence on organizations. The campaign against genetically modified organisms in the United Kingdom mentioned earlier led to the total withdrawal of genetically modified foods from many supermarkets. Those at the forefront of research in this area, for example Monsanto, had to modify their plans for development as a result and even now are not able to move forwards as swiftly as they would wish given ongoing protests.

The on- and offline media as reflectors of public opinion are vital to public relations because the very same channels are often used by public relations as a means of information and engagement. Dissonance between the two is fuel for further media interest for good and bad. The media often define and crystallize the public mood, although sometimes its influence can be overestimated.

It is certainly true that these media can fatally damage the reputation of an organization or individual. Sometimes this is because the organization is genuinely at fault, in which case the media is doing its job of serving the public interest. Sometimes, as libel cases attest, there is little ground for their attacks.

It is also the case that the media can massively enhance the reputation of an organization by, for example, endorsing its products or by favourably reporting on its performance. This is especially true if comment is made in influential media which are regarded as authoritative reference sources such as the *Financial Times* if a financial matter is being reported, or in the tabloids, consumer press and online magazines if a consumer product is being promoted.

Timescales

Obviously timescales are critical when determining public relations programmes; this topic is discussed in detail in Chapter 8, but covered briefly here. Sometimes the practitioner has the luxury of planning a programme over a self-determined period of time. However, external or internal restraints, or both, can determine when activities can be performed.

- *Externally driven timescales.* Some external factors are fixed and totally outside any individual or collective organizational influence, for example, planned parliamentary timetables: if an organization wants to change a clause in some proposed legislation, it has to undertake its lobbying within the time frame laid down by Parliament. Financial results are regulated by the Stock Exchange rules. Thanksgiving is on the fourth Thursday in November in the USA. These are known external factors, but sometimes programmes have to be altered because of unknown factors which then require a reaction. For example, information regarding competitive activity may lead to pre-emptive action within very precise time limits. A breaking news story may provide an unexpected opportunity to action the programme earlier to good effect.

- *Internally driven timescales.* Examples of internally imposed deadlines are the introduction of a new product or service, a decision to build a new production line, achievement of an international quality standard, staff awards and so on.

Resources

The level of resources put into a public relations function or department clearly determines the level and scope of activities that can be undertaken. The resourcing of specific programmes is discussed in Chapter 8. However, it is appropriate here to cover it briefly.

Normally there are two approaches. The first is to determine an appropriate departmental structure along with the relevant activities that need to be undertaken, and to provide the human and financial resources to implement them.

The second approach is to devote a budget to public relations determined by some internal resource allocation model. The trick then is to prioritize the public relations activities and to carry out those essential elements of the programme within budget. It is this second approach that is the most common.

It is surprising how many public relations campaigns are undertaken without a full appreciation of the context in which they are to take place and this is a significant contributory factor to failure. While the first six areas give an overall context to public relations, it is true to say that timescales and resources are controlling factors on activity. Nevertheless, those factors together define the operational constraints that public relations has to operate within.

Notes

1. Freeman, R E (1984) *Strategic Management; a stakeholder approach*, Pitman, Boston, MA
2. Grunig, J E and Hunt, T (1984) *Managing Public Relations*, Holt, Rinehart and Winston, New York
3. Gregory, A and Willis, P (2013) *Strategic Public Relations Leadership*, Routledge
4. Conversation reported to the author.

03
Starting the planning process

Responsibilities of practitioners

Having looked at public relations within the organizational context and recognizing the ways in which public relations can make a contribution to the organization and how it can be structured and conducted, we can now look at planning campaigns in detail.

Public relations practitioners as members of their organizations have two sets of responsibilities. First of all they have organizational responsibilities like anyone else who works in that environment. They are public relations specialists and are responsible for discharging their specialized work to the best of their abilities. In addition to this, if they hold a management or supervisory role they have to handle budgets and people, run an effective department or consultancy, control suppliers, ensure quality standards are met and so on. In fact, all the skills required of any manager are required of public relations professionals.

There are also a number of other pressures. Much of the work is high profile. A mistake made when working with a journalist or influential blogger has very public consequences. In fact, most of the activities of public relations professionals are by definition 'public'. It's a profession where there are very few ground rules: the practice is not highly prescribed as it is for other professions, such as accountancy and law. The work is often driven by deadlines and demand. When dealing with an issue or crisis it is impossible to predict how large 'the job' will be. There are severe qualitative and quantitative pressures on practitioners.

The public relations brief is a large and complex one: to manage the relationship and reputational interface between the organization and all its publics, either as a department or with others.

Hence, a systematic, efficient approach is essential. As far as possible there have to be ways of asserting some control, although total control in the dynamic world of public relations is impossible and not even desirable.

Public relations policy

Given that public relations practitioners are not solely responsible for building relationships with stakeholders and publics, the first requirement is for a clear public relations policy to be laid down. This should define the remit of public relations activity and set the ground rules for operation.

The idea of a policy is not to be regulatory and restrictive, but to give the rules of engagement so that everyone knows where responsibility lies, where the lines of demarcation are and, ultimately, who is accountable for what activities. It also gives some security to those non-public relations staff who will be communicating on behalf of the company.

Policy statements need not be long or complicated, but they must be clear.

Figure 3.1 shows an example from a FTSE 100 retailer in the UK. The company has a group (corporate) communication function which deals largely with company-wide matters and which agreed this media policy with senior management.

FIGURE 3.1   FTSE 100 retailer corporate media

Media policy

1	As a FTSE 100 retailer we receive a large amount of media attention. The amount of press attention we receive reflects the enormous public interest in our Company.
2	It also represents a tremendous opportunity for us to work with and through the media to communicate with our customers and stakeholders.
3	It is important that we work in a coordinated way, with one voice, to get positive coverage on our stores, products, people, and the contributions we are making in our communities.
4	Handling the media in the right way requires sensitivity and skill. We need to make sure that they receive the correct information at the right time. This is essential if the media is to run balanced stories on our company and is crucial to our success.
5	We have an experienced Corporate Communications team whose responsibility is to manage our relationships with the media, and to provide support in any media dealings. To ensure that we manage our media relationships professionally, to help make the most of these relationships, and to protect you and the Company, we have a comprehensive Media Policy and Guidelines.
6	**Central to these Guidelines is one key principle:** All media calls must be passed onto the relevant media team before making any comment or agreeing to an interview or meeting. More guidance on this is given within this document.

The team

- Corporate Communications comprises of Internal Comms, Public Affairs, Investor Relations and three different press teams. Each of the press teams covers a specific area:
- The Corporate PR Team handles all media enquiries on price sensitive information, and any news or business stories that concern the whole company including the company's brand and our people.
- The Product PR Team handles all queries relating to the products that we sell.

Objectives

- To manage our relationships and dealings with the media in a way that supports our business strategy and plans
- To deliver clear and consistent messages
- To provide the media with the correct facts and agreed Company messages, therefore ensuring that we receive balanced coverage and opinions
- To communicate to the media our news and achievements
- To provide an easy and clear channel of communication for both media and staff by directing all media calls through the relevant media team

Media guidelines

1 Share Price Sensitive Information

As a FTSE 100 company we are listed on the UK Stock Exchange. We are owned by our shareholders who each have a financial investment in the Company.

As such, some of our Company news and information is 'share price sensitive', which means that it can affect the share price and impact on the value of the Company.

The type of news and information which is deemed 'share price sensitive' includes:

- Our company performance – Trading Statements, Interim and Full Year Results – even at a store level
- Strategic announcements
- Future plans for the Business – Including store openings, remodels and closures
- Key Management appointments
- New product and marketing initiatives

As all of these issues can affect the share price, **only** the Corporate PR Team, Company Directors or others specifically authorized should speak to the media on the Company's behalf.

All media calls regarding any of the above should be immediately directed to the Corporate PR Team. Journalists calling to speak to you on any of these issues should be given the direct number of the **Corporate Press Office**: 0XX XXXX XXXX.

A member of the Corporate PR Team is on duty 24 hours a day, 7 days a week to handle such calls. The duty press office can be contacted at anytime, including out-of-office-hours via: 0XX XXXX XXXX.

These rules also apply for any written or emailed communication from the media asking for information.

2 National Media

All other enquiries from national newspapers and magazines, broadcasters (TV or Radio) or online media, should be redirected to the relevant press office:

- *Specialist Media Calls*
  Specialist or trade magazines that cover areas like IT, e-commerce, Human Resources or Property, may make direct contact with employees requesting quotes or interviews. Please pass any such requests onto the **Corporate Press Office**: 0XX XXXX XXXX

- *Interview Requests*
  Please pass any requests for Interviews onto the Corporate Press Office before committing or agreeing to take part. The team will decide whether it is appropriate to take part and if it is, they will manage the interview to protect you and the business.

  They can prepare you in advance, support you, help with any sensitive questions and do any necessary follow-up work after the interview, ie answer any additional questions, communicate the Company's key messages, find out when the article/programme is to run, provide relevant visuals, etc.

- *Product Calls*
  Media enquiries about products should be put through to the **Product PR team**: on 0XX XXXX XXXX.

3 Regional PR

Due to the volume of calls and emails that Corporate Press team receive from the national press, we have appointed three PR agencies to act as our PR Partners and manage proactive and reactive regional media relations on behalf of our stores.

These specialist agencies work from eight different offices across the UK and Ireland, and are all specialists in working on the ground at a regional level. Their role is to deal with the local press on your behalf.

They are also there to advise on whether activity and stories are appropriate for our Company, so please call them before you begin planning. It is vital that we make sure any messages or stories that go out externally are on brand and consistent.

- **Proactive Regional PR**

  Our PR Partners have been briefed to work closely with our stores to seek out and develop proactive, positive stories for the local press that are appropriate for our Company.

  Please feel free to discuss any opportunity with your local PR partner. Once you've worked with them to select and get involved in an activity, they can then work with you to develop material and messaging that is appropriate to the cause and to our Company.

- **Reactive Regional PR**

  Our PR Partners have also been tasked with responding to all regional media enquiries that come directly into our stores. They are the experts in handling potential media issues – which can be very tricky – and are best placed to develop appropriate company responses.

This could include:

- Temporary store closures due to weather, flooding, fires

- Customer incidents – including theft, accidents and fatalities

- HR-related incidents/issues

- Protests

- Requests for comments on local issues – BIDs, funding, congestion, etc.

Again, this is by no means everything that you may be approached on, so please forward all direct calls from your local or regional newspapers, radio stations or websites to your relevant PR Partner.

The most effective way to do this is to take their contact details and details of their request and to say 'I'll pass your request on to our Corporate PR Team and ensure that someone gets back to you as soon as possible.' Do not feel under pressure to give any other response.

And finally...

Given the interest in our Company, it is inevitable that journalists may call you from time to time. If they do please don't panic!
Just remember to:

- Take their name, number, the publication they are writing for or the television/radio programme that they are researching for, the top line details of their request and the deadline to which they are working.

- Pass these details through to the relevant Press Office or PR Partner.

And please don't:

- Ignore a journalist's call, delay passing it on, or bury their request.

- Say 'no comment' – this will be printed! Instead, offer to have the appropriate person get back in touch, and pass on the details to the relevant Press Office immediately.

- Be bullied into talking by aggressive or persistent journalists – just pass them on to the relevant Press Office.

The way we manage our media relationships can enhance – or damage – our Company's brand and reputation which makes it essential for all employees to follow the guidelines outlined in this Media Policy.
If you have any queries at all about these guidelines or would like to learn more, please don't hesitate to contact the Corporate Press Team on 0XX XXXX XXXX.

Once public relations policy has been confirmed, activities can be planned with a level of confidence that the right people will be handling the right area of work.

Why planning is important

It is quite legitimate to ask 'Why plan?' There is always so much to do and the world of public relations requires such responsiveness, why not just get on and do it?

Apart from the vital fact of putting some order into working life, as discussed in Chapter 1, there are several other good reasons for planning:

- *It focuses effort.* It ensures the unnecessary is excluded. It makes practitioners work on the right things. It helps them to work smart instead of just working hard. It enables them to operate efficiently and effectively because they are concentrating on the things that are important, not just urgent.

- *It improves effectiveness.* By working on the right things, agreed objectives will be achieved. Time and money will be saved because effort isn't being diverted into worthy but less important tasks. Importantly it makes saying 'No' to unplanned things much easier. Or at least there can be discussion along the lines of, 'If I take on this task, which of my other prioritized jobs should I drop?' or, 'If this task is necesary, we need to employ extra support'. In other words, working to planned campaign objectives gives targets to aim for, a sense of achievement when they are reached, and effective benchmarks for measurement.

- *It encourages the long-term view.* By definition, to plan requires looking forward. This forces a longer perspective than the immediate here and now. It requires a look back to evaluate past achievements, a look around at the organization and its priorities and at the broader organizational context, and it helps produce a structured way forward to meet future as well as current needs.

- *It helps demonstrate value for money.* If there is a fight for budgets or a need to indicate a return on investment, then demonstrating past achievements and being able to present a powerful, costed, forward-looking and realistic programme gives a point from which to argue a case for money.

- *It minimizes mishaps.* Careful planning means that different scenarios will have been considered and the most appropriate selected. It means that there will be meticulous contingency planning and all the angles will have been covered. As far as possible all the potential problems and issues will have been identified and addressed.

- *It reconciles conflicts.* When putting together a programme or a campaign there are always conflicts of interests and priorities. Planning helps practitioners confront those difficulties before they arise and to work them through to resolution. Sometimes this can mean difficult discussions with and decisions about other colleagues in different departments, but better to sort that out at the planning stage than in the middle of a complex, time-constrained campaign. Furthermore, if external stakeholders and publics are involved in planning campaigns, their potential issues and conflicts can be addressed at an early stage.

- *It facilitates proactivity.* Practitioners setting their own agenda is vitally important. Of course public relations work is about reacting to media demands or responding quickly to a crisis, but it is also about deciding what is important – what actions should be taken, and when. Planning a comprehensive and cohesive campaign helps achieve this.

Planning applies to everything, whether it is to complete campaigns and programmes lasting one or several years or even longer, or to individual activities such as an event or a new publication.

Basic questions in planning

The planning process has a number of logical steps that break down into a manageable sequence. It is helpful to ask five basic questions:

What do I want to achieve?	(What are my objectives and desired end-point?)
Who do I want to talk to?	(Who are my stakeholders and publics?)
What do I want to say?	(What is the content I want to get across or the dialogue I want to initiate?)
How shall I say it?	(What mechanisms shall I use to get my content or dialogue across?)
How do I know I've got it right?	(How will I evaluate my work?)

The purpose of campaigns is to influence attitudes, opinions or behaviour in some way. It is also to listen to stakeholders and publics to see whether the organization needs to change in order to maintain support and approval.

To answer the questions posed above there are two major requirements:

- *Information.* Finding out everything there is to know about the task in hand – careful research and analysis and turning into useful intelligence.

- *Strategy.* Using that intelligence to identify the guiding principles and main thrust of the programme.

From these two requirements comes the tactical programme that can be evaluated for effectiveness.

At this stage it should be noted that the list of questions above includes questions about information-seeking and research (objectives, publics, messages and evaluation), but only one question about the actual doing.

This is about the right proportion of effort that should go into the planning process. Get the research and analysis right, and the programme should then virtually write itself. Please note, it is not being suggested that 80 per cent of the time spent on *implementing* a programme overall should be put into information-seeking. That is plainly wrong as nothing would be achieved on time. However, 80 per cent of the effort put into *devising* an appropriate programme should go into the first stages. Once having put all that work into planning, the implementation has a much greater likelihood of running smoothly and effectively.

All planning models follow a similar pattern, whether they are for the strategic management of an organization or for a public relations campaign. There are four basic steps as shown in Figure 3.2.

US academics Scott Cutlip, Allen Center and Glen Broom1 visualize the planning and management of public relations programmes as shown in Figure 3.3.

FIGURE 3.2 The strategic management process

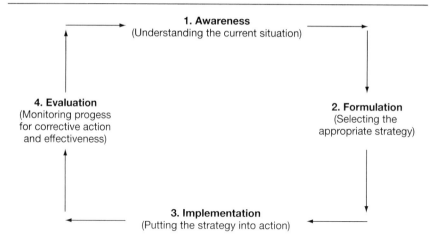

1. Awareness
(Understanding the current situation)

4. Evaluation
(Monitoring progess
for corrective action
and effectiveness)

2. Formulation
(Selecting the
appropriate strategy)

3. Implementation
(Putting the strategy into action)

FIGURE 3.3 Cutlip, Center and Broom's planning and management model

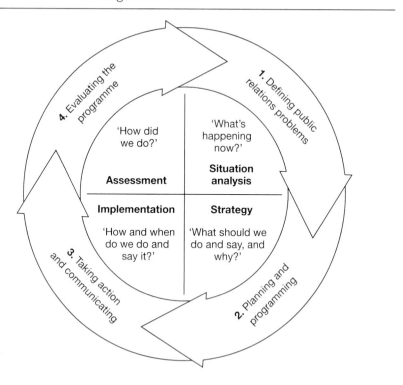

4. Evaluating the programme

1. Defining public relations problems

'How did we do?'

'What's happening now?'

Situation analysis

Assessment

Implementation

Strategy

'How and when do we do and say it?'

'What should we do and say, and why?'

3. Taking action and communicating

2. Planning and programming

The 12 stages of planning

To expand on the above, we can look at a sequence of planning steps that will ensure an effective programme (an ongoing employee relations programme or individual campaign) is put together:

- analysis;
- aims;
- objectives;
- stakeholders and publics;
- content;
- strategy;
- tactics;
- timescales;
- resources;
- monitoring;
- evaluation;
- review.

The UK Government has agreed a planning template that it now uses across all Departments called OASIS[2]. The schematic it uses is given in Figure 3.4.

FIGURE 3.4   The UK Government's communication planning template, OASIS

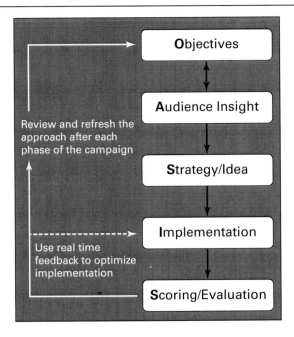

FIGURE 3.5   The planning process in logical steps

```
┌──────────┐      ┌──────────┐      ┌──────────┐
│ Analysis │◄────│  Aim(s)  │─────►│Objectives│
└──────────┘      └──────────┘      └──────────┘
                        │
                   ┌─────────────┐
                   │ Stakeholder/│
                   │   Publics   │
                   └─────────────┘
                        │
                   ┌──────────┐
                   │ Content  │
                   └──────────┘
                        │
                   ┌──────────┐
                   │ Strategy │
                   └──────────┘
                        │
                   ┌──────────┐
                   │  Tactics │
                   └──────────┘
                        │
                   ┌───────────┐
                   │ Timescales│
                   └───────────┘
                        │
                   ┌───────────┐
                   │ Resources │
                   └───────────┘
                        │
                   ┌────────────┐
                   │ Monitoring │
                   └────────────┘
                        │
                   ┌────────────┐
                   │ Evaluation │
                   └────────────┘
                        │
                   ┌──────────┐
                   │  Review  │
                   └──────────┘
```

The planning process is illustrated in Figure 3.5.

Sometimes the analysis and objectives are in reverse order. An organization might give its public relations department or consultancy a list of objectives it wants them to achieve. However, these objectives must be carefully scrutinized in order to see if they are appropriate and to ensure the objective is a public relations objective or whether it masks a problem that cannot be solved by public relations alone. For example, the organization may say it has a problem recruiting good new staff, in which case the public relations objective would be to help attract new recruits and could commission a communication campaign designed to do just that. However, after careful analysis, the public relations professionals may discover that the real problem is not recruitment, but retention of good staff, thus the objectives of the programme will have to change and an internal rather than external campaign will have to be mounted which addresses employment policies and perhaps cultural issues within the workplace. These problems will require more than communication to solve them.

The planning process looks quite straightforward when laid out as it is in Figure 3.5. However, there are often problems in practice. Sometimes there is a lack of detailed information on which to base the plan. This may be because senior managers are sometimes reluctant to share all the context or details of the situation, or it may be that a client only wants to give a consultancy limited information for reasons of confidentiality. Perhaps the campaign itself is very complex or fast moving, for example a complicated takeover bid. It could be that the plan is being executed under extreme time pressure, in a crisis even. It is often the case that the resources devoted to campaigns are less than ideal and so corners have to be cut or the campaign pruned. There also is the possibility that there are other issues that emerge part-way through the campaign that require energy and resources to be diverted from the original course of action.

However, the scheme outlined gives a solid basis for planning and the template can be followed whatever the scale of the task. If the programme is particularly large it may be necessary to split it down into a series of smaller projects that follow the same steps. Thus there might be a public affairs campaign and a community relations campaign, each with focused objectives and different publics, which feed into an overall programme with wider objectives and broader stakeholders, publics and messages. This is illustrated in Figure 3.6.

FIGURE 3.6 Splitting a multi-faceted public relations programme into manageable strands

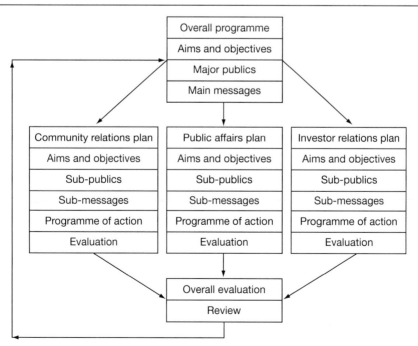

There are two things that should be noted. First, objectives need to be tied into organizational objectives (see Chapter 5). Second, as described here, the planning process could be perceived to be mechanistic and inflexible. This is not the case. The process described gives a framework for planning. In reality, time and events move on, sometimes very quickly, and public relations practitioners must be prepared to respond to changing circumstances. All the best-laid plans must be capable of being flexed or developed, and indeed scrapped altogether if necessary. Furthermore, it can well be that if an activity has become somewhat routinized, for example an AGM may have a specific format that is adhered to year on year, then the planning template can be used more as a mental checklist to ensure that all the usual areas are covered and to ask sensible questions about whether certain elements have changed or need refreshing.

When working with other colleagues, having a framework that conforms to recognized planning disciplines does provide structure and coherence. The absence of a plan can otherwise indicate the lack of a strategic approach and sometimes a lack of capability. A plan indicates professionalism and accountability. It is an indicator of good management and not only assures the organization that public relations will make a valuable and agreed contribution, but provides boundaries that offer some protection and stability for the practitioner.

It is important to stress that planning is an aid to effective working and not an end in itself. It is not meant to be a straitjacket; neither does it guarantee success. A good plan in and of itself will not make unimaginative or poorly executed programmes work. In addition, as suggested earlier, flexibility and adaptability are essential. In public relations, of all disciplines, there has to be a capability to react and adjust to the dynamic organizational and communication environment. Sometimes objectives and tactics have to change – rapidly. That is a factor of organizational life.

Plans are made to ensure that priorities are focused on and achieved. The planning process holds good, even if programmes themselves have to be adjusted. The steps given in Figure 3.2 can be followed whatever changes are made.

Linking programme planning to the bigger picture

To illustrate the links between the planning sequence described in this chapter with the wider organizational context discussed in Chapters 1 and 2, Figure 3.7 provides an example.

The best campaigns are not planned in isolation. There is a clear golden thread linking the organization in context, organizational imperatives and campaign approach and objectives. Without this link, questions have to be asked about the necessity for the campaign. Campaigns should be

FIGURE 3.7 A comprehensive planning model

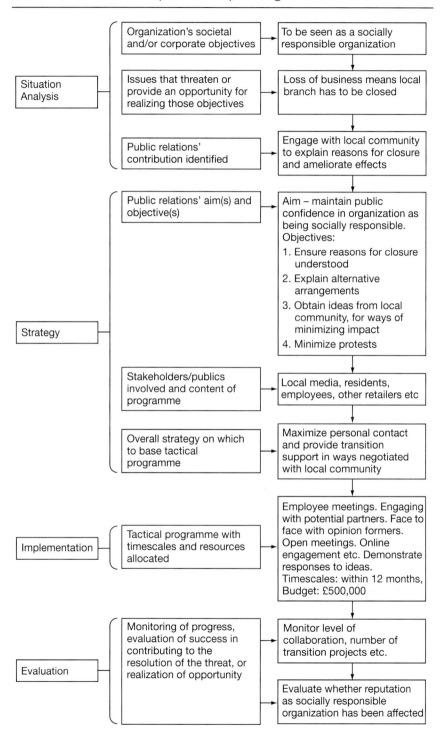

impact-oriented and have a defined purpose. Without this they may well be just activity for activity's sake.

Note

1 Cutlip, S M, Center, A H and Broom, G N (2010) *Effective Public Relations*, Prentice-Hall International, Upper Saddle River, NJ, 10th edn

2 Government Communication Service (2014) *A Guide to Campaign Planning*. Available at https://gen.civilservice.gov.uk/wp-content/uploads/2014/05/Guide-to-campaign-planning_May14_v2.pdf

04
Research and analysis

Before going into more detail about the elements of the planning process outlined in Chapter 5, it is vital to stress the importance of research. A hallmark of strategic public relations programmes is that they are founded on research and that research permeates the whole process.

Embedding research in the planning process

In recent years there has been a drive in both the public and private sectors, to have evidence-based inputs to decision making. It is true that some insightful entrepreneurs have 'hunches' that work, but even here, the evidence is that they are finely attuned to what their stakeholders' aspirations are, and that comes by being deeply informed about stakeholders themselves and what is going on in the wider world that is affecting stakeholder attitudes and behaviours. Most people do not have that intuition, and even if they have, intuition should be tested to determine whether it is based in reality.

Again, within organizations, those proposing plans are expected to present a 'business case', or a compelling argument for why their plans should be accepted. For public relations this will not just be about resources, but there will be an evidence-based case for why particular issues should be addressed, which relationships should be invested in, and what the requirements are if the organization's reputation is to be protected, maintained or enhanced. Furthermore, once the plan is implemented, it will be expected that the promised 'returns' can be evidenced as being realized. Public relations plans should therefore follow these expected disciplines. Indeed, research should be seen to inform all stages of the plan if it is to stand up to scrutiny. Combining the four major stages of planning suggested by Cutlip, Center and Broom in Figure 3.3, with the 12-step planning template given in Figure 3.4, provides a model for describing the type of research needed for any plan, as Figure 4.1 demonstrates.

FIGURE 4.1 Embedding research in the planning process

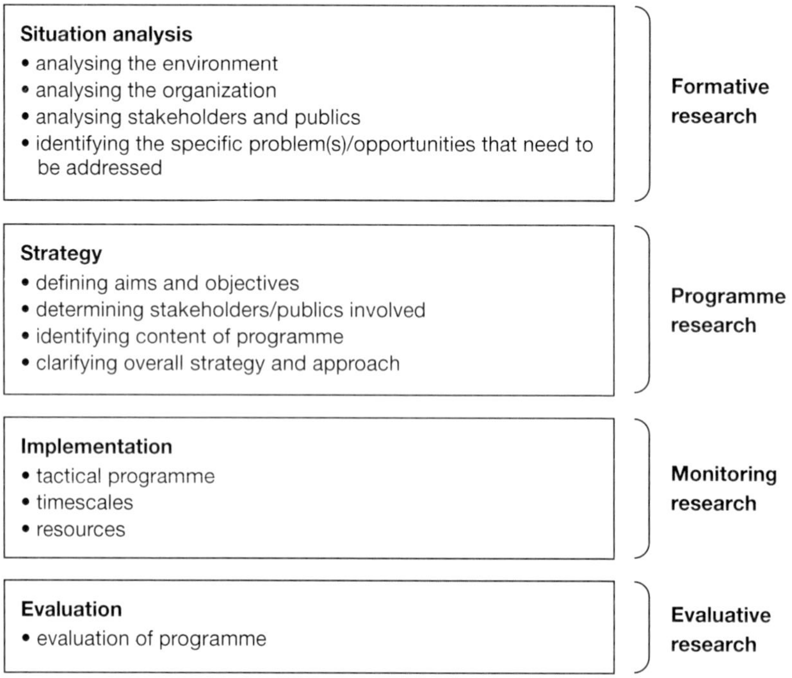

Formative research is undertaken to gather and interpret the data (intelligence) that helps to identify the real issues, problems and opportunities within a specific time and events context. A proper understanding of the situation is the essential foundation of any strategic plan. Key questions at this stage are 'what', 'why' and 'who'. What is going on, why and with whom?

Programme research aims at ensuring that the proposed plan of action is properly thought-through and informed. Key questions here are 'who', 'how' and 'what'. Who is it we need to engage with? How will we engage with them? What are our objectives and how will we measure success at the end of the programme? How are they likely to respond? What are the intended and unintended consequences of our engagement? This will involve, for example, pre-testing ideas, research on the suitability of the channels of communication to be used, pilot testing of content, testing of reactions to the proposed programme: all research-based activities.

Monitoring research is designed to check whether the programme is on-track as it is being implemented. Key questions here are 'what' and 'how'. How is the programme developing and what are the responses? How do we need to adjust the programme? Questions should also be asked about programme management: are the timescales likely to be achieved? Are resources adequate or too much? Can we make management of the programme more effective and efficient by cutting out what appear to be redundant activities? What will the impact of that be?

Evaluative research determines whether the programme achieved its declared objectives, or outcomes. Key questions are 'what' and 'why'. What did we achieve? Were our objectives realistic? If not, how should we have framed them, or were there other factors to take into account? What did we do well? What did we not do well and why? What lessons can we learn? What can we build on for the future? What were the unintended effects and why did we not identify these? What have we contributed to the organization as a result of this programme? A hard look at the evaluation techniques used also needs to be undertaken at this stage. Did they produce the information required for correct judgements about the success of the programme to be made, or would other types of evaluation have been more appropriate? Were there other unexpected outcomes that also need to be evaluated, and if so, how? For example, it may be that a consultancy was aiming a recycling campaign at people taking packed lunches to work, but an unintended and good effect is that their children also became enthusiastic about recycling, and contributed significantly to the results of the campaign.

Having outlined the role of research in the whole of the planning process, it is now appropriate to focus on the formative research element: situation analysis.

The first planning step

Analysis is the first part of the planning process. This entails research in order to identify the context and issues on which to base public relations programmes. Without getting to the core issues there will not be a credible or effective programme, or one that supports organizational objectives. Issues-based campaigns are effective, because, as was explained in Chapter 2, publics collect around issues. Furthermore, to stimulate interest, framing concerns or aspiration on issues that have direct, immediate relevance is a powerful way to gain engagement.

If a core issue is that the organization and products are regarded as old-fashioned and therefore it is losing credibility and market share, the programme will have to be about demonstrating that the organization is forward looking and that products are modern and leading edge (provided that they are), not that they are cheaper than their competitors.

There isn't room in this book to look at the whole area of research in public relations. Complete volumes have been written on the subject. However, it is possible to give an overview.

When setting up a department or a full programme from scratch (for example, following a large merger), the contextual research outlined in Chapter 2 is vital. However, if the public relations function is established and the planned programme or campaign is a continuation of an ongoing activity, then a judgement will have to be made about how much of the full analysis should be made. Nevertheless, a mental check-through of the process is necesary, even if it is just a case of confirming that a full exploration of all the steps is not necessary. It should be borne in mind, however, that it is important and illuminating to conduct this contextual research from time to time and some of it (for example, online monitoring and checking stakeholder perceptions) should be ongoing anyway.

As indicated at the beginning of this chapter, for new campaigns or programmes it is vitally important to undertake a situation analysis – formative research. This research falls under four headings: a) analysing the environment; b) the organization; c) stakeholders and publics; and d) identifying and clarifying the specific issues (positive and/or negative) that need to be addressed.

If a new department is being established or all public relations activities are being reviewed, this sequence will be the one to follow to determine which programmes and campaigns need to be undertaken. Sometimes, however, an issue is apparent or the practitioner is presented with an issue to solve. Here it is important to undertake some initial clarification of the issue, while using the first three steps to provide context, deeper understanding and a measure of the task in hand. For example, suppose a charity is experiencing a decline in the number of volunteers and public relations is asked to mount a campaign to reverse the trend. The analysis sequence and questions might be something like this:

Initial clarification:

- How long have numbers been declining?
- What are the demographics of our volunteers (eg age, gender, geography, income)? Can we draw conclusions about which groups in the volunteer community are declining?
- What are the travel patterns of our volunteers?
- What type of work is most/least popular, etc?

Analysis of the environment:

- What are the broader social changes that might affect volunteering?
- Are there pertinent economic changes?
- Are there regulatory constraints? For example, new legislation affecting those who interact with vulnerable adults? And so on.

Analysis of the organization:

- Have there been changes in the organization that might affect volunteers, eg the way we communicate, travel expenses policy, management changes, changes in the location of premises, working hours, etc.

Stakeholders and publics:

- Who is involved? Do we have a deep understanding of our volunteers and of their issues and aspirations? Why do they volunteer? Why do they think numbers are declining?
- Who else is involved? How? Why? What is the nature of their stake?
- Who else should be involved? How? Why? etc.

Having given a brief example, therefore, of the analysis that might be undertaken by this charity, it is appropriate to take a more detailed look at each of these steps in turn.

Analysing the environment

The analysis of both external and internal context is called 'environmental monitoring' in the public relations literature. It is important because wider issues in the environment often require organizations to act or react and action always has a communication dimension. Furthermore, the changing external environment, usually outside the ability of any one organization to control, often affects employees in their other lives and shapes the future. For example, the impact of information technology now has to be factored into the way organizations make their decisions and those who ignore this imperative will find themselves in difficulties.

Thus, the external environment might be described as containing the 'big picture' issues that set the organizational context. They arise from the actions of governments, and other regulatory organizations, from economic and social trends and from developments in science and technology. The macro environment is external to the organization and it is important to know about the external forces that are impacting on both the organization itself and its internal and external publics. These pressures, issues and imperatives and provide the context for the attitudes and decisions of publics need to be known by the public relations practitioner so that he or she can frame a programme with these matters taken into account. The external environment is of course both a very large and complex concept. Thus, to help frame thinking in this area, tools from the business literature can be borrowed.

PEST analysis

A commonly used and immensely valuable technique for analysing the external environment is PEST analysis. PEST divides the overall environment into four categories and covers most things that can affect an organization. The four areas are: Political, Economic, Social and Technological.

The main questions to ask when undertaking a PEST analysis are:

- What are the environmental factors that affect the organization?
- Which of these are currently most important?
- Which will be most important in the next four years?
- Are there any emerging factors that might affect us in the future? How? When?

For public relations practitioners other questions need to be asked:

- How will these factors impact on our reputation?
- How will they impact on our existing relationships? Will we need to develop new ones? With whom?
- Will these factors mean we have to change the direction or stance of our organization?

The grid on the next page gives some headings that could be considered under the four areas.

POLITICAL	ECONOMIC
Environmental legislation	Interest rates
Employment legislation	Inflation
Trade (including overseas) legislation	Money supply
Change/continuance of government	Levels of empoyment
Political alliances within and between countries	Disposable income
	Business/economic cycles
	World business/economic conditions
	Energy costs
SOCIAL	TECHNOLOGICAL
Population shifts and growth	New discoveries
Lifestyles	Pace of change
Levels of education	Investment in technology
Income/wealth distribution	Spending on research and development
Consumer purchasing trends	Obsolescence
Social attitudes and concerns	Impact of and access to new technologies
Purchasing habits	

Some experts recommend an expanded version of PEST, believing the original no longer does justice to the complex environment in which modern organizations operate. A popular acronym is EPISTLE. Here, as well as the four elements of PEST, separate consideration is given to Information, the

Legal (or regulatory) aspects and the physical (or Green) Environment. Information, as they say, is power. Thus the access to and availability of information is critical to organizations. The ubiquity and power of the internet and its ability to empower and connect stakeholders and publics makes this element of the environment even more potent. Conversely, it also means that those without the skills or access to technology will become increasingly disenfranchized. It also makes the communication challenge with these people and groups even more important to remember.

The legal environment in which organizations operate is increasingly complex and apart from national considerations there are transnational regulations such as EU law and international agreements such as those made by G20 and G8 members. Furthermore, there are quasi-legal restraints, including the 'moral' undertakings that governments make, such as the commitment to reduce greenhouse gases, in which organizations have a part to play.

The physical environment in which we live is judged to be one of *the* major concerns of the 21st century. The impact of global warming, pressures to radically alter transport systems, sustainability, waste disposal, etc, are all 'hot' topics and organizations will need to be aware of the drivers for change and the issues facing them as a result.

In addition, some analysts recommend that 'culture' merits specific consideration. Organizations need to recognize and take into account the diverse religious, ethnic and social cultures prevalent in the different countries in which they operate or trade. Also, sensitivity is required in organizational culture which in itself reflects these differences and the different norms and values that mark out the 'distinctiveness' between organizations that work even within the same sector. Virgin is very different from Singapore Airlines.

The point of doing such analyses is to identify the main drivers that will impact on the organization. These drivers will be different, depending on the country, industry and organization being analysed – there are no stock answers.

It is also important to establish the interrelationships between these drivers. World economic trends may affect political decisions and technological developments may affect social aspects of life. For example, the technological developments in games technology has transformed the lives of many young people, especially boys, and has social consequences that have prompted political action. Gaming has also opened up opportunities in education and training and the sophisticated simulations generated by the industry have spilled over into military as well as civilian applications.

Having generated a list of possible external environmental influences, the most relevant ones have to be identified, and it is imperative to be as specific as possible to the organization under consideration. So, for example, someone working in the higher education field in the Western world will have to consider the following three drivers among others. The first is to do with demographics; the proportion of people under 21 is decreasing so the higher education system will have to compete more fiercely for this 'traditional' source of students. The second is that the use of technology in teaching is transforming the traditional teacher/student relationship. Teachers are becoming facilitators of learning, helping students to navigate a whole range of alternative sources of information, often at a distance rather than in the traditional classroom. Third, the requirement for the population to constantly update their knowledge and be retrained for different careers means there will be more mature students in the higher education system requiring a different educational experience from 'traditional' learners. This will demand greater flexibility and a wider range of skills of teaching staff, and the funding of these students will be on a different basis.

The PEST analysis process can also identify how external influences can affect organizations in different ways. So a company that traditionally sources its raw materials from a number of countries is less likely to be vulnerable to a political crisis than a company that sources its raw materials from a single, cheaper supplier in a country with a less stable political regime.

Some organizations are more affected by one of the four PEST areas than others. For example, the political context is vitally important to local government, whereas economic factors may be more important to retailing organizations.

Some of the 'big picture' issues facing most organizations and with profound communication ramifications are: globalization; the impact of technology (especially the internet); a culture of consumerism and consumer attitudes; diversity; individualism; the fragmentation of the media; mass migration and demographic changes.

Issues management

PEST analyses are done at particular points in time – something that is sometimes forgotten. They should be undertaken for the current situation and for different situations that might occur in the future. So in scenario planning, the most likely key drivers are given different weightings and alternative futures are envisaged, together with associated plans of action.

By carrying out a thorough-going PEST analysis, which looks not only at current but also future developments, it is possible to identify the potentially most significant issues that might affect the organization and to track those issues. A number of organizations such as universities and Think Tanks, eg The Work Foundation, DEMOS, Royal Society of Arts, and research companies such as Ipsos MORI, undertake regular futures research. In addition, the media monitoring companies now offer an issues analysis service. They not only track what are the most prevalent issues of the day overall (for example, views on current economic performance), but also spot those issues that are emerging on to the agenda because they are beginning to attract on- and off-line comment and media coverage.

Forward-loooking companies spend a great deal of time and effort on issues management. They constantly scan the wider environment to determine which issues they should be paying particular regard to. Issues that are not identified or not taken seriously have a nasty habit of coming back as crises.

Issues management works in two ways:

- It identifies those issues over which the organization can have no control, where public opinion is inevitably going to move in a particular direction and therefore it would be foolish for the company to maintain or take up a position that flies in the face of the prevailing view. It would be very odd if an organization in the West were to promulgate the view that large families are to be encouraged when a major concern is overpopulation.

    In this situation an organization has to examine its policies and practices, and bring them into line with public opinion, or it risks losing the sympathy and support of its stakeholders.

    Organizations that are adept at issues management not only handle current issues, but also predict the likely public reaction to emerging concerns and position themselves as leaders by changing their policies and practices or adopting new ones ahead of anyone else. They can be seen to be leading the field rather than being forced to react because of prevailing opinion. They do this not just to get ahead, but because they are progressive, ethical, responsive to the likely demands of their stakeholders and sensitive to the wider responsibility they have to society.

- It detects those issues where the organization can have an input into the emerging debate and therefore shape its outcome in an ethical and beneficial way. An example of this was Rhone-Poulenc Agriculture's 10-year, independently verified experiment looking at organic versus conventional farming (ie farming with agro-chemicals), which provided scientific evidence to determine the best farming method, economically, environmentally and in food quality terms. By establishing the facts about both systems, the company was able to make a definitive contribution to the debate.

Thus issues analysis works in both directions: detecting those external factors, political, economic, social or technological that require the company to change; and identifying those areas where it might have an input into the public debate and influence the outcome.

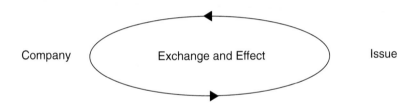

Any comprehensive long-term public relations programme must address long-term issues. Individual public relations campaigns must also identify any relevant issues which, depending on the nature of the campaign, may be long or short term. Obviously a campaign to launch an individual car care product will not require such a wide-ranging examination of the issues as a five-year programme to relaunch and reposition a charity.

A note of caution on undertaking research on the external environment. This is a difficult and complex job and can be too large for a single individual or public relations department to undertake alone. Working with other colleagues in the organization, or employing skilled external consultants to help, both with the collection of information and, very importantly, its interpretation, can be a wise investment.

In summary, it is important to know the broad organizational context, the issues affecting the organization now and into the future and to make informed decisions about how the organization will act in the face of these issues.

Having looked at the external context it is now appropriate to look at the internal context: the organization itself.

Analysing the organization

The second element of situation analysis is the investigation of the organization. Chapter 2 provides some detail on the types of question that need to be asked when looking at the organization as a whole. It goes almost without saying that any assessment of the organization must be both thorough and honest.

In addition to the areas identified in Chapter 2, there needs to be an assessment of the organization's performance. Is it good at what it does? What are its aspirations and are they realistic? Also germane is an assessment of the organization's culture – the way it does things and the 'set of conscious and unconscious beliefs, values and patterns of behaviour (including language and symbol use) that provide identity and form a framework of meaning for a group of people'.[1] Is this culture conducive to the achievements of the organization's objectives? Does it align with the expectations of the organization's external stakeholders? An analysis of this will reveal the extent of the internal communications task, although clearly it will also identify issues that may be to do with the organization's structure, processes and practices, which also need to be resolved and which are not amenable to communication solutions alone.

Following this kind of analysis, the public relations planner can begin again to categorize the analysis in a structured way, similar to the way that EPISTLE organizes thinking for external analysis purposes.

One way to approach this is to divide these considerations by undertaking a SWOT analysis. The first two elements, Strengths and Weaknesses, can be seen as internally driven and particular to the organization. The other two, Opportunities and Threats, are normally external and will have been largely identified through the PEST analysis. The four elements can be seen as mirror segments in a quadrant. A brief example follows.

STRENGTHS	WEAKNESSES
Financially strong	Conservative in investment
Innovative	Limited product line
Good leadership	Traditional and hierarchical
Good reputation	Complacent
Loyal workforce	Inflexible working patterns
OPPORTUNITIES	THREATS
Cheap supplies from Eastern Europe	Reputational issues arising from potential accusations of exploitation
Expand into China	Danger of being overstretched
Acquire competitors	To be taken over by a larger conglomerate
Diversify product line	New and aggressive competitors

It is sometimes useful to apply SWOT analysis to categories of activity, for example corporate, product, internal and so on.

Again, the purpose of the SWOT analysis is to identify and then prioritize the major issues that face the organization in order to design public relations programmes that will address these issues. By definition, the analysis will identify those issues that have strategic importance since they isolate those areas that have corporate significance for the organization. By addressing those areas, the public relations function will be able to demonstrate its strategic contribution to organizational sustainability.

A legitimate question might be why should the public relations person be involved in all this external and internal research, after all their business is relationship building through communication? It is precisely because this is their business, that practitioners need to be alert to the drivers affecting an organization – probably as much if not more than anyone else in the organization. The purpose of having a public relations function is to help an organization meet its objectives. If a public relations professional is not aware of the drivers that frame company objectives, how can he or she fulfil the boundary-spanning communication role described earlier (see Chapter 1)?

Taking the above analysis into consideration we can see from the SWOT example that the public relations programme will have a number of jobs to do in support of corporate objectives. For example, to mount a marketing communications campaign if the product line is to be expanded. An internal communications programme will be needed to assist in managing change.

An international corporate and government relations campaign will be required to support expansion into China, and a financial relations programme will certainly be needed to preserve a strong reputation, raise capital to fund expansion and combat takeover possibilities.

Having determined from an organizational point of view what the key issues are and the organization's stance on them, it is then the public relations professional's job to create a public relations programme with objectives that address those issues.

Analysing the stakeholder

The third element of situation analysis is to investigate the current state of stakeholder and publics' attitudes, opinions and behaviours towards the organization.

Smith[2] calls this 'analysing public perception' and says there are two elements to this:

> **Visibility:** that is the extent to which the organization is known.
>   Do people know about it? What do they know and is this accurate?

> **Reputation:** how do people regard the organization? Their perceptions will be based on 'the verbal, visual and behavioural messages, both planned and unplanned, that come from an organization'.

If an organization has good visibility and a strong reputation, it will be easier to build on this. If it does not, then the reverse is true.

Lerbinger[3] calls the type of research that defines stakeholders and publics and finds out how they perceive an organization before, during and after a campaign 'public relations audits'. If the view that stakeholders have of an organization differs from the reality, there is an issue that needs to be addressed. The problem may be lack of information, or wrong information, that can be countered quite easily. The problem might be more profound or complex, for example, the organization might have a reputation for being a bad employer because it made 50 per cent of its workforce redundant to survive several years before and the legacy of how badly that was done lingers on.

Then the task is to discover if a real communication problem exists, what the actual problem is, with whom (which stakeholders), what needs to be communicated, how it should be communicated and whether or not there has been effective communication in the past. Lerbinger calls the kind of research that evaluates whether or not content has got through to the targeted publics 'communications audits'. 'Social audits' research the consequences of an organization's actions on its publics and monitor corrective actions; this kind of research may need to be done before a campaign starts, particularly if the campaign is required as a result of organizational action that has had an adverse effect, as is often the case in crises. Once again, detailed research into stakeholders and publics will reveal any issues that need to be addressed.

This detailed investigation into internal and external environments and of stakeholders and publics is vital to obtain a complete understanding of the issues that need to be addressed. Issues then need to be drawn together, examined to see where there are linkages, and prioritized according to the extent to which they either enable or block the organization achieving its objectives now or into the future. These issues then form the *raison d'être* of specific public relations programmes. Figure 4.2 shows the process and an example of how these issues can be linked.

FIGURE 4.2   Prioritizing and linking issues

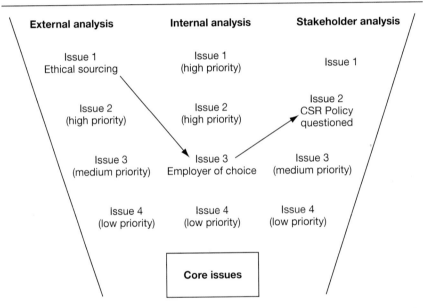

In this example the organization understands that there are external societal pressures which increasingly require that companies should ensure that they source their raw materials ethically – wood from sustainable forests, cloth produced by companies that do not employ child labour, etc. They also identify that although quite well respected as an employer, they are not the employer of choice by graduates. Their stakeholder analysis also reveals that there are questions about their corporate responsibility commitments, possibly because they have had suspect environmental policies in the past. It is clear that there are linkages between these issues and that they should have a high priority. An analysis undertaken from a public relations perspective reveals connections which then should be drawn to the attention of senior management. If they address the area of sustainable sourcing, which could then make them both an employer of choice and address some of their stakeholder concerns on their corporate social responsibility (CSR) policies. However, without this detailed analysis they would not have a rounded picture of the issue, neither would they understand the extent to which it affects the reputation and potential relationships of the organization, or of the potential benefits they would achieve by tackling it.

Although research around the topic in hand needs to be rigorous and objective, it need not necessarily be expensive – it depends on the task. If what is needed is to find out the views of the local community, it is a simple matter to walk the streets and ask, to go to the local cafes, to ask local community groups (actual and virtual) and to speak to local community leaders. This might be all that is required. If, however, the task is to launch a major campaign aimed at changing the country's eating habits, much more detailed and sophisticated research will be required.

The principles behind formative research are the same whether they are for major, strategic, long-term programmes or short campaigns. Research helps to establish what the real issues are and the nature and size of the public relations task.

Who should undertake the research?

Given that whole programmes or campaigns are based on research, it is important that it is carried out properly. It is not good enough to instruct the most junior member of the public relations team to contact a few customers to find out what they think of the existing corporate identity. Those involved in serious research must understand what is involved. Getting biased or incomplete answers will lead to ill-founded programmes. Investment is needed to become competent at collecting basic information and interpreting it accurately and fully, but this need not cost a fortune. There are several excellent short courses and textbooks on conducting research.

Obviously, an established research consultancy or trained in-house people will know all about undertaking valid research, which involves, for example, selecting a sample that genuinely reflects the universe being studied.

Sometimes it is entirely legitimate to do a 'quick and dirty' study of, for example, reactions of personal finance journalists to a new pension plan, as long as the limitations of that study are recognized and it is not used as anything other than a fairly superficial survey of a very particular group of people.

The benefits of using trained in-house researchers are that they know the business and will need little briefing except for the specifics of the research problem. On the downside, they may be seen to be less objective than external researchers.

External researchers can offer skills in specialized research areas, including communication. They may be perceived to be more objective, but are often (although not necessarily) more expensive because they build in learning time, overheads, profits and so on.

Of course, it is perfectly possible to mix the two: internal administration and collection of results, with professional advice on questionnaire design, and analysis of results.

It is worth bearing in mind that interpretation of results is critically important and if savings have to be made, it is advisable not to make them here.

Research techniques

Quantitative, qualitative, mixed and tracking research

There are several different types of research. Quantitative research collects data that is then expressed statistically giving results in numbers or quantities. Qualitative research investigates non-quantifiable variables such as opinions, reactions and attitudes. Thus, measuring how many people have blue, green or brown eyes or who will vote for a particular party at a general election would require quantitative research; finding out what views an individual has on the policies of the major political parties is a qualitative research task.

Many situations require a mixture of qualitative and quantitative methods. The public relations planner needs to know how many people are involved, what their attitude or behaviour is, and why. Segmentation is used to group people with similar characteristics together. This reveals how many are in the group and what their key attitudinal and behavioural drivers are.

Continuous or tracking research is where the same group of people or people of the same profile are asked the same questions at regular intervals. Building societies regularly survey groups of people on a one-off basis, but with the same characteristics, to find out what awareness of the various societies is. Advertising and public relations research companies track stakeholder awareness of communication: what they recall and how they interpret it etc. Satisfaction surveys track whether or not customers are happy with the performance of a company, product or service over time.

The large research companies frequently conduct Omnibus surveys to discover all kinds of things, from views on the economy to opinions on executive pay. Surveys are undertaken on just about anything from food preferences to what people thought of various countries' performance in the last football World Cup.

Continuous or tracking surveys are particularly helpful when trying to measure something like consumer trends or changes in attitude over time.

One-off surveys are useful if factual information on which to establish a campaign is needed. For example, what proportion of the population buys watches and who they are will need to be known before a new kind of watch is launched.

Primary and secondary research

Information can be collected in two ways: via primary or secondary research. Secondary research is often called desk research and entails collecting information from already published sources. There is an enormous amount of published data that can be accessed. The trick is knowing where to find it. Public and university libraries have knowledgeable librarians able to point to material on companies and industry sectors, social trends and so on and they are connected to international information databases which are expensive for individuals to acquire. They also have newspapers and magazines archived on virtual and hard copy databases, as do trade libraries run by professional bodies such as the Law Society. Government departments hold statistics on subjects relevant to them and the National Statistics Office in the UK holds an enormous bank of information. Company reports and corporate and product information are available from most organizations. The internet also provides huge access to information from individuals, aggregators and organizations worldwide and the use of various search engines to identify and aggregate information is an invaluable resource. Furthermore, the potential that big data offers is enormous, especially with its predictive capabilities.

Several research companies are capitalizing on the almost insatiable appetite for information. The large research companies such as Mintel, Ipsos MORI and Gallup conduct their own surveys on various topics, and listings are available online so that their reports can be bought very easily, either as hard copy or electronically. Of course desk research takes time and hiring the services of a professional researcher who knows where and how to look could make the task much easier if time means money. However, research that has already been conducted is often a great deal cheaper than doing the work from scratch. A search and a small fee to a research organization to find out what's available could save a great deal of money.

The benefits of secondary research are that it is available quickly, it is usually more comprehensive and cheaper than doing it personally and it provides a basis on which to conduct further specific research if necessary. Some of the problems with secondary sources are that the quality is sometimes suspect, the quantity can be overwhelming and integrating data from different sources can be difficult. It is also not tailored to particular requirements.

Primary research is finding out the information at first hand by going directly to the source. There are various empirical techniques for obtaining primary data, some of which are listed below.

Self-completion questionnaires

These are a relatively cheap way to contact a large number of people over a geographically widespread area (or even a small number of people in a geographically tight area). They are excellent for obtaining information from people who are difficult to contact (maybe they are shift workers) and they allow time for people to consider their answers carefully before responding. It is useful to include an incentive (for example, free entry to a prize draw) to encourage a good response. Self-completion questionnaires need to be clear, simple and as short as possible. They can be distributed and collected by post, in person or via another medium such as the internet or a magazine, and are usually completed by the respondent without supervision. If a questionnaire is more complex it can be issued to groups, with a trained researcher supervising the session or answering questions that may arise.

Questionnaires are often used to obtain a mass of quantitative data, but can also be used for qualitative material. Good questionnaires that are unbiased, unambiguous and which collect all the information that is required are very difficult to design. Professional help must often be sought from trained researchers.

One-to-one depth interviews

This survey technique is excellent for collecting qualitative data. Interviews are obviously time consuming for the researcher and the interviewee.

Omnibus surveys and syndicated studies

Omnibus surveys may be run by one of the larger research organizations. They often undertake regular surveys on specific groups such as teenagers and industry sectors like motoring, and on particular products such as computer games. A few questions can be added to the survey and they charge per question. Results from these interviews can usually be turned around very quickly, often within a few days.

There are also syndicated studies where the results are available to those who subscribe to the service. The survey mentioned earlier where building societies track awareness is a syndicated study with the participating building societies obtaining the results for a fee. These omnibus or syndicated studies are more suited to quantitative questions, but it is possible to ask a few, very well crafted qualitative questions that will require explicit interpretation.

Although relatively expensive, the quality and quantity of information that can be gathered from tailor-made one-to-one interviews can be superb. Again it is important to stress that interviewing is a particular skill and training is required to get the best from the opportunity. Interviews can be structured so that specific information is collected, unstructured where the questions are developed as a result of the answers given, or somewhere in between – semi-structured.

Interviewing allows the researcher to explore views and opinions in depth, and the reasons why those views are held. When trying to get to the heart of difficult issues it is an excellent technique to use. Computer packages are now available to analyse text, picking out key words and phrases, and facilitate quantitative as well as qualitative analysis of interview data.

Telephone interviews

This technique is particularly suitable for collecting structured information. They are a kind of halfway house between face-to-face interviews and questionnaires. They don't allow as much probing as the face-to-face interview or the reflection of the questionnaire, but they are a relatively speedy way to collect information from a broad or narrow section of respondents. The Computer Aided Telephone Interview (CATI) system allows researchers to input answers to questions very quickly and instant analysis is possible. CATI systems also provide call management facilities such as organizing calls, redialling engaged numbers and keeping statistics of failed contacts. A danger of this technique is that many people resent the intrusion of telephone research, particularly when at home, and the data gathered can be biased with the respondent giving answers to satisfy the researcher or in an unconsidered way to get the researcher 'off the phone'.

Focus groups

Focus groups are discussion groups comprising carefully selected individuals (maybe with the same profile, for example 20- to 25-year-old Asian women, married with children, all born in the UK and living in Cardiff; or maybe of the same age, gender and location, but with very different backgrounds). Running a successful focus group is highly skilled and requires a competent co-ordinator to guide discussion and to ensure all the relevant questions are asked. The idea behind a focus group is that the responses from the participants prompt and develop responses from other participants. Properly done, focus groups can obtain far more information than one-to-one interviews. There are difficulties associated with this technique: selection of participants, length of time needed, facilities required (room, recording equipment), expense (travel costs, refreshments), danger of bias, particularly if there is a participant who is persuasive of others, but the depth of insight that can be acquired is a rich reward.

Online

As well as gathering information from various sources on the internet, it is very easy to undertake one-to-one or group research. For example, visitors to a website can be asked to fill in a short questionnaire or to make comments on particular subjects. Bulletin boards or chat rooms can be hosted on a site. A virtual campaign could drive traffic to a particular site or forum for discussion and comment. Twitter is also a good source for instant and 'quick and dirty' research that may provide prompts for more extensive work that needs to be undertaken, but it should never be regarded as proper, scientific evidence since it is a self-selecting community and could not be replicated.

The use of e-mail, Facebook, Skype and so on means that contacting and obtaining the views of specific groups of people, for example employees or suppliers, is simple and fast. Of course, the temptation to go back to these sources repeatedly (to the point of annoyance), because it is so easy, must be resisted. On the other hand, the opportunity to set up a genuine and ongoing dialogue with stakeholders in which research is an integral part is something that it would be irresponsible to miss. The use of simple survey tools such as Survey Monkey in association with rapid access to groups means that obtaining and analysing data is now infinitely simpler than in the recent past.

Observation

Watching what people do is very enlightening. People can be asked what they do and they can describe it more or less accurately. However, seeing them in context reveals all those things that even they are not aware of, for example, the influence of others, the way in which they work or complete a task, what they find hard or easy to accomplish. Observation can be undertaken over a long or short period of time. For example, anthropologists may live with and observe groups for extended periods to understand their way of life and cultures. Such a level of detail can be invaluable but may be unnecessary. On the other hand, observing just a few meetings of the CEO with staff will provide enough data to advise him or her on their presentation techniques, and will be far more informative than extended interviews with them and their staff.

Observation can either be non-participant – that is, no part is taken by the researcher, or participant – that is, the researcher will intervene to a greater or lesser extent. For example, they may just ask questions to clarify points, or they may become a fully operational member of the activity or team. Mystery shoppers play the part of a 'proper' consumer, although they may be briefed to enact a particular role, for example, a difficult customer, or one with a specific disability, to test the responses of the objects of the research. In these kinds of cases, careful thought has to be given to the ethics of research: indeed, the ethical conduct of research must be considered in any research programme.

The benefit of primary research is that it can be tailored to the public relations researcher's specific requirements. It can delve into attitudes, opinions and behaviours and answer the question 'why' – a key to understanding communication issues, and essential to decisions about how the researcher would like people to respond, either attitudinally or behaviourally. It can fill gaps left by secondary research and it can be used to test initial reactions to ideas and proposals. Its disadvantages are that it is usually more expensive than secondary research, often time-consuming, and it is easy to miss vital questions, which leaves the research incomplete. Problems also arise if the primary research indicates conflicting evidence from secondary research – who has the right answer?

Informal research

Apart from formal research techniques, there are all kinds of informal ways of obtaining information about issues and organizations. Chance encounters and informal discussions with the whole range of publics associated with an organization such as competitors, specialist journalists, neighbours and suppliers can be very enlightening. Getting a feel for the organization by attending its annual general meeting or social events helps. A trap is to talk to the obvious people: cleaners, secretaries and security people are very well connected and have a 'sense' for the organization, and are often more honest and realistic than senior people with a vested interest. Regular reading of the press, online searches, listening to and watching general interest and current affairs programmes, even discussions with friends and colleagues in social situations, help to build an all-embracing overview of the context and the specifics of any particular situation, and help make connections between issues and organizations that might not be available via formal research.

Informal, or 'quick and dirty' research, has its value. A very successful campaign to save a London hospital was based on the public relations executive walking the streets surrounding the hospital asking people about it and talking to people in the pub. Not a procedure recommended as exemplary, but time was pressing and it provided essential information about the strength of local feeling from a broad spectrum of people.

Media research

It is important not only to know the organization and the relevant issues, but to investigate the channels of communication too. The written and broadcast media provide information on readership profiles, circulation, effectiveness of advertising, reaction to copy and so on. Organizations such as Technorati and Google do the same for the internet. Other media such as direct mail, advertising, posters and sponsorship can also be analysed. The various media have their own trade bodies that can provide detailed information on their use and effectiveness, and this should be carefully considered when deciding which channels should be used for particular publics.

Communication audit

Apart from researching the issues affecting an organization or the facts surrounding a particular campaign, it is vitally important for the public relations professional to examine in detail the communication process itself. This is done via a communication audit. In brief, a communication audit identifies those publics vital to an organization's success. It investigates the scope of communication to determine whether all existing or potential publics are being covered. It examines their current attitudes and behaviours to assess whether or not work is required to confirm or change them and what other engagement is required. It appraises critically the nature and quality of the communication between the organization and its publics, looking carefully at the content to see if it is what is required, its frequency and the techniques that are used to transmit it, as well as the effectiveness of the communication. It identifies communication gaps and unexploited opportunities, as well as the information needs of all the key publics. It also looks ahead by examining future information requirements and new methods of communication that should be used. An audit also pinpoints the resources and skills needed to run a successful programme or campaign, and whether or not these are available to an organization.

To undertake an effective audit requires extensive research of the organization's context, within an organization, with the whole range of personnel responsible for communication, and with the stakeholders and publics of the organization to investigate the opinions of those who are in contact with it.

Interpreting the findings

Collecting data can be a complex task but what should be done with it once it has been obtained? At the risk of becoming repetitive, it is important to stress that analysing and interpreting data is a highly skilled job. All too often very simple analysis is done on very rich data. Wrong and obvious conclusions are drawn from statistics when analysed by the statistically illiterate. It could be that 30 per cent of a sample said no to questions, 45 per cent said yes, but 25 per cent said maybe. It is true that most people said yes, but the majority said either no or maybe and they may be more inclined to no rather than yes. There is no clear confirmation of a positive answer. It could well be that enlightenment will come from using information from other parts of the survey, but more detailed investigation may be required. The golden rule is: once having paid good money for research ensure full, interpretation and professional help may be required for that.

Investment in research pays – two cases in point

The point of doing research is to enable public relations programmes to be undertaken more effectively. Identifying what the real issues are and the best way to go about executing a programme is, of course, vital to its success.

Research sometimes throws up the unexpected and drives practitioners to conduct programmes in a way that might not have been anticipated. This is good news because if programmes are conducted on hunches, rather than the way that research dictates, the end result is wasted time, effort and money, and not achieving or at best only partially achieving your objectives. An example of how research guided a campaign is given below.

CASE STUDY   Love Food, Hate Waste, a research-based campaign by WRAP (Waste and Resources Action Programme)

This case illustrates how rigorous research has underpinned each step of an unfolding campaign aimed at preventing food waste. It also shows that having a solid research basis against which to benchmark progress, helps in the ongoing monitoring and evaluation (see Chapter 9 for more on this).

Background

Preventing food waste has been a key priority for WRAP and for the Government of the UK for many years and since 2007 WRAP has run a consumer facing campaign called Love Food, Hate Waste (LFHW). From the beginning the campaign used research to make the main argument against food waste.

In 2009 WRAP's *Household Food and Drink Waste in the UK* report established that in 2007, 8.3 million tonnes of food waste was generated in UK homes every year and 5.3 million tonnes could have been consumed, ie was avoidable. Without action, the figure was set to increase.

Some of the key facts were:

- £3 billion is wasted on good food that is thrown away: that is £430 per person every year.

- 5.1 million potatoes, 4.4 million apples, 2.8 million tomatoes, 1.6 million bananas and 1.2 million oranges – all perfectly wholesome, are thrown away every year.

- One in three bags of food purchased ends up being thrown away.

Astoundingly consumers were unaware of food waste as an economic issue, and 90% of them claimed not to waste food.

The factors associated with food waste and our relationship with food is complex, as the research showed (see Figure 4.3). A simple, glib approach just telling people to cut down on waste would not be at all appropriate. To add complexity, this type of campaign had not been undertaken before and responses to it were very difficult to predict. How would consumers react? Would there be opposition from consumer groups and food producers? Would it be seen as another example of the 'nanny state' preaching to the public? Again, a deep understanding of consumers' relationship to food gained through the research was critical to getting the content and the tone of the campaign right. Positively, the research also found that once alerted to the problem, consumers were keen to do something about it.

FIGURE 4.3   The complex relationship with food

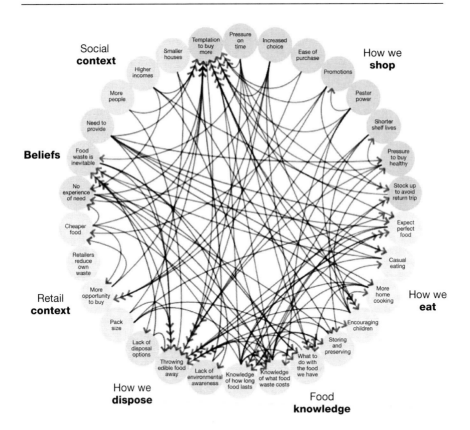

The big task was to work with consumers, owners of food brands and retailers to connect them with the issue of food waste and to stop it reaching landfill sites. In response to the task, Trimedia (now Grayling) devised Love Food, Hate Waste (LFHW), the world's first campaign encouraging consumers to reduce food waste in the home.

Objectives

In 2007, the client (WRAP) had four objectives and these remain the same up to the present day:

- raise awareness of food waste and the LFHW campaign;

- encourage consumers to review their own attitudes and behaviour;

- reduce the amount of food going to landfill sites by 100,000 tonnes, by summer 2008;

- provide a solution to the problem and a means to access these solutions.

Target audience

All consumers, but especially families and 'foodies'.

Planning

Some of the complex and potentially conflicting issues related to waste were also carefully thought through. For example, the Government is encouraging people to eat five portions of fresh fruit and vegetables a day and ironically it is vegetables and fruit that are wasted most. Care had to be taken not to blame families for wanting to eat healthily and much of the advice and practical guidance therefore focused on storage and use rather on discouraging good eating habits. There were also ready and controversial discussion points on supermarket practices, such as 'buy one, get one free' offers which can encourage people to purchase more than they need, but undoubtedly also encourage people to eat more vegetables.

Implementation

The key tactics employed were:

Stage 1: Pre-launch

Based on research into food wastage, a number of editorial ideas were developed for the key media, highlighting the 'shocking facts' about waste. This was complemented by a range of practical ways to reduce waste so that consumers could take action.

Solutions that were proposed included:

- keeping fruit in the fridge

- using up leftovers

- better portion control

- home composting

Stage 2: Recruiting supporters

Recognized food industry experts were also identified through research and recruited to the campaign, including the ex cookery editor of *Good Housekeeping* magazine, who helped with recipes and in offering practical solutions to the problems of food waste. The majority of the UK's leading chefs and food writers gave their support and a Love Food champion's community project was initiated with the Women's Institute, who provided practical advice and feedback from local communities.

Stage 3: The launch of LFHW

Launch day was staged at London Borough Market, a venue synonymous with the campaign's values and attended by thirty journalists, crews and key stakeholders. Celebrity chefs acted as campaign advocates to provide mainstream and 'foodie' appeal. Cook offs and web stations showing a information-packed and advice-filled website, provided the interactive elements and a show reel of chefs and celebrities who all gave their time for free was played. This not only brought the practical advice to life, but brought emotional depth and personal connections to the issue.

Stage 4: Maintaining momentum

After the launch it was imperative to ensure the campaign stayed in the front of consumer's minds. To help sustain and embed the campaign, the following happened:

- BBC Good Food Show regional radio show;

- a Christmas to February campaign focusing on the 230,000 tonnes of festive food waste, worth some £275 million, providing new stories, tips on leftovers and advice on making meals go further;

- an April burst, focusing on fruit and vegetable waste using the banner 'an apple a day gets thrown away', to highlight the million apples that are discarded daily;

- in May, launching the research based Food We Waste report to media and stakeholders which for the first time in the UK identified how much food in their various categories we waste – from whole chickens and yoghurts, to cans of lager and chocolate gateaux.

Evaluation

The results of the initial campaign demonstrated significant success. By the end of 2008 the following had been achieved:

- 555 pieces of coverage (Objective 1);

- 100% penetration of key media, with 99% of all print coverage favourable and 98% including at least one core message (Objective 1);

- 43 leading chefs, foodies, journalists and celebrities have actively contributed to the campaign, free of charge (Objective 1);

- 1.45 million households committed to throwing away less food (Objective 2);

- reduction of 500,000 of carbon dioxide equivalents (Objective 2) and

- translates into savings for consumers of almost £240 million (Objective 2);

- reduction of food waste going to landfill of some 100,000 tonnes (Objective 3);

- 154,000 people visited and contributed to the LFHW website (Objective 4);

- 54% of all print coverage included practical advice (Objective 4).

By November 2011, WRAP was able to announce a reduction in total household food and drink waste of 1.1 million tonnes and avoidable food and drink waste had decreased by 950,000 tonnes, although not everything could be put down to the campaign because at that time increasing food prices and difficult economic conditions also played a part.

In 2012 the research results showed that avoidable household food waste has been cut by an impressive 21% since 2007, saving UK consumers almost £13 billion over five years. However, despite this significant drive to reduce food waste, UK households were still throwing away 4.2 million tonnes of avoidable household food and drink waste annually; the equivalent of six meals every week for the average UK household.

Developing the campaign

As well as its ongoing national campaigns (see www.lovefoodhatewaste.com for details of the current campaigns), WRAP has also mounted some more specific and targeted campaigns. In 2012/13 Greater London Authority and WRAP worked in partnership to deliver the Recycle for London (RfL) programme, a cross-London initiative supported by the London boroughs.

Objectives, target audience and message

The objectives remain broadly the same for the ongoing campaign:

- raise awareness of food waste;

- encourage consumers to review their own attitudes and behaviour;

- reduce the amount of food going to landfill sites;

- provide a solution to the problem and a means to access these solutions.

Based on national research, the core message of the London LFHW campaign, aimed again at all consumers was 'You could save up to £50 per month by throwing away less food'.

Implementation

Activities during the campaign period included:

- **Radio advertising** – a 30 second radio advert ran on 8 London radio stations for 2 weeks reaching 60% of Londoners aged 25–44 (2.6 million people), who each heard the advert an average of 7 times.

- **Digital adverts** – including banner adverts on a range of websites, and adverts linked to search terms on Google which were linked to lovefoodhatewaste.com to direct people to the website.

- **London Underground advertising** – LFHW adverts ran on 465 poster sites across the London Underground networks for one month. The posters reached 23% of Londoners (1.85 million people) who each had an average of 32 opportunities to see the posters.

- **One quarter-page advert was placed in the _Metro_ newspaper reaching** an estimated 17% of Londoners (1.42 million people).

- **Digital adverts** appeared on the Transport for London online Journey Planner for one month.

- **Social media** – RfL actively used social media channels, such as Facebook and Twitter, to engage directly with London residents about LFHW. This included promoting key messages in line with national campaign activity, and promoting London events. Between October 2012 and March 2013 there were a total of 1,122 updates via RfL social media. The number of people reached through Facebook during this period was 12,483 and 648 tweets generated 1.39 million impressions and had a reach of 555,648.

- **Lovefoodhatewaste.com** – the national website included a section dedicated to the London campaign, which was promoted as a banner on the home page. There were 89,199 visits to the LFHW website from Londoners (based on IP address locations) of which 73% were new visitors to the site.

- **Press releases** – were used to support each of the key bursts of activity. Unfortunately there was little pick up in the printed media, although ITV news covered the London LFHW campaign twice.

- **Events** – RfL ran events to raise awareness of the LFHW campaign including the 'Food Waste Challenge', working with Londoners to challenge them to reduce the food that they throw away. Other events included the Alternative Valentines Banquet and the 'Feaster' banquet in partnership with Food Cycle which involved meals being made from surplus food. These events reached 226 people including direct engagement with 52 Londoners through the food waste challenge, 80 people attended the Valentines Banquet and 90 people attended the Feaster event. The reach of the food waste challenges was extended to 131,402 people through social media (#FoodWasteChallenge).

- **Food Waste Champions** – London-wide recruitment and training of 2,397 'Food Waste Champions' to cascade messages to local communities about how to reduce the amount of food thrown away and save money. Once trained, Food Waste Champions are encouraged as a minimum to pass messages on to friends and family and to identify opportunities for reaching wider audiences. Estimates are that Food Waste Champions cascaded the messages to a further 39,795 Londoners.

- **Internal communications** – a range of internal communications were delivered within the Greater London Authority (GLA) and public organizations including the London Fire Brigade and the Metropolitan Police. Within the GLA, 750 employees received an internal newsletter.

In addition to the London-wide activity, one focused campaign was in the six boroughs of the West London Waste Authority area (WLWA). Activity here focused on raising awareness of the issue locally and community engagement to influence relevant behaviours. Activities were planned to amplify the impact of the national and London-wide activities and comprised:

- **Local radio adverts** – radio adverts placed on LBC Radio, followed by adverts on Radio Jackie, Hayes FM and Sunrise Radio in March 2013. The minimum reach of these is estimated to be 1.1 million people.

- **Let's Get Cooking Clubs** – 28 Let's Get Cooking Clubs were set up across West London, engaging 800 people. The purpose of the Clubs is to provide practical cookery skills and information to enable people to make the most of the food that they buy.

- **Internal communications** – targeting staff within the boroughs of West London through internal magazines and the intranet at key points throughout the year and targeted 9,000 staff members.

- **Social media** – WLWA delivered an ongoing programme of social media with residents about LFHW; 99 LFHW related tweets were put out by WLWA.

- **Local online advertising** – LFHW digital adverts included the websites for local news, linked to the LFHW website to direct people to the national campaign. *Harrow Times* and *Richmond and Twickenham Times* website gave 113,634 page impressions with 609 people clicking on the link and following through to lovefoodhatewaste.com.

- **Website** – nine articles were published on the WLWA website relating to LFHW with a direct link to the national website.

- **Press adverts and advertorials** in the local press/borough magazines – half page adverts were placed in four of the borough magazines, with half page adverts placed in the local press for the other two boroughs (for which borough magazines were not available). The local newspaper and borough magazines would have reached 689,445 people.

- **Vehicle livery** – LFHW vehicle livery on eight refuse vehicles in the London Borough of Harrow.

- **Posters** – posters were displayed in local shops and community noticeboards to promote key messages.

- **Bus adverts** – 65 bus-back adverts were displayed for a period of 8 weeks, including 53 adverts which remained for 14 weeks.

- **Outdoor adverts** – 24 six-sheet adverts were placed across the six boroughs for a period of two weeks, and ten four-sheet adverts were placed for four weeks.

- **European Week of Waste Reduction (EWWR)** – there was a focus on food waste prevention during European Week of Waste Reduction (November 2012), through the local zero waste challenge run by WLWA. This challenged local residents to reduce their waste in general and food waste in particular in a number of different ways.

- **Roadshows/community engagement activity** – WLWA delivered 50 roadshows and community talks, directly engaging 900 residents, providing information to residents primarily about food waste prevention but also included how to recycle their food waste and distributing 2,245 engagement resources. These events were primarily focused on waste prevention.

- **PR** – regular press releases to support local and London-wide activity. Unfortunately, as with the London-wide PR there was little media coverage.

Evaluation

The results in the West London boroughs were carefully evaluated by two independent research companies, who looked at two specific measures:

- measurement of changes in the amount of food waste generated by West London households using waste compositional analysis (with informed consent of the participating households); and

- investigation into changes in attitudes, awareness and behaviour relating to household food waste using a face-to-face quantitative survey (household interviews).

The research team surveyed the same households before and after the campaign enabling the results to be linked. The results showed that:

- avoidable food waste for those households surveyed decreased by 14% and

- unavoidable food waste reduced by a staggering 24%. The latter figure was affected by the fact that more people were using their leftovers, less food was being prepared from scratch (partly because more leftovers were being used and because there were some changes in cooking practices, for example less food being prepared at home);

- 14% of households stating that they had seen the campaign and food-waste messaging and were doing something different as a result;

- if all the changes could be attributed to the campaign alone, the reduction in avoidable food waste in West London is equivalent to 5,250 tonnes per annum;

- purchasing that amount of wasted food would have cost West Londoners £14 million and

- to dispose of it would have cost West London boroughs £559,000.

Building on success

Following the success of the West London campaign, WRAP is rolling out 10 UK specific food waste prevention campaigns to cover the period up to 2016. WRAP's consumer food waste strategy calls for a major combined effort with retailers, brands, governments and consumers to work together towards the common goal of halving avoidable food waste by 2025 compared to when LFHW started in 2007. They will be working with a range of organizations to deliver this programme including local authorities, community groups, charities, the public sector, local businesses, and the grocery industry. The city specific work will run in parallel with a wider awareness campaign across the UK. This intends to overcome the key barrier that many people still do not believe that they waste food, and if they do, do not recognize the financial or environmental value associated with it.

WRAP's core activities will be:

- **LFHW cookery classes** that provide practical cookery skills and information to enable people in each city to reduce food waste. WRAP will directly contract with the delivering organizations in each city and manage their delivery to ensure consistency, impact and value for money;

- **LFHW kitchen skills programme – Save More** – will be rolled out in each of the 10 cities, working with disadvantaged groups. This will be done at two levels. Firstly through working with national organizations who can embed the programme in their day to day delivery, and secondly through the printing and distribution of packs to local groups/people in each city. It will be promoted at a local level through the LFHW cascade training and volunteer network to reach groups and people who work with those who can benefit by learning budgeting and planning skills around food to save money;

- developing and managing a **volunteer network of Food Champions** across each city via its cascade training programme;

- providing an overarching public relations and events plan for the 18 months of activity in each city working closely with its partners to identify opportunities.

Useful resources about the campaign

The Love Food, Hate Waste website: www.lovefoodhatewaste.com
Evaluation of the six West London boroughs campaign: www.wrap.org.uk/sites/files/wrap/West%20London%20Food%20Waste%20Campaign%20Evaluation%20Report_1.pdf

Points about the campaign

- Careful research has underpinned this campaign at every step.
- The research is independent which makes it difficult to refute.
- Facts are presented in a compelling yet human way. The facts about food waste, our relationship with food, consumer habits, industry practices and practical solutions connect with consumers without prompting an adverse reaction.
- The campaign clearly lends itself to a staged roll-out. Critical to success was obtaining feedback about the points of traction and what actually changes behaviour over time.
- The raft of tactics is relatively limited, but they are impactful because they focused on deep engagement: necessary where behaviour change is required.
- The mix of rational and emotional appeal is good. The 'killer' facts were simple and easy to grasp, while being shocking, but there was also a range of solutions readily available to capitalize on both the rational and emotional response.
- The case demonstrates that good research not only ensures a good campaign is well founded, but it demonstrates progress along the way and which direction the campaign has to move in to gain maximum impact and efficiency.

CASE STUDY The Sleep Pod Hotel Media Tour conducted by Argyle Communications for GlaxoSmithKline (GSK) Consumer Healthcare

Background

Many Canadians believe that nasal strips are used to relieve snoring and by athletes to improve breathing during training and events. However, their broader benefits include relieving night-time nasal congestion, resulting in a better night's sleep. Argyle Communications' brief from GSK was to design and implement a strategic media relations programme to increase awareness and understanding of the benefit of using their Breathe Right® nasal strips focused on the major cities of Montreal, Ottawa and Toronto.

Research

The main target audience was adults aged 25–54 who were looking to solve night-time nasal congestion that affected their sleep. The target consumer used a toolbox of solutions to deal with the problem, including cough-cold, allergy, medicated and non-medicated products. The imperative was to make Breathe Right nasal strips part of this toolbox. The issue for the client was that the target consumer had a lack of product familiarity and/or did not associate it with sleep. The key was establishing this familiarity and connection.

Through brand team meetings, and a news and social media review, Argyle identified a number of considerations that would influence programme success, including:

- A crowded discussion on the topic of sleep. Analysis: In much of the preceding period, sleep had been a popular topic in both news and social media. Many consumer brands were also engaging consumers on the topic of sleep, with new products designed to improve sleep quality or create a better sleep environment. Insight: Argyle saw a need for a 'new' angle that would differentiate the campaign from others already in the market to cut through the clutter and gain traction. With October being Healthy Workplace Month, the team decided to focus on the link between sleep and workplace wellness to capitalize on story opportunities related to the national health promotion campaign theme.

- Limited understanding of product benefits. Analysis: While the GSK/Argyle team wanted to focus on sleep quality, research suggested this product benefit was poorly understood by the market. As indicated earlier, nasal strips are more commonly recognized as a way to reduce snoring and are used frequently by athletes to improve breathing. Insight: The Argyle team saw a 'way in' to the discussion about sleep by taking advantage of the programme timing on the cusp of cold and flu season. Argyle's key messages would tap into the collective irritation people feel when they are congested at night, positioning the strips as an ideal, drug-free solution that could be used along with other medication.

- Spokesperson endorsement linked to increased product sales. Analysis: During a previous media relations programme for the same product, Argyle had employed an alternative health professional, Bryce Wylde, as a third-party brand spokesperson. The team noted a clear correlation between these interviews and sales. Insight: The use of credible, recognizable spokespeople would help to engage audiences and encourage the desired action – ie, product purchase and trial.

Goals and objectives

Communication goals	Programme objectives
Earn national share of voice for Breathe Right within the news coverage on sleep as part of a strategy to improve sleep quality and therefore work productivity.	Secure a national feature story reporting on Breathe Right-branded research into the prevalence of sleep challenges, ideally with a syndicated columnist or newswire reporter to enable publication across Canada. Total audience reach objective of 12 million impressions.
Drive local-market awareness of Breathe Right in Montreal, Ottawa and Toronto via branded media coverage of the pod hotels.	Secure one major print and broadcast news story per local market. Secure two spokesperson interviews per local market. Secure media coverage in English and French news outlets.
Position Breathe Right nasal strips as an ideal solution for relieving night-time nasal congestion and improving sleep quality.	Ensure media coverage included: at least one key message about sleep health (100 per cent of stories); one spokesperson quote (80 per cent); and one direct brand mention (80 per cent), with the third objective being the most critical.

Planning

- Sleep pod hotels in major cities. To dramatize the importance of sleep and connect it to the Breathe Right brand, GSK's all-agency team developed and promoted attention-getting Breathe Right 'sleep pod hotels' in high-traffic locations in Toronto, Montreal and Ottawa. Consumers could 'book' their time in the pods online or drop by for a nap pending availability, and the unusual sight would spawn many images in both news and social media.

- A unique local media experience. The team would capitalize on the presence of sleep pod hotels in Montreal, Ottawa and Toronto to drive local media interest and have some fun with reporters. The pods had a high novelty factor, as most people had never seen one before, let alone slept in one. Reporters were invited to visit the pods in anticipation that the fun factor of the experience would lead to branded media coverage.

- New research and fresh voices on timely sleep topics. To expand and extend coverage, the campaign was tied to Healthy Workplace Month and Argyle commissioned fresh research into how sleep affected Canadians' ability to function at work, supplemented with expert spokespeople. The aim was to uncover surprising facts about how poor quality sleep resulted in loss of productivity and absenteeism, and what trade-offs Canadians would accept for better sleep.

Implementation

- National advance feature story. In an increasingly competitive news environment, a key reporter was selected for her interest in seeing the survey research in advance of its wide release. Misty Harris, consumer trends, social science and demographics reporter for the national Postmedia print and online network was chosen and offered an exclusive first look at the research.

- Customized local-market media materials and outreach. A national news release and survey data summary were prepared, along with customized media invitations for the pod hotels in Montreal, Ottawa and Toronto that included detailed information about hours of operation, spokesperson availability and media nap times. The team conducted national media outreach to support the survey data release and contacted all local media outlets in advance of the pod hotel's arrival to ensure key reporters and outlets were aware of the pods' arrival and could book interviews for the week when the hotel was live.

- Expert spokespeople. Two expert spokespeople were identified to address the health/wellness and workplace productivity story angles separately – and effectively. Alternative health expert Bryce Wylde would speak on the importance of sleep when recovering from illness and offer tips for improving sleep (including the use of Breathe Right nasal strips). Executive coach Sophie Lamarche would speak on the impact of sleep on workplace wellness and productivity, and offer tips for improving performance at work, noting the impact of sleep on career success.

Results

Objective	Results
Reach: National feature news story reporting on the Breathe Right sleep research. Target: 12 million impressions.	An advance feature story opportunity was secured with Postmedia. The story was published online at Canada.com, and appeared online and in select print editions of eight daily newspapers across Canada. Total audience impressions – 24,157,010.
Local awareness: Pod hotel coverage in Montreal, Ottawa and Toronto. One print + one broadcast story per city; two spokesperson interviews per city.	14 interviews were facilitated for the campaign spokespeople, resulting in 25 secured stories. An additional 11 stories were secured, but did not include a spokesperson interview. The sleep pod hotel was featured on eight local television stations, including an in-studio sleep pod and an on-site live broadcast.
Branded coverage: Position the strips as an ideal solution for relieving night-time nasal congestion and improving sleep by breathing better.	98 per cent of coverage including at least one key message. A spokesperson quote was included in 71 per cent of all media coverage, both slightly below our admittedly aggressive goals. Most significant of all, however, media coverage was heavily branded with 96 per cent of coverage including a branded product mention – far in excess of our goal or the client's expectations.

Points about the campaign

- A popular device, a survey, was used to generate media interest, but an insightful link to Healthy Workplace Month gave it extra usefulness not only for the media, but for the client who operates in the healthcare market. This helped to add more popular credibility to a product whose range of uses was poorly understood.

- Use of a respected social science and demographics reporter gave added credence to the survey results.

- The survey on its own might have been strong enough, but the use of the sleep pods gave added visual impact especially for those media more dependent on the visual.

- Those looking for a non-medical solution to nasal congestion would be reassured by endorsement by an alternative medicine expert.

- Each element of the campaign supported the other making it efficient as well as effective.

This case shows how scientific research can be used effectively with the media, not only to start it off, but as part of a media event itself.

Notes

1 McCollum, M (1997) The culture of work organizations, *Academy of Management Review*, **19**, 836–39

2 Smith, R D (2009) *Strategic Planning for Public Relations* (3rd edition), Lawrence Erlbaum Associates, Mahwah, NJ

3 Lerbinger, O (1972) *Designs for Persuasive Communication*, Prentice Hall, Englewood Cliffs, NJ

05
Communication theory and setting aims and objectives

Knowing where you're going

Setting realistic aims and objectives is absolutely vital if the programme or campaign that is being planned is to have direction and demonstrably achieve something.

One of the things that is rife in the public relations industry is poor objective-setting, specifically over-promising. This applies to both in-house departments and consultancies. It comes partly from an eagerness to please, but largely from a lack of understanding about what can actually be achieved.

Ultimately the aim of public relations is to influence levels of awareness (ie what is thought about something), attitudes or opinions (ie what is felt about something) or behaviour (ie what is done about something). Thus, the objective might be to encourage someone to buy a newly introduced furniture range, or keep their holdings in a company, or to speak up for the company when it is under attack, or to support nursery provision even if the target group doesn't have children. However, there are several steps along the way to influencing awareness, attitudes or opinions and behaviour and it is only very occasionally that someone who is dedicated to opposing something or who has no particular opinion at all will suddenly become an ardent supporter.

Attitude is all important

Of course one of the things formative research will have shown is whether stakeholders or publics are aware of an organization. It may appear that by definition they should be, but not everyone that the organization does or will affect will be aware of them. For example, a supermarket may intend to open a new store in a region of a country where they have no previous presence. Not everyone will be aware of them and even fewer will be aware of their intention, but will everyone be aware of that intention or of the impact it will have on them? Usually, stakeholders or publics are aware or not aware of an organization, that is quite simple, yes or no, but their level of awareness will vary. Attitudes or opinions are more difficult to unpick. Exactly what the attitudes of various stakeholders and publics are will have been investigated during the formative research stage. Attitudes and opinions are complex and will probably have been built up over time and from a variety of sources and experiences. Knowing exactly what attitudes and opinions stakeholders and publics have provides a benchmark measure of the task in hand and this is vitally important when planning a programme. It is a much easier and less time-consuming job to reinforce favourable opinion than to neutralize hostile ones. In fact it may be that it has to be admitted that it is impossible to neutralize ingrained opinions, particularly if they are based on deep-seated prejudice or beliefs.

So, how are attitudes formed? All kinds of influences impact on people:

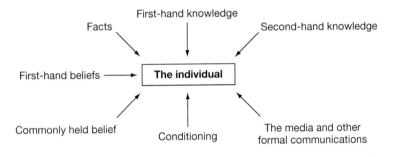

- *First-hand knowledge* is a very powerful attitude former. If a car is bought from a certain garage and the car itself, the sales and after-sales service has been excellent, then the purchaser will have a favourable attitude towards it.

- *Second-hand knowledge* is also a strong influence, particularly if gained from a friend or a 'person like yourself',[1] trusted colleague or an authority of some kind. If an individual hears from a friend about a certain country that knowledge, coupled with good ratings on a consumer website and good feedback via social media may present a persuasive argument for us to holiday there.

- *The on- and offline media* is a potent influence, particularly if a topic is one of heightened public interest such as the concern over standards in public life. Companies also communicate via other formal methods such as annual reports, websites and product literature.

- *Conditioning* influences the way people look at everything they come into contact with. How they have been brought up, their education, religious beliefs, political views, what they view and read, age, sex and social position are all part of the baggage people bring with them when thinking about any subject.

- Then there are *commonly held beliefs.* For example, people may believe, even though they may not own one or know anyone who does, that Aston Martins are superb cars or that Italian suits are especially well designed and made.

- *First-hand beliefs* can be defined as the way the mind puts together a structure to create a frame of reference for understanding. Beliefs can be divided into core or central beliefs and peripheral beliefs.[2] Central beliefs are those concepts that are most important to individuals such as fairness, integrity etc and these may support more peripheral beliefs such as equality at work legislation and transparency in work practices. Peripheral beliefs can also be held in isolation. For example I believe this can of beans is best. Central beliefs can be equated to values and are more difficult to change than those at the periphery.

- *Facts* also affect attitudes. Knowledge that New Zealand is geographically isolated means that will make us disbelieve anyone who says that they can cycle there in half an hour.

Usually attitudes are formed via a combination of all these factors. Some attitudes are very firmly fixed and supported by significant personal experience, like views of the service received from a bank, while other attitudes may be much more loosely held, for example views of the Canadian government by non-Canadians.

The communication chain

To set realistic objectives, apart from understanding what the attitudes of various stakeholders and publics are, there also needs to be an understanding of the communication process. Assumptions along the lines of 'If I tell it loud and long and they hear it, eventually they'll believe it' are naive in the extreme. There are several models describing communication between individuals, groups and the media. Just a few are outlined here to indicate the complexity of the subject.

Real communication involves the two-way exchange of information and an interaction that may result in either or both parties changing in some way. However, many public relations practitioners in effect still believe that the one-way, linear communication model whose underlying principles were formulated by Shannon and Weaver[3] in 1949 is what happens in real life. The underlying pattern of the model is like this:

SENDER $\longrightarrow$ MESSAGE $\longrightarrow$ CHANNEL $\longrightarrow$ RECEIVER

The idea is that the sender is active, the receiver is passive and that the message is somehow decanted into the receiver's mind through a channel of communication and that it will be fully understood. Furthermore, no distinction is drawn between communicating with individuals, groups, mass audiences or via third parties.

The above model could apply to individuals, but what's missing is any notion of feedback. Senders need to know if the message has affected the receiver at all by receivers making them aware of something changing or reinforcing attitudes, or making them behave in a particular way. For example, the sender could leave a note (channel) saying that dinner is in the oven (message), but they will never know whether the receiver has understood or acted on the message unless they inform the sender or if the dinner is eaten. Feedback closes the loop. A much more realistic model is the fairly well-known one shown in Figure 5.1.

FIGURE 5.1 The communication process model

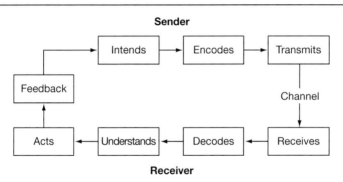

The underlying principles behind this model were developed by Osgood and presented by Schramm[4] in 1954.

The sender intends to communicate and articulates or encodes that intention, bringing with him or her all the conditioning and belief baggage mentioned before. He or she then chooses a channel through which to transmit the communication. This may be the radio, a tweet, a comment on a website, a text message or a gesture, and the recipient receives that communication.

The actual transmission of information is fraught with danger. It may be that the message has associated channel noise. The radio may be crackly, the tweet may be difficult to interpret, the receiving mobile phone may be in a poor reception spot, or the website may be difficult to navigate. There may also be psychological noise. The sender might be using the wrong body language or the corporate message from the chief executive may be intimidating rather than informative. Then there is language noise, where the language itself can be misinterpreted. 'Do not cross while light is flashing' can mean do not cross when the light is flashing or do not cross until the light is flashing.

Having once received the message, the recipient then needs to decode it so that it can be understood. He or she also brings all his or her conditioning and beliefs into the decoding equation. There is then normally some sort of action following on from the communication, which might be encoded or explicit. For example, this might be a simple grunt of recognition or a positive and vehement tweeted rejection of the idea proposed, accompanied by threats. This action then has to be decoded by the receiver and acts as feedback. The loop is then closed, since the sender is looking for a reaction to the message that demonstrates communication has taken place. This allows the possibility of the sender adapting either his or her message or way of communicating, to help understanding and enhance communication, or maybe deciding to escalate conflict, or to discontinue contact. An important feature of this model is that the sender and receiver are seen as essentially equal and both are involved in encoding, decoding and interpreting. This, in fact, has led to some criticism of the model: it intimates a feeling of equality between the communicating parties. However, observation demonstrates this is not the case, there are sometimes large differences in motivation, power and resources between the participants, although the internet is reducing the capability of the advantaged party to wield that advantage.

More recent models of communication have emphasized the cyclical nature of the process. Rogers and Kincaid[5] developed the 'convergence' model, in which the participants in communication give and receive information and explore their understanding of it to the point where there is such a level of mutual understanding (which does not need to be complete) that further exchanges are not necessary. Of course, it is doubtful that complete understanding is ever obtained, but the notion is that there is sufficient understanding of each other's position to be able to make reasonable judgements.

In this model concepts such as the sender, message, receiver are superceded by concepts such as participants, joint activity, co-creation of meaning and joint understanding, where the beginning and end of the process are less clear and who initiated it becomes less important.

The models so far are particularly applicable to one-to-one, interpersonal communication, where there can be relatively easy checks on understanding and where there is feedback, for example, one-to-one briefings. They are less suitable as descriptions of what happens between organizations and groups or between organizations and mass audiences or groups reached through a third party such as the media, where there can be relatively little feedback or direct personal interaction.

Communicating with groups

There are several models available describing communication with groups; one that is quite widely accepted in public relations circles is the 'co-orientation model'.[6] This is particularly applicable where the organization is involved in a genuine dialogue – two-way, interactive communication in which the organization is prepared to change its position to accommodate its publics. It is not applicable where the organization is just giving out pure information or is undertaking a persuasive exercise only.

Without going into the fine detail of the co-orientation model, its principal features are accuracy, understanding and agreement. An example will illustrate the idea. Suppose a company wishes to set up a plastic re-cycling plant in a town. It thinks it will provide employment, stimulate the local economy and serve a laudable 'green' cause. Local residents, however, may see this development as bringing heavy lorries to the district, polluting the air and taking up space that could be used for much-needed housing. Each party may have a quite inaccurate perception of the views of the other; they may not understand each other's point of view and they certainly don't agree.

The company, realizing that there is a potential major problem, begins to communicate openly with the residents, explaining its motivations for opening the plant. The residents, too, express their reservations. Through the process of discussion, more accurate perceptions of each other's position are achieved. Both sides gradually adjust their understanding as they proceed: they co-orient themselves. They may not like the position of the other side, they may agree to disagree, but at least there is common understanding. From this position, the aim would be to discuss how they can compromise and come to a mutually acceptable solution, even if both sides have to give ground in the process.

Communicating with mass audiences or via the media

When dealing with mass audiences there are many receivers and it is impossible to influence people in a uniform way. People select information depending on their various states of knowledge or their predisposition. Receivers talk to each other, they are influenced by opinion leaders and so on. This recognition has led to the development of the two-step communication model[7], where the information is received by key 'gatekeepers' (normally opinion leaders), who further interpret for the mass audience.

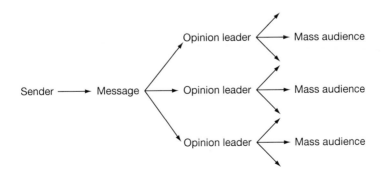

Thus, for example, if a public relations practitioner sends out a media release, the targeted journalists and bloggers perform the role of opinion leaders and interpret the information on behalf of their readers. Again, some uniformity of interpretation is assumed.

In reality this model is too simplistic. People receive information from all kinds of sources and this often bypasses the opinion leader. Communication is multi-faceted, multi-step and multi-directional.[8]

All this communication is overlaid with individual and group attitudes, psychological variables, channel noise, feedback from various sources and the knowledge base of all those involved. Little wonder, then, that communication with mass audiences is an immensely complex and open-ended business.

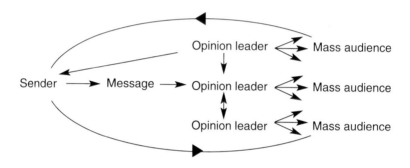

Rogers and Kincaid's convergence model (see page 94) has particular application to communication between individuals, but there are certain principles at play here that also apply to groups. It is essentially a network model because the effect of the communication comes from joint activity and affects all those involved. Network models have a number of features that are important in understanding what is happening in communication:

- Connectedness: an analysis of how highly connected individuals are to a network, will give an indication of how quickly information will flow through it. Highly connected networks are tight communities, whereas more loosely connected networks have members who are more isolated: they may not receive information, or receive it more slowly.

- Integration: this provides an indication of the type and number of linkages between members of the network. So, for example, if members share social networking sites, text, phone and e-mail each other regularly, they have many channels of communication and this can be useful to the public relations practitioner.

- Diversity: if the network is diverse, there will be several routes into the network. If it is not diverse, it will tend to exclude those who do not conform to the characteristics of its membership.

- Openness: if the network is open to external contacts and influences and is well linked to the environment, it will be easier to reach than those that are closed.

By taking into account these features, the public relations practitioner can plan communications better. Through examining the nature of networks the practitioner can also understand why there are blockages in communication: for example, it may be difficult to break into a network because it lacks diversity, thus the only way to enter it is to work with third parties who are acceptable to the membership. For example, activist groups are normally unreceptive to those who do not share their views, hence a way to gain the opportunity to communicate with them is to work with a third party who they may respect as being sympathetic to, or even a member of their network.

Undertaking an analysis of networks forces public relations planners to look at the structure of a whole network and is particularly useful when looking at online communities. It reveals information about the membership of the network and identifies key roles within it. There will be individuals who fulfil the liaison role – they link individuals or clusters within the network. There will be stars who are linked to large numbers of other individuals. Isolates are linked to very few individuals and boundary-spanners make links to the wider environment. Bridge individuals create links between the group and other groups, whereas non-participants just get on with their work without communicating. They may, for example, set up links to other websites, which just 'appear', without telling everyone they have done this.

Recognizing these roles enables planners to understand how communication will move around a network. Stars are the planners' friend (or enemy), since they are very well connected and will have great reach into the network. Isolates may need particular attention since information may not reach them and they in turn will not pass it on to many others in the network. These people may represent 'hard to reach' individuals who may have particular importance even though they are not well connected. Bridges will be ideal for passing information from one network to another.

Network analysis can be used as a tool to understand how information flows around a particular community. Networking itself, whether on- or off-line, can be used as a communication strategy. Linking in to particular networks can be the most effective and authoritative way of connecting with certain groups, especially those who are hard to reach. It has been used to great effect by Cumbria County Council, when handling the difficulties surrounding the Appleby Horse Fair.

The Annual Appleby Horse Fair is an unofficial event held in the northern town of Appleby in the UK. Every year, Travellers meet to renew friendships and trade horses: highly symbolic and useful animals in the Traveller's life. There is a tense relationship between the residents of Appleby whose town is filled with Travellers during the week of the fair. Residents complain of drunkenness, litter and other anti-social behaviour. Travellers on the other hand, believe their traditional way of life is becoming increasingly threatened and do not want to see the Fair banned, which was an option being considered by the Council.

By undertaking a careful analysis of the Traveller community – their way of life; membership of their network; who the influencers are inside and outside; how the network operates (stars, bridges and boundary-spanners) – Cumbria County Council were able to plan a communications campaign that put clear boundaries around acceptable and unacceptable behaviours, explain the facilities that were available for use by the Travelling community and open up avenues for contact if any issues arose that needed to be discussed. They then used the network itself as the primary means of communicating these things. The result is that in 2015 several public sector agencies now support the event. There is an official website (**www.applebyfair.org**) and relationships between residents, tourists, Travellers, Council and other agencies have greatly improved.

One-to-one, one-to-many, many-to-one, many-to-many, machine-to-machine

Developments in communication technology have resulted in many permutations of connective possibility. Apart from Network theory which includes the connection between networks (many to many), those outlined above are largely based on one-to-one, one to group or group to one communication. However the world is changing rapidly. There are an increasing number of connections between humans and intelligent systems. Often websites no longer have details of a human contact and many interactive systems, for example online shopping, exclude human interaction from any part of the transaction. The internet of things promises non-human to non-human interaction as a matter of course.

Mapping and outlining the theorizing on all these permutations is beyond the remit of this book, but the implication is clear. Public relations professionals now have to work much harder at plotting the course of the communication link between themselves and their 'audience' while carefully thinking through where their communication may be routed beyond that audience and its potential impact. They also have to consider where they might effectively make their interventions if they wish to engage in dialogue. Those interactions that exclude all human contact also exclude the possibility of building personal relationships, although it has to be acknowledged that enormous strides have been made to personalize the information that is both pushed and pulled automatically to those who are online.

What also has to be acknowledged is the unprecedented access that publics, stakeholders and audiences have to other sources of information, whether they be deliberately sought, accidentally discovered or deliberately targeted at them while they conduct their personal, business and public lives on line.

Implications of communication theory and recent developments

These discussions on public relations and communication developments theories lead to a number of conclusions:

- Transparent, two-way, proactive and interactive public relations is the only sensible way to operate: there are too many other sources of information to permit any alternative to transparency. In addition, being seen to be a useful information resource and providing transparent access is regarded as a positive indicator of social responsibility.

- As indicated in Chapter 2, publics can be seen as collecting around issues rather than as homogeneous blocks such as 'customers'. Because issues can remain on websites or social networks for prolonged periods, the choice of when to react is in the hands of publics. Issues can re-emerge at any stage, maybe years later, as different groups of people gather round the issue and form a 'new' public. (See Chapter 6 for more detail on issues-based publics.)

- Online channels are the friend of *active* and *aware* publics, who are information-seekers. They are potentially the greatest friends of an organization as well as its greatest 'problems'. (For a full explanation of active and aware publics, see Chapter 6.)

- The thought to action continuum often stimulated by ongoing contract and much desired by organizational communicators can be reinforced or broken by users accessing alternative information sources (many of which may be unknown to the organization) or taking other communication routes from the plethora of options available.

- This continuum is time-contracted, as information for decision making is readily and swiftly available. Prompts to action in support of or opposition to an organization can be stimulated when a user is part of a like-minded and supportive community (witness the 'Arab Spring' uprisings, which were largely organized through online communications).

- Lack of information from organizations is a potentially serious problem because there will be several, readily accessible alternative sources, not all of which may be supportive. Not providing information can be regarded as secretive and in itself can create an issue around which a public can gather.

- Online, mobile technologies change the power relationships between stakeholder networks because smaller interest groups can present their case as well as large organizations and can interact directly with other stakeholders. These technologies are an activist's friend.

- Individual opinions have equal weight; no one is more important than anyone else. Opinions are formed in a different way, as traditional opinion-formers give way to new ones. As a result, the traditional opinion-formers, for example the offline media and community leaders, are less influential than they were.

- Increasingly, communication is direct, without the mediation of, say, journalists or other traditional opinion formers. This changes not only power relationships, but also the speed and reach of communications: sometimes to groups unknown to the object of the communication.

- With their knowledge of stakeholders and their management, public relations professionals are uniquely placed to be the knowledge managers for their organizations. This new role for the public relations professional is at a higher level. They are neither technicians nor managers, but communication executives who will be regarded as the peers of the highest executives in the organization.

How 'receivers' use information

A consideration of how those who receive communication from public relations practitioners is clearly important and the process is complex. Much investigation and theorizing has been done on this topic. Many public relations practitioners want to believe in the Domino Theory[9] of the effect of communication.

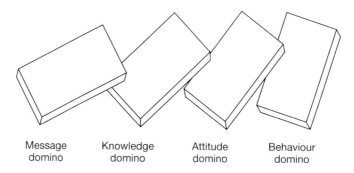

| Message | Knowledge | Attitude | Behaviour |
| domino | domino | domino | domino |

This is reflective of early marketing theory which was based on the AIDA model. First of all people become **A**ware of an idea or product or service but have little knowledge about it.

Then they develop an **I**nterest and seek out more information. Then they become persuaded of the benefits of the idea or product or service and develop a **D**esire to buy it. Finally they show their support by taking **A**ction and buying the product or service.

Sometimes this simple progression is achievable, but often it is not. In fact, Grunig and Hunt state that the chances of someone progressing through the dominos from the point where the message is received to behaving in a desired way are 4 in 10,000. An audience or public might learn about an organization and form a negative rather than a positive attitude, or they might develop an attitude but not take the desired action. The portrayal of wars and famines often engenders strong sympathy in the minds of television viewers and newspaper readers, but they might not make a charitable donation as a result. There is certainly no proven causal link between people thinking about something, forming an attitude and then acting in a predictable way. Public relations people may provide and present in an attractive manner all the information an individual needs to think or act in a particular way. However, the way those individuals form their attitudes and behave is usually very specific to them and their particular situation, and is not entirely predictable.

Furthermore, people are very adept at holding incompatible beliefs. For example, individuals may be vociferous supporters of measures to combat climate change, but may own a car. They will therefore argue differently depending on the situation they are talking about. One thing is very clear; if someone is very firmly of a particular opinion and acts to support it, it will be very difficult to persuade him or her to a different point of view. Just giving people lots of positive information will not necessarily change their attitudes or behaviour. Changing deep-seated central beliefs is very difficult, whereas peripheral beliefs are easier to alter. It is one thing to change someone's belief that a certain brand of baked beans is better than another. It is quite another thing to change their beliefs on what constitutes integrity. The leverage points have to be identified and worked upon in order to make productive shifts in awareness, attitude or behaviour and these need to be emotional as well as rational. If there are no leverage points which can be worked on persuasively, the argument is lost from the start (more on this in Chapter 6).

There are other theories that provide a more sophisticated insight into how people receive information than the Domino Theory. Uses and Gratification Theory states that receivers of communication select the content that is most gratifying or useful to them. Thus, readers of an internal employee newsletter, will look at the material that most fulfils their individual social and psychological needs. Hence, if sport plays no role in their life and they find no gratification in reading about it, these items will be of no attraction.

The original formation of Uses and Gratification Theory equated 'needs' with Maslow's hierarchy, but more recent work[10] includes other kinds of gratification, including:

- information: obtaining advice, learning, orientating with different parts of the environment;
- personal identity: self-knowledge, reinforcing personal values, finding attractive models of behaviour;

- integration and social interaction: finding out about others, discovering how to relate to others, discovering how to play a role, building social interactions;
- entertainment: relaxing, escaping from problems, passing time, satisfying intellectual, physical and social needs.

Thus, receivers make a judgement about the value of the received information based on the gratification, or need-fulfilment they get from it; either immediately or for the future.

A distinction can be drawn between those people who value communication for its outcome (ie need fulfilment) and those who value it as a process (ie people enjoy the act of communication itself). Of course a mixture of the two is also quite common. However, the public relations person needs to be aware of this distinction. Some individuals and groups are satisfied with a to-the-point, 'no nonsense' communication that provides unambiguous content. Others have a need to engage in lengthy discussion or correspondence and gain gratification from that process. The implications of both cases are obvious.

While Uses and Gratification Theory is useful in identifying how receivers of communication select the content they find most useful, it does not explain how that content is interpreted, or given meaning. Reception Theory attempts to explain how people do this. The idea is that meaning is not somehow 'fixed' in the content of communication by the sender, but it needs the receiver to co-construct it on reception. Often this involves an iterative process where meanings are checked and adjusted (see also Rogers and Kincaid's convergence model), and is undertaken within the particular social and cultural environment that individuals or groups inhabit, and their own backgrounds. Thus, individuals and groups construct 'frames' or lenses through which to interpret the content of communication. They will hold these frames more or less in common with other individuals and groups and the more these frames are shared or understood, the greater the chance of a common understanding being reached. This 'cultural' understanding of what happens in the act of communication allows for the fact that content is always amenable to several interpretations and is likely to evoke different reactions; support, rejection, or a place in between. Thus, a deep knowledge of the individuals and publics that are the objects of communication is a requirement when planning public relations programmes (more on this in Chapter 6).

Setting realistic aims and objectives

Bearing all this in mind, then, we can now look at setting purposeful, stretching yet achievable aims and objectives.

First, a note on definitions; an aim is a broad statement of what the communicator wants to achieve. It does not have any specifically measurable outcomes. Objectives on the other hand are the concrete, measurable steps and activities that will help to achieve that aim. They are highly specific and, in their totality will ensure achievement of the whole aim. A simple example illustrates the difference:

Aim: maximize shareholder attendance at the next AGM

Objectives:

- identify a location for the AGM that is most accessible to shareholders 10 weeks in advance of the AGM;
- identify the best time for the meeting by sampling shareholders 10 weeks before the AGM;
- undertake a phased and integrated on- and offline communication campaign in the eight-week period prior to the AGM;

and so on.

Aims

Setting the overall aim, or aims for a public relations campaign, is not easy. First there has to be agreement about what the contribution of public relations will be to solving a particular issue, or capitalizing on a specific opportunity. Second, there may be different opinions about the scope of the campaign and over the best way to approach the issue.

To achieve consensus on these issues, it is advisable to work collaboratively with those who are commissioning the work because they will have the biggest stake in the outcome. It must be borne in mind that the eventual programme will be judged on whether or not it has achieved its aim(s). If these are not agreed at the outset, the programme could well be judged on other criteria.

There must also be clarity over outcome and process aims. Outcome aims are those concerned with what you want publics to do: the results of the communication. Process aims are orientated around what the practitioner does to achieve the aim. 'Maximize shareholder attendance at the AGM' is an outcome aim. The aim could have been stated as 'use all available mass communication techniques to maximize shareholder attendance at the AGM'. This includes a process as well as an outcome. The two are related, but should be separated.

There are some general principles to bear in mind when setting aims:

- Make them singular (one aim at a time), clear (specific) and readily understandable.
- Frame them in terms of outcomes and describe the process by which they will be achieved in overall terms if necessary.
- They should be able to be evaluated at the end of the programme by turning the aim into a question. Hence, the aim 'to improve

relationships with the University's business partners' becomes the evaluative question 'did the University improve relationships with its business partners?'

It may be possible to have just one overall aim for a campaign with a relatively simple outcome, such as 'Maximize attendance by shareholders at the AGM', but if the programme is complex, multi-layered and has a number of publics or stakeholder groups involved, a number of aims will be needed, each having objectives to support their achievement. For example, in a flu outbreak, the aim for the general public could well be about the importance of vaccination; for hospitals and doctors it will be about identification and treatment of flu victims; for those in the hotel industry, it will be about safety of the staff and guests. Of course all these aims could be subordinate to the overarching aim of ensuring the well-being of the nation; but the point is made, in this case the specific programme will need different aims for different publics.

Finally, aims need to be linked to organizational objectives, and targeted at societal, management or specific programme issues, or any combination of the three. That way a direct link to organizational contribution can be made.

Objectives

Objectives are the specific, measurable statements that break down the aims into the steps that must be achieved if success is to be realized. They are effectively the project milestones.

As has been stated before, public relations is purposive; communication usually has some persuasive element. The communication continuum has at one end making people aware of something, and at the other getting people to behave in particular ways with working at the attitude and opinion level being somewhere in between. There is an accepted hierarchy of objective setting then, which mirrors these three levels: awareness, attitudes and opinions, and behaviour.

- *Awareness* – getting target publics to think about something and trying to promote a level of understanding. Awareness objectives focus on information and knowledge. These are often called *cognitive* (thinking) objectives and are to do with attention, comprehension and retention. An example could be the government wishing to make citizens aware of a change in tax rates.

- *Attitudes and opinions* – getting target publics to form a particular attitude or opinion about a subject. Attitudes are concerned with how people react to information. These are often called *affective* (feeling) objectives and are to do with interest and acceptance or rejection. An example could be a pressure group wanting moral support for changes in mental health provision.

- *Behaviour* – getting target publics to act in a desired way. These are often called *conative* (acting) objectives and are to do with promoting a desired response involving action. An example could be a local police force using local radio to ask drivers to change their route home away from a major accident site.

Bearing this in mind, there are three things that are very much in the practitioners' control which helps them achieve their objectives.

- The level of objective needs to be chosen carefully. If a new or difficult idea is being introduced, practitioners might work at the awareness level first before moving on to the higher levels; planners should not try to obtain a behavioural response immediately unless they have legislation to back them, or their 'offer' is so powerful as to be irresistible.
- Planners can choose who the priority target publics are and, furthermore, planners can enlist the help of those individuals or groups within those target publics who are already favourably disposed towards them or who could be readily enlisted (more of this in Chapter 6).
- The persuasion doesn't need to be all one way. As stated several times, the organization can change too and sometimes relatively small changes in organizational attitude or behaviour can result in major positive effects on target public.

The principle to remember is that it is a much larger and more difficult task to get someone to act than it is to get them to think about something. So the kinds of objectives public relations programmes might have could be:

Awareness level:

- create awareness;
- promote understanding;
- inform;
- confirm a perception;
- develop knowledge.

Attitudes level:

- displace prejudice;
- encourage belief;
- overcome misunderstanding or apathy.

Behaviour level:

- act in a particular way.
- stop acting in a particular way;
- sustain participation.

Golden rules of objective setting

There are a number of imperatives that must be borne in mind when setting objectives:

- *Ally to organizational objectives.* Public relations programmes and campaigns must support organizational objectives, otherwise effort will be dissipated on interesting but essentially unimportant and tactical work. If a corporate objective is a major repositioning of the company in its market, then the public relations effort must be directed to supporting that.

- *Set public relations objectives.* Again it is a tendency of public relations professionals to set objectives that public relations cannot deliver. It is not reasonable to say that public relations should increase sales by 20 per cent if that depends on the salesforce too. It is reasonable to say that presentations should be made to 50 per cent of key retailers to tell them of new product lines and to try them. It may well be that as a result sales do increase by 20 per cent – but it is outside of the public relations practitioners' control to promise this.

- *Link to aims.* All objectives should clearly support the aims and contribute to their fulfilment.

- *Be linked to specific publics.* Vague aims around 'the general public' are just that. Be specific about the publics being worked with and what is to be to achieved.

- *Be outcome focused.* Objectives will form the basis of future evaluation so be sure to focus on outcomes, not on the process used (such as number of hits on the website). It is admissible to have process objectives but be clear that this is specified and differentiated from outcome objectives.

- *Research based.* Objectives should have an evidence base around them. If it is known that 60 per cent of a public act in a particular way, it may be reasonable to create an objective around increasing that to 70 per cent. However, setting a 70 per cent target based on no research is very dangerous. Benchmarking against similar programmes or obtaining information from others who have worked with the target groups closely will help determine what is realistic.

- *Be singular.* Focus on the separate steps to meet the aims. Objectives with more than one element are difficult to evaluate.

- *Be precise and specific.* Objectives need to be sharp. To create awareness is not good enough. Creating awareness of what, with whom, when and how needs to be clearly spelt out.

- *Do what is achievable.* It is better to set modest objectives and hit them, than to aim for the sky and miss. Wherever possible evaluate the likely benefits of ideas and pre-test or pilot schemes. If a major part of the programme is to contact all investors to inform them of a particular development, there must be certainty that it can be done within the Stock Market rules.

- *Quantify as much as possible.* Not all objectives are precisely quantifiable, but most are. If the aim is to contact particular audience groups say how many. Quantifying objectives makes evaluation much easier. Furthermore, make sure that what is being quantified is important and worthwhile. As Albert Einstein said, 'Not everything that counts can be counted, not everything that is counted counts'.

- *Work to a timescale.* Know when delivery is required then work can be phased or help brought in as needed. Be explicit about delivery dates.

- *Work within budget.* A good planner and manager knows exactly how much things will cost, and will design objectives with that in mind. Penetration of a particular public by 100 per cent may not be achievable within budget.

- *Work to a priority list.* Prioritizing objectives enables planners to see where the major effort is to be focused. Have enough to achieve the aim, but more than that is unnecessary and inefficient.

Remember the SMART acronym for objectives: **S**tretching, **M**easurable, **A**chievable (given other activities), **R**ealistic (having the resources to achieve them) and **T**imebound.

Examples of workable objectives are as follows:

Corporate:	Inform 10 targeted investors of reasons for management buyout before the AGM. (awareness level)
Trade:	Ensure 50 top dealers attend annual dealers' conference. (behaviour level)
Consumer:	Increase levered editorial coverage of service by 20 per cent over 18 months. (process objective, purpose is to increase sales – a behaviour-level objective)
Employees:	Maximize branch acceptance of corporate clothing by December. (90 per cent is target for acceptance) (behaviour level)
Community:	Increase support for accepting new waste recycling scheme by 10 per cent in 12 months. (attitudinal, leading in future to behavioural level)

Constraints on aims and objectives

Of course it would be nice to plan without any form of constraint, but there are usually a number of factors that have to be given careful regard. These are either internally or externally generated.

Internal constraints

- *Who should do the job?* The capabilities of the people assigned to the task need careful assessment. Are they able to carry it out? If not, will this mean that the demands of the task will have to be limited? Alternatively, is it possible to enlist the help of other people such as a public relations consultancy? Are there enough people for the task? Again can extra hands be drafted in or will the scope of the task need to be reduced?

- *How much will it cost?* No one has an open-ended budget so what are the effects on a prioritized programme of any budgetary constraints? What can be left out if necessary or for what should a case for additional resources be made? Can some elements be delivered via partners to save costs?

- *When does it need to happen?* Sometimes an internal timetable will require that the public relations task has to be carried out at a certain time, for example, the announcement of a major company restructure or the introduction of a new process.

- *Who makes the decisions?* Are the public relations professionals able to decide on the appropriate courses of action or is the power elsewhere, such as with a marketing director?

- *Is the support in place?* Is there the right administrative back-up and physical resources such as IT and video production, to support the programme?

External constraints

- *Who is the programme trying to reach?* What is the range of publics or audiences? How many are there? What are their preferred media? What about their socio-economic grouping?

- *What are the socio-cultural differences?* What are the different media conventions in the various countries being operated in? What social and cultural differences and protocols have to be observed?

- *What infrastructure support is there?* What facilities such as mobile phone network coverage or access to catering facilities are available?

- *Time frames?* Are there certain calendar dates such as New Year or a national holiday that have to be met? What about other key events such as the Grand Prix or the Cannes Film Festival?

Different levels of aims and objectives

Aims and objectives can, of course, apply to whole programmes or individual projects. They can also operate at various levels: societal, corporate and programme.

The example below shows how the issues that an organization faces translate into aims and objectives at the various levels.

ISSUE	AIM	OBJECTIVE
Company seen as old-fashioned (reputational)	Position as company that is innovative	Promote product as exemplar of innovation to opinion formers
Company not seen as contributor to local communities (societal)	Position as company that takes public responsibility seriously	Introduce company-sponsored recycling scheme in community
Company to be seen as caring employer (managerial: retaining good employees)	Demonstrate company's ongoing commitment to employees	Promote enhanced well-being scheme

The setting of good, realistic aims and objectives is fundamental to the success of public relations plans. They provide the whole basis of the campaign by clearly setting down what the key achievements must be. They become the rationale behind the strategy, set the agenda for the actions to be taken and provide the benchmark for evaluation further down the road. When put into practice, they also guide management decisions, such as where to cut resources if necessary, or where to expand the budget and put in extra resource.

The temptation to over-promise must be resisted. That is not so say that public relations practitioners should set themselves soft targets; they should be as rigorous, but based on careful research. They must, however, recognize the complexity of the communication process, and be realistic about what shifts in attitude and behaviour can be achieved.

Campaigns that aim to produce radical shifts in attitude and behaviour usually take a great deal of time and are bound initially to meet with a limited amount of success. There are, of course, exceptions that break the rule, and these are often triggered by a crisis or the creation of a 'hot issue' that is fuelled by the media. For example when the British celebrity Jade Goody died of cervical cancer, there was a spike in screening uptake by women under 30 who had previously been reticent to take up the offer. Generally speaking, however, the most successful programmes start from the point of where the publics are, and attempt to make incremental shifts which, over a period of time, can be seen to have made considerable progress. The reputations of the best companies have taken considerable time to build. Public relations activity is to do with building reputations, too, and that is a slow and painstaking business.

Notes

1 See Edelman Trust Barometer 2015. Available from www.edelman.com/insights/intellectual-property/2015-edelman-trust-barometer

2 Rokeach, M (1960) *The Open and Closed Mind*, Basic Books, New York

3 Shannon, C and Weaver, W (1949) *The Mathematical Theory of Communication*, Universty of Illinois Press, Urbana, IL

4 Schramm, W (1954) How communication works, in *The Process and Effects of Mass Communication*, ed W Schramm, University of Illinois Press, Urbana, IL

5 Rogers, E M and Kincaid, D L (1981) *Communication Networks: Towards a New Paradigm for Research*, The Free Press, New York

6 First proposed by J M McLeod and S H Chaffee (1977) in Interpersonal approaches to communication research, *American Behavioural Scientist*, **16**, pp 469–500, but since then refined and applied specifically to public relations

7 First proposed by E Katz and P F Lazarsfeld in *Personal Influence*, Free Press, Glencoe

8 See Windahl, S, Signitzer, B with Olson, J (2009) *Using Communication Theory*, Sage, London, for further explanation

9 Grunig, J E and Hunt, T (1984) *Managing Public Relations*, Holt, Rinehart and Winston, New York

10 See Windahl, S, Signitzer, B with Olson, J (2009) *Using Communication Theory*, Sage, London, for further explanation

06
Knowing the publics and messages

Who shall we talk to and what shall we say?

Having answered the question 'Where am I going?' by setting achievable aims and objectives, the next question to ask is 'Who shall I talk with?' Please note it is 'talk with' not 'to' if we are seeking genuine communication.

By undertaking formative research for the proposed programme an analysis of the attitudes of each of the stakeholders and publics that relate to the organization will be available. Now the closer stakeholders, referred to as publics because of the organization's specific relationship with them around specific issues, need to have a priority order put on them and a decision made on how to interact with them. Sometimes the priorities are fairly obvious. If there is to be a launch of a new product, the primary audiences are going to be existing and potential customers. However, sometimes dialogue needs to be started with groupings with whom the organization has had little or nothing to do. If the organization is a private company seeking a stock market listing for the first time, then it will need to speak to the City, specialist financial journalists and opinion-formers in the sector who influence potential investors, and will have to begin from scratch.

There are groupings of publics that are fairly common to most organizations. These are shown in Figure 6.1.

Figure 6.1 shows a typical approach to grouping, or segmenting publics, but it has to be borne in mind that organizations do not exist in isolation. Consideration has to be given to the networks in which they exist so that potential stake-takers are identified: that is those who will take an interest and exercise it in some way once they become aware of the activities and decisions that the organization is making. In particular, online stake-takers need careful thinking through.

FIGURE 6.1   Publics common to most organizations

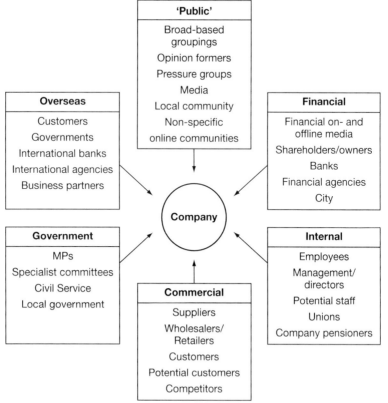

Again it is a common failing of public relations practitioners that they perform a rather simple and crude chopping up of the publics that organizations have. They believe that a particular grouping contains individuals who all act in the same way.

In Chapter 5, where objective setting was discussed, it was shown that radical shifts in attitude and behaviour are very difficult to achieve. It is vital therefore that there is understanding of what can be achieved with particular audiences or publics and the different sub-groupings within them.

What is public opinion?

It is worth spending a little time discussing public opinion since sometimes what practitioners are trying to achieve is not only to shift the balance of opinion of the various publics interacted with, but to shift public opinion as a whole. It has already been noted that understanding the broader context that publics inhabit is essential. Public opinion can be broadly regarded as the prevalent view held by the majority of people. It is against this background that work with particular publics takes place. One definition of public opinion is as follows:

> Public opinion represents a consensus, which emerges over time, from all the expressed views that cluster around an issue in debate, and that this consensus exercises power.[1]

Public opinion works two ways: it is both a cause and effect of public relations activity. Public opinion, strongly held, affects management decisions. For example, increasing concerns for the environment has affected the motor and furniture industries. Noxious emissions from cars have been cut and there are an increasing number of electric and hybrid cars. Trade in non-replantable hardwoods is frowned on. Public relations practitioners ensure management are aware of public opinion so that they can make decisions in the light of it. Practitioners also publicize the fact that their organizations care for the environment and thereby attempt to gain public support.

On the other hand, a stated objective of many public relations programmes is to affect the general public and often this means or implies affecting public opinion, often by mounting a media relations campaign. The commonly held view is that public opinion is 'what is in the media' and if what the media says can be affected, public opinion will also be influenced because the media help to set the public agenda.

Most people have opinions on most things, they only have to be asked. These opinions may be strongly or weakly held as explained in the discussion on beliefs in Chapter 5. The fear of many public relations practitioners is that these opinions could be drawn together and focused by the media against their organization. The hope is by getting an organization's message out to as many people as possible mass opinion will be supportive. Thus many public relations programmes adopt a scattergun approach, spreading very general messages via mass online and traditional communication channels to very broad publics.

Recent research in the USA[2] has shown that contrary to earlier thinking media consumption was dividing according to generational or political differences, it is the topic and spread of the story that principally determines where people go for news. Most people use a mix of sources to keep up to date including newspapers, TV, radio, computer and mobile phone. Three quarters of Americans get news every day, and this includes six out of ten who are under 30.

What can be concluded is news consumption is fragmenting as people use a plethora of sources to obtain news. In addition, most people have neither the time nor the energy to be involved in everything. They are selective and devote time to those things that they are involved in, and where they feel they can make a contribution.

Uniform public opinion occurs very occasionally and well-informed public opinion occurs even more rarely. What uniformity there is is increasingly under threat as people turn to many different sources of news, each with very different editorial stances and some with no pretence of being objective.

Having said this, the media still play a role in setting the public mood and agenda and the mainstream media are often the primary sources of information for online opinion formers, so their influence is still extensive.

The media do not always determine what people think; but they do provide a platform for discussing issues and they can reinforce and 'steer' the 'public' view if a particular issue catches the imagination.

However, what appears to be a small proportion of the total population (for example students) concerned with a particular issue (emerging nation indebtedness) can be a large group when all banded together and can affect the mission of a large organization (eg the banks).

Opinions are very interesting phenomena and can operate at different levels. Asked for a view of something in the news, most people will offer an opinion. That might be superficial and not always thought-through. These views might be called perceptions. At a deeper level people may have an opinion about a particular issue such as hanging, which has been well thought-through and for which they can produce arguments. They can be said to have a particular attitude towards that subject. At an even deeper level attitudes can turn into forms of behaviour. At the most extreme, this could take the form of direct action which could be against the law, such as some of the activities of the more militant animal rights groups.

To make things even more complicated, as indicated earlier, people can hold two conflicting opinions at the same time. For example, they might think animal experiments are wrong in general, but also believe that certain types of drugs should be tested on animals before being used on human beings.

Types of publics

In general terms, publics can be divided into active or passive. James Grunig[3] defines four sorts of publics:

- *Non-publics*, which are groups that neither are affected by nor affect the organization. For example, a retailer based in southern India will have no effect on and will not be affected by publics based in northern India. Broadly speaking, these publics can be ignored and are often not even identified.

- *Latent publics*, which are groups that face a problem as a result of an organization's actions, but fail to recognize it. For example, a haulage company planning on expanding its business may as a consequence increase local traffic levels, yet the local residents may be unaware of this.

- *Aware publics*, which are groups that recognize that a problem exists. In our haulage company example, the local residents may read a tweet from an employee that tells them about the intended expansion.

This apparently theoretical approach is useful, since if an organization identifies its issues-based publics it will pinpoint those who are likely to be the activists on any particular issue. This is particularly important when dealing with online communities, which we have seen (Chapter 5) form around issues.

From this it is clear that active publics are the most likely to use information from public relations programmes as a prompt for their behaviour. They will only be a proportion of the targeted population; however, it is important to identify them since communication effort should be focused on them.

A further note of caution is needed. Grunig says that if attitudes or behaviour objectives are changed (remembering that awareness will have been raised already), don't expect to affect more than 20 per cent of the target group and remember that some of these will be negative in their response. The importance of researching the attitudes of various publics, what they think of the organization and how they act enables organizations to determine how they can understand and communicate more effectively, cannot be overemphasized.

It is, of course, eminently sensible to put together the traditional way of segmenting publics into consumers, employees, etc, with Grunig's approach. The broader categories can be analysed for those subgroups that are likely to be active, aware and latent. It brings a very potent communication perspective and helps prioritize the actions of the communicator.

Grunig's work has been criticized as not being sensitive to cultural or diversity issues, that it does not properly engage with the differences in power between the communicating partners or the fact that people have relationships with organizations at many levels and in many different types of situation. Nonetheless, it does promote a good starting point for considering publics and, particularly the fact that publics collect around issues is a seminal insight.

Using other segmentation techniques

Apart from Grunig's method of identifying publics there are others that are used by public relations practitioners. There are several ways publics can be segmented or categorized and the best way will be determined by the nature of the programme. For example, a government wanting to promote responsible driving may segment by age, gender and type of car. A youth club wanting new members may segment by age and proximity to the club. An online clothing retailer will segment by age, income, lifestyle and gender. There are many ways to segment publics:

- by geography – where people live, work, go on holiday;
- by demographics – age, gender, income, social class;
- by psychographics – attitudes, opinions, beliefs;
- by group membership – of clubs, societies, professional associations;

- by media consumption – of newspapers, magazines, websites;
- by type of power:
  - overt: religious leader, opinion former
  - covert: influence, connectedness;
- by role in decision process – financial director, CEO, parent, head teacher.

A common segmentation technique is to identify the two most important variables for the situation being addressed and to create a matrix with these two variables as axes.

One of the most popular is the power/interest matrix used by strategic business planners.[4]

FIGURE 6.2   Power/interest matrix

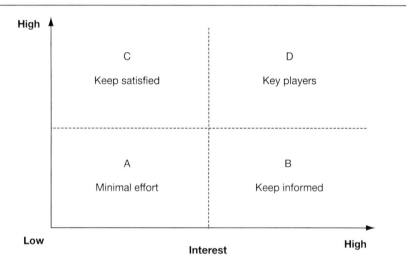

The author has seen other variables such as credibility and reach, resources and influence used in a similar way.

The power/interest matrix categorizes publics according to the amount of power they have (and that needs to be defined; is it resource power, influence over others, power by virtue of their role, political power etc?) and the level of interest they have in the issue that is the focus of the public relations programme (and interest needs to be defined: is it personal interest, do they represent others and is the interest positive or negative, etc?). The more power and interest they have, the more likely they will impact on the organization: hence their label – key players have most power and most interest.

It is possible and desirable at times to move publics from one segment to another. For example, shareholders often reside in segment C, their interest being limited if the company is performing well financially. However, in times of crisis, it might be desirable to stimulate their interest so that they become positive and active supporters of the company, in which case increased communication will be used to move them to segment D. Similarly, activist groups can often be placed in segment B; they have a lot of interest. By keeping them informed and addressing their issues as far as possible, it may be possible to move them towards segment A, or at least prevent them from seeking means to achieve power and hence becoming key players.

When applying this model to the public and third sectors, care is needed. Groups without power or interest are usually given minimal attention in the private sector: they are regarded as unimportant. However, in the public or third sectors it can be the reverse. Many charities exist to give a voice to those who have little power or have no interest in issues that might affect them. In the public sector, hard to reach groups who have little power and whose interest is blocked by practical issues such as an inability to read or to speak the dominant language, can be found in this segment.

By carefully plotting publics in the grid it is possible to identify who potential advocates or opponents are and how communication should be used to engage with them. For example, more information may empower a group. By focusing on issues that concern them specifically, it will be possible to stimulate their interest. A visual tool such as this helps to identify more easily who should be repositioned on the grid and where they are relative to other players. By exploring scenarios it will help to show how stakeholders may move as the scenario develops. Their potential movement may or may not be desirable and preventative action can then be considered.

In social marketing campaigns, which are designed to stimulate behavioural change about some of the larger issues that affect society as a whole, a detailed examination of target publics is undertaken in order to gain Insight: a technical term meaning a profound understanding of people that is then used to identify the mechanisms that will change their behaviour. This is a three-stage process involving data collection (the what), obtaining key understandings (the why) in order to identify the key levers that will generate behaviour change (the how).

Data collection comes from four sources: an environmental analysis (outlined as EPISTLE in Chapter 2), existing studies (for example from databases), commissioned research (for example, through a questionnaire) and then an in-depth understanding of the publics whose behaviour the organization is wanting to change (obtained, for example, from observation).

In addition to this, a detailed understanding of who exactly the target publics are (demographics), their attitudes and opinions (psychographics) and what they do (behaviours), will provide a rich picture.

Drawing all this information together, analysing it and synthesizing it then leads to some fundamental understandings of the issue, how people associate with it and, specifically, how they can be motivated to change – this last part is the resultant Insight.

Insight is vital in behaviour-change programmes. It helps to develop that 'killer' proposition that makes people want to change their behaviour. For example, in the early 2000s there was a problem with young people, in particular, not wanting to use rear seat belts. They felt rear seat belts were restrictive and uncomfortable, wearing them indicated distrust of the driver, seat belts were for little kids and rear passengers were not as vulnerable as those in the front. Research also revealed that many drivers were killed by unbelted rear seat passengers, who, if there was a collision from the front, smashed into them from behind.

The insight arrived at from the research and a deep understanding of the target publics was that they certainly did not want to be responsible for the deaths of drivers, people who they often knew and loved. A campaign built around this insight increased seat belt use by that group by 23 per cent over just one year.

So what about the media?

Earlier the role of the media in influencing public opinion was played down, but it is obvious that it does have a powerful impact in our lives. Here are some general observations.

The media are more likely to create a public when the information is negative. People react against child abuse or government officials being overpaid expenses. If the coverage is extensive and the topic catches the imagination it is possible that a hot-issue public could be created.

Hot-issue publics often react to the thing of the moment without necessarily thinking things through carefully, and once media interest dies down, so does theirs. However, if an organization handles a hot issue badly it could turn hot-issue publics into longer-term active ones by forcing them to think more deeply about the issues concerned. The growing support for 'natural foods' is a case in point.

Media campaigns to promote organizations are most likely to reach active publics who positively seek out any information about the organiza-tion they are interested in. This includes those who are opposed to them as well as those who may support them. Thinking through the consequences and likely reactions of those who feel negatively about the organization when seeking media coverage is, therefore, very important.

The implications for targeting publics

The implications of all this are fairly obvious. Don't devote too much time on publics that are not interested in what is being done or said, but always keep an eye on them just in case. Of course, if the aim is to reach a disinterested public, practitioners will have to be creative about how they reach them and it will usually take more time and effort to accomplish objectives. There will be a need to research what channels and issues there are that are important to them and to attach to those interest points. Active publics are the 'communicators' friend'. They positively seek out and want to understand information. On the downside while it is possible to keep a low profile with them, if they are not supplied with information, they will seek it from elsewhere and that could have negative or positive results.

It is unrealistic to expect changes in attitude and behaviour from huge numbers of publics or for it to happen quickly. Only a proportion of active and aware publics are likely to respond. However, they can act as catalysts for change and their power should not be underestimated.

How to prioritize publics

If initiating or rebuilding a public relations department from scratch the practitioner will need to make an assessment about which publics are most important and how much time and resource should be devoted to them.

The easiest way to categorize publics is to move from the general to the particular. First of all define broad categories to identify their overall connections with the organization. Divide these broad categories into particular groups. As indicated earlier in this chapter, this could be done on the basis of geography or the level of activity likely from the group, or on the power and influence of that group.

An example of how time (and resources) can be prioritized is given in Table 6.1 (the groupings are very broad, but the principle holds). For individual programmes or campaigns the same principles can be applied, although the headings will be different depending on how the various publics are segmented.

TABLE 6.1 Proportioning out the public relations effort to different publics

Grouping	Percentage of communication effort required
Corporate	25
Shareholders (active)	10
Shareholders (latent)	2
Government ministers (active)	4
Government ministers (aware)	3
Opposition front bench (active)	3
Opposition front bench (aware)	1
Senior civil servants	2

TABLE 6.1   *continued*

Grouping	Percentage of communication effort required	
Customers		25
ABC1 householders (current purchasers)	10	
ABC1 householders (potential)	5	
Retail shops (active)	7	
Retail shops (new)	3	
Employees		20
Executives	3	
Supervisors	7	
Shopfloor workers	7	
Trade union leaders	3	
Community		15
Neighbours	4	
Community leaders	5	
Schools		
Headteachers	2	
PTA	2	
Governors	2	
Suppliers		9
Raw materials		
major suppliers	6	
minor suppliers	3	
Services		6
major suppliers	4	
minor suppliers	2	

The amount of effort and time that is required for each public will be determined by the configuration of factors specific to the situation, including importance, urgency, power, legitimacy and how communicative the organization wishes to be.

The overall level of activity is likely to be limited by budget.

Remember that individuals or groups can belong to more than one category so there needs to be identification and monitoring of the cross-overs to ensure that publics are treated equitably, and so that there is conflicting content is not available, even if there are differences in emphasis or different content depending on the needs of different publics: co-ordination is vital.

What shall we say?

Devising the content of a programme or campaign is a complex business and very specific to the individual situation. There are a number of considerations that need to be taken into account. First, the nature of the campaign itself.

The nature of the campaign

There are three main types of campaigns.

Information campaigns: seek to transmit information and do not encourage dialogue. They are essentially one way. It is perfectly legitimate to conduct an information campaign. For example, a doctor's surgery may wish to inform patients about extended opening hours. In essence this is a transmission of factual information. Clarity and the use of appropriate channels are the key elements for success here.

Persuasion campaigns: seek to persuade people to a particular view, ie to affect their attitudes or to influence their behaviour in some way. Social marketing campaigns fall into this category. The originating organization presents a case as persuasively as possible, in order to evoke a specific response. Use of appropriate channels is obviously required and a level of dialogue is to be anticipated as arguments develop.

Persuasive campaigns are often the purpose of public relations activity, and some of the descriptors the industry uses, for example, lobbying or advocacy, underline that. Persuasive campaigns cover the whole gamut of public relations activity, from consumer campaigns promoting products, industry associations putting a case for fracking to election campaigns, to government campaigns wanting to promote certain behaviours such as online submission of tax returns, to activist groups promoting their particular cause.

Dialogue-based campaigns: in these types of campaign organizations and groups communicate as peers, the one learning from the other, seeking mutual benefits and sharing on an equal basis. Dialogue can promote understanding, joint decision making and action, and deepens relationships, reputations and respect. Well-conducted dialogue is essential for relationships of trust to develop.

It must be borne in mind, however, that not all dialogue results in the positive. Sometimes, dialogue reveals deep differences and divisions, but if this occurs, dialogue can help to promote an understanding and hopefully a respect for the other point of view, even if the end result is an agreement not to agree. Hence, dialogue can have a twin purpose: to build coalitions where there is consensus, and/or to identify areas of potential conflict and then work towards a resolution of the issues involved.

Clearly dialogue requires open and two-way channels of communication. The content will be emerging, developing and multi-layered as people strive to make sense using the frames alluded to earlier in the book. Dialogue could well involve persuasion as each party makes their case, sometimes forcefully, but it will also involve conceding points and a willingness to be persuaded.

'Deliberative engagement' is a phrase used to describe dialogue-based campaigns that result in decision making by the target public, together with the organization initiating the dialogue. It is a technique being used increasingly by the public sector in the UK, an example being how community-based projects should be prioritized and run.

Constructing the content

Having decided what the nature of the interaction will be, the content then has to be developed accordingly. It is generally accepted that communication is made up of both rational and emotional elements.

Rational content

The use of rational arguments to persuade goes back to Greek times. The rhetoricians used logic and reason to invest their arguments with power. Smith[5] has put together a summary of the main arguments contained in the research on persuasive communication and concludes the following: the primary idea behind a persuasive speech, advertisement, e-letter or other communication vehicle is called a proposition.

There are four kinds of proposition:

- *Fact:* based on what actually exists or is the case and is provable. Facts are often used to enhance awareness or understanding. For example it is a fact that more women than men in the UK are involved in gaming[6].

- *Conjecture:* based on what it is reasonable to conclude given the evidence and inviting the identified public to agree. Conjecture is used to gain acceptance and/or support. For example, given all the evidence on climate change it is reasonable to conclude that coal-fired power stations should be as coal-efficient as possible.

- *Value:* these types of proposition focus on the virtue or intrinsic worth of something. This aims to increase interest or build positive opinions. For example, the merits of giving asylum to a persecuted minority may be argued on virtue grounds: everyone should be able to live without fear of persecution.

- *Policy:* argues for the adoption of a new policy, and is aimed at forming opinions and affecting behaviour. For example, advocating an increase in the school-leaving age.

Propositions are backed by strong arguments and proof wherever possible. Where action is required they are also accompanied by the removal of any barriers. Smith goes on to say that physical evidence to support propositions is the most compelling, but in many situations that is just not available, in which case other types of 'evidence' can be used:

- *Analogies:* using familiar situations and illustrations to draw parallels so that understanding is facilitated. Analogies are often presented as similes or metaphors. So, for example, tweeting can be likened to gossiping, only online.

- *Comparisons:* by identifying a particular characteristic or value relating to an issue and then making positive or negative association with something familiar. Comparing political parties' records on education with one another will put one or the other in a better light.

- *Examples:* the public is able to draw conclusions because of examples that are relevant. For example, you know this product is reliable, because the other six in the range have all been so.

- *Statistics:* to provide reliable evidence that claims are true. For example, this is a good school because we have statistics to prove excellent pupil performance over 10 years.

- *Testimonials and endorsements:* testimonials are provided by people who have used services and products. Endorsements are provided by people who are prepared to back the cause or the ideas of the organization. For example, testimonials about services provided by a firm of accountants are a common feature of their publicity material. Endorsements are often sought from celebrities, for example celebrities supporting fundraising efforts on YouTube videos.

- *Case studies:* detailed examples provided by users of services or products, or of causes that have been supported that encourage adoption by others.

- *Visual evidence:* such as photographs, charts, blogs, online videos, animated websites, diagrams, illustrations and so on all add power to content.

- *Demonstrations, presentations, exhibitions:* often provide a way to present first-hand experiences of products or services.

Emotional content

Human beings can sometimes respond to rational arguments alone. However, most human beings require a mixture of both rational and emotional content to evoke a reaction. The public relations planner will have to make a judgement on the correct mix of rational and emotional appeal that they need to put into the campaign. It is likely that campaigns about returning tax forms promptly will be more rational in nature, whereas campaigns about engagement rings will be more emotional.

On occasion there are deliberate cross-overs from what might be regarded as more naturally rational campaigns, to draw people in emotionally and so encourage sales. For example, toilet rolls are a commodity product, but Andrex have used their puppy Labrador for years to create an emotional attachment to the product via a cute and vulnerable dog.

Emotions are used either positively or negatively. Smith provides four examples of positive emotional appeals:

Love appeals: these focus on the many aspects of love – family, pity, compassion, sympathy, bittersweet, etc. Love-based images are very powerful and are often used by charities for fundraising.

Virtue appeals: these can be used rationally, but they can also be used emotionally. Linking campaigns to the community and individual sense of what is right and proper is very powerful. Hence, calls to enlist during wartime, for organ donation and volunteering all draw on appeals to virtue.

Humour appeals: good for reinforcing existing attitudes and behaviours, but not very effective in changing them. Humour makes the originator more liked, but rarely more credible. Humour should be used to complement a message, not as a substitute. It also needs to be tasteful and genuinely funny.

Sex appeal: a difficult area. Sex appeal can range from the suggestive to the outrageous. Sex appeal content can demand attention, but great care has to be used to ensure it is appropriate to the target group and that it is not offensive. An issue with sex appeal is that often the sexual content is remembered, but not the brand. Footballer David Beckham has famously modelled underpants, but fewer people remember that the brand was Armani. The most effective way to use sexual content is if there is a strong link to the product or theme, for example links to contraceptive devices or underage sexual activity.

Smith also provides two examples of content based on negative emotion:

Fear appeals: these aim to affect behaviour directly. Fear appeals must be accompanied by an easy and immediate solution to the problem. The key to effective fear appeals is that they must be proportionate. Put too strongly and people can avoid the issue or defy it. Also, without a ready solution, no matter how great the fear is, people will feel powerless and remain inactive. Source credibility is critical in fear appeals, and the source is best when it is quite dissimilar to the target public. Hence, use of scientists, unknown to the public, is a common ploy. Obviously, if the issue is important or significant to the target public, it will also have more effect. The thought of a large refuse tip being located within smelling distance of their houses is likely to galvanize community action.

Guilt appeals: aim at promoting a sense of personal guilt or shame. As with fear appeals, guilt should be used in moderation and providing a route from feeling guilty towards a more positive frame of mind, such as feeling fair or just, is the mirror of offering a solution in fear appeals. For example, people may feel guilty about poverty in Asia, but also want to feel they can help to solve that by being generous and fair.

One final thought: as Smith points out, when conducting fear or guilt campaigns, careful consideration must be given to any ethical implications.

Content and messages

Earlier in this chapter information and persuasion campaigns were discussed and it was argued that there are right and proper uses for these types of campaign. Often campaigns of this type have messages that the originator wants to get across. Even in dialogue-based communication there may again be some core content, which may be described as messages, that each party will want to register as important, or even as non-negotiable.

The different kind of engagement with publics mainly assisted by online technologies is driving public relations towards being dialogue-based; however, the notion of core content or messages does have relevance, but requires careful thought.

Messages have utility for two additional reasons. First of all they are an essential part of the awareness and attitude-forming process. If publics play back to the originator the message that the originator has initiated, it is a clear indication (a) that the message has been received and (b) that the message has been taken on board and is in some way being used. That may be just as a part of the thinking process, or it may permeate as far as actions.

The second reason is that they help to demonstrate the effectiveness of the communication. They are an essential part of the evaluation process. If distinct messages are utilized directly by the press, or if they are repeated in evaluative research such as attitude surveys, that clearly shows the messages have been assimilated.

Content and the messages within it are often under-crafted, but they are vitally important. They are the point of contact between an organization and its publics in communication terms. They are what are 'given' by the organization and 'received' by the public and vice versa. Messages and the way they are conveyed are the starting point of the thinking, attitude or behavioural change that the organization is seeking. Badly done, they can be the end point too.

Crafting messages

There are four steps in crafting effective messages:

- *Step one* is to take existing articulated perceptions. For example, it may be that an organization's products are regarded as old-fashioned and this has been identified in earlier research.

- *Step two* is to define what shifts can be made in those perceptions. If, in fact, the products have been substantially upgraded this needs to be said loud and clear.

- *Step three* is to identify elements of persuasion. The best way to do this in this case, as indicated earlier, is to work on the basis of fact. The organization might be making major investments in upgrading their plant. It could be that there has been a series of new technology initiatives. Maybe they have won an innovation award recently. These are all facts that falsify the view that their products are old-fashioned.

- *Step four* is to ensure the messages can be credibly delivered through public relations rather than some other means, such as salesforce training.

Messages can be general in nature. Sometimes they have an overall corporate thrust. Advertising pay-off lines or company straplines such as Audi's 'Vorsprung durch Technik' are a good example. The organization's message is that it is at the forefront of technological advancement.

These general messages are often backed up by very specific sub-messages which may pinpoint a particular piece of information or a specific service that an organization wants to put across.

For example, the Royal Mail has a main message on its commitment to the local communities.[7]

It also has various sub-messages to illustrate the main message: 'Royal Mail invests around £10 million directly in UK communities', 'Our Articles for the Blind scheme provides a free delivery service for blind and visually impaired people', 'We hold the Guinness World Record for payroll giving' and 'We aim to raised at least £2 million for our charity of the year – Prostate Cancer UK'.

Again, as mentioned earlier, it is important that messages do not conflict as people can belong to more than one public. It is perfectly feasible for there to be differences in nuance, or for messages to differ from one public to another, but the overall thrust of the messages must be in broad alignment with each other.

How the message should be presented

The integrity of a message is affected by a whole host of things that determine whether it is taken seriously or not:

- *Format.* How is the message put across? Are there visual images that are associated with it? The care taken with the physical presentation of a corporate identity is a good example of this. The appropriate words, even typeface, must be used to get across the impact of the message. Bold, joking messages often use brash, elaborate typefaces, serious material uses serif typefaces. A financial institute is probably not going to use funny cartoons to put across a death benefit product.

- *Tone.* Choice of language is very important. All messages need to have careful attention paid to the mood, atmosphere or style that they are trying to portray. The mood might be upbeat or sombre. This point is carefully linked to the format issue.

- *Context.* The context in which a message is seen is vital. If, for example, an organization announces its company results on the day a stock market slide occurs, its performance will be commented on in the light of this.

- *Timing.* It is no use pumping out information about the special Christmas offers if Christmas was last week.

- *Repetition.* Obviously the more often a credible message is repeated, the more likely it is to be heard and picked up. However, familiarity can breed contempt and care has to be taken not to repeat messages for the sake of it or they will become devalued. Using a raft of communication channels can help, since in the mind of the receiver there can be a reinforcement of credibility if they see the message in different contexts and endorsed by different media and other third parties.

On top of these points there are three things that need to be said about the source from which content or messages emanate:

- *Credibility:* the source of the message or content should be credible, that is they must be believable. A credible source is one that is seen to have the right to speak because they have the expertise or knowledge, are of the right status and are seen to be a person of honesty and integrity. Recent research by Edelman[8] has shown that the most credible spokespeople are academics or industry experts and company technical experts. The least credible are CEOs and Government officials or regulators.

- *Personability:* the source needs to be seen to be sympathetic or empathetic to the issue. It also helps if the public sees them as a person they can relate to.

- *Control:* a source may need to be able to demonstrate a measure of control over the situation in hand. Some sources do have power and authority. For example, at the end of the day a government can legislate to change behaviour and/or punish those who do not conform. The ability to stand up to, or for something and not be found wanting is a key element to reputation and relationship building.

Having command over all these factors is likely to be a tall order: a meticulously planned media event can be ruined bcause of a breaking news story, more positively there are always opportunities that suddenly occur which can be taken advantage of even if the context is not the best possible.

Sometimes the choice of media in which content is relayed is restricted and not seen to be ideal. An annual report is a legal document and some of the information in it is strictly regulated. At other times the message imperative will dictate the communication channel. A product recall dictates that advertising and online will be used to get the message out as quickly and in as controlled a format as possible, despite the fact that the world will know about the problems, even those who haven't purchased the product.

It is often the case that content and messages are not given the meticulous attention they deserve in public relations programmes. General messages are all very well in themselves, but particular publics should be served by carefully researched and constructed messages set within the proper context and medium if the communication is to do a specific job of work. Vague content in communication brings about vague results. Carefully researched, sharply refined and aimed content and messages may have an opportunity to deliver the desired effects.

Notes

1 Cutlip, S M, Center, A H and Broom, G M (2006) *Effective Public Relations*, Prentice-Hall, Upper Saddle River, NJ, 9th edn

2 The Media Insight Project 2014. An initiative of the American Press Institute and the Associated Press – NORC Center for Public Affairs Research. See www.america-pressinstitute.org/publications/reports/survey-research/personal-news-cycle

3 Grunig, J E and Hunt, T (1984) *Managing Public Relations*, Holt, Rinehart & Winston, New York

4 Johnson, J, Scholes, K and Whittington, R (2007) *Exploring Corporate Strategy*, Pearson Education, London, 8th edn

5 Smith, R D (2009) *Strategic Planning for Public Relations*, Lawrence Erlbaum Associates, Mahwah, NJ, 3rd edn

6 Internet Advertising Bureau UK (2014) *Gaming Revolution*, Internet Advertising Bureau UK

7 See www.royalmailgroup.com/community-supporting-our-communities

8 Edelman Trust Barometer Global Results (2015) See www.edelman.com/insights/intellectual-property/2015-edelman-trust-barometer

07
Strategy and tactics

The fourth basic question in the planning process asked in Chapter 3 was 'How shall I say it?' – what mechanisms shall be used to communicate? The answer to this question falls into two parts: strategy and tactics.

Getting the strategy right

Moving immediately from objectives or content to tactics is a temptation planners should resist. Devising the strategy for a plan or campaign is the most difficult part of the planning process. If the strategy is right, everything else rolls off the back of it.

Rather than thinking of a cohesive and coherent strategy, many practitioners move straight to tactics, the 'What shall we do?' part of the campaign, rather than considering carefully how the overall approach should be shaped. They then end up with a fragmented, unfocused effort which lacks any underpinning direction or driving force.

Strategy, like planning, applies at all levels: to the overall approach to communication, to full ongoing programmes and to individual campaigns. It's important because it focuses effort, it gets results and it looks to the long term.

What is strategy?

Strategy is the cohering approach that is taken to a programme or campaign. It is the coordinating theme or factor, the guiding principle, the rationale behind the tactical programme.

Strategy is dictated by the issues arising from analysis of the information at the planners' disposal (see Chapter 4). It is not the same as objectives and it comes before tactics. It is the foundation upon which a tactical programme is built. Strategy is the principle that will move the planners from where they are now to where they want to be. It is sometimes called 'the big idea'. Sometimes it is: it can be an all-embracing concept. Sometimes it isn't, and planners shouldn't be overly concerned if they can't come up with a big idea. They should, however, be very concerned if they don't have a clear rationale.

A very clear if somewhat dated and unpleasant example of 'strategy' and 'tactics' was demonstrated in the war conducted by the combined forces which moved against Iraq following that country's invasion of Kuwait (a particularly appropriate example bearing in mind the military origins of the two words):

The objective: to get the Iraqis out of Kuwait
The strategy: according to General Colin Powell was to
                   cut them (the Iraqis) off and kill them
The tactics: pincer movement of ground forces to cut the
                   Iraqis off from Iraq, carpet bombing, diversionary tactics,
                   cutting bridges, jamming communications and so on

Further examples of the relationship between objectives, strategy and tactics are given in Table 7.1.

Strategies can be built around a number of propositions. For example, sometimes a strategy is clearly borne out of the necessity to use certain kinds of channel or tactics. For example, given that gaming is prevalent in the under-18 population, it could well be that a game becomes the focus of a campaign with other elements of activity being based on it (toys of the characters, apps, clothes etc). If the issue is credibility, then endorsement by

TABLE 7.1   Examples of objectives, strategy and tactics

	Example one (single-objective, short-term campaign)	Example two (longer-term strategic positioning programme)
Objective	Publicize new product or service	Establish as market leader
Strategy	Mount media relations campaign in trade press	Position as industry voice of authority
Tactics	Press conference Press releases Interviews Advertising Advertorial Visuals/copy for online Mags	Research-based reports Quality literature Media relations Thought-leading web content Webinars Google hang-out Speaker platforms Industry forums Award schemes etc

indirect channels (third partner) may be the strategy chosen. Sometimes the strategy is to focus on a particular theme or message. The long-running road safety campaigns in the UK revolve around the message, 'Think!' – think before you drink and drive; think by keeping distance between you and the driver in front; think about driving when you are tired, etc.

In a nutshell, strategy is *how* you will achieve an objective and tactics are *what* you will do. For large programmes with several elements, eg community relations, employee relations and customer relations, there may well be strategy for each part of the programme.

From strategy to tactics

Tactics are the methods or activities that are used to implement the strategy.

It goes without saying that tactics should be clearly linked to strategy. When developing a tactical programme all the powers of creativity need to be deployed, but there are one or two key factors that should be borne in mind:

- *Use strategy to guide brainstorms.* Strategy should not act as a straitjacket, but it does help to keep focus on the job in hand.
- *Reject non-strategic activities.* Brainstorms are marvellous and stimulating, and all kinds of exciting ideas can emerge. However, no matter how good the idea, non-strategic activities should be discarded: if they don't fit in with the strategic thrust of this programme, they need to be put on one side and saved for another day.
- *Relate tactics to strategy and strategy to objectives.* There should be a definite logical progression. Objectives give the overall direction to the programme – what needs to be achieved. Strategy provides the driving force, the 'how to', and tactics give the activity programme in detail, what will be done on a day-to-day basis.
- *Test tactics where possible.* It is always advisable to find out as far as possible if a particular tactic will work. There may be a reasonable expectation it will work because similar things have been done before, in a slightly different context. Test feasibility as far as possible. Thus, if the idea is to run a series of competitions online, there needs to be some kind of online trial to find out if there is support for the idea.

The link between strategy and tactics is crucial and two things should be borne in mind. If the strategy has been carefully thought-through and it is clearly the right one to use, tactics should be changed before strategy. It is likely that something is wrong at the tactical level if a programme is not working as it should. Changing strategy means that there is probably something wrong at a fundamental level, maybe with the conclusions on the main issues or with the objectives that have been set, or maybe there is something missing in the data collection or the analysis that has been done.

Of course, there must be some flexibility of approach. Sometimes when moving on to the tactics of a campaign it is realized that a particular tactic, or group of tactics, should become the strategic thrust of the programme. For example, maybe a company has a problem with name recognition (people remember the products but not the organization). It could well be that the strategy is to project the company name more prominently on its promotional material. Tactically, new literature is recommended that has stronger company branding together with a revamp of the website and making the company name larger on the products. Putting this into practice may lead the public relations professional to the conclusion that a rethink of the company's corporate identity is required, and this then becomes the strategy, giving coherence, direction and a framework around which to hang the communication programme as a whole.

While the classic way to plan is strategy first and then tactics, it is sometimes the case that some tactics just stand out as being obvious and should be core to the programme. For example, with scientific communities evidence is required, hence research-based activities are an obvious tactic. Back-rationalizing this thinking could lead to the planner concluding that a strategy based on a number of research reports on key issues is correct. Tactics would then focus on the exploitation of these reports and associated activities.

What tactics should be employed?

It would be easy to think up a series of clever ideas and put them together into some kind of programme. Too often the techniques themselves become the focus of attention rather than the objective they are meant to achieve.

A programme with a variety of publics and objectives will need a variety of tactics.

One way of looking at public relations programmes is to regard them as 'contact and convince' or 'contact and dialogue' programmes. The first task is to identify and contact the relevant target publics, which entails selecting the publics and choosing channels of communication through which to contact them. Second, convince them, through the power of communications, that they should think, believe or act in a certain way, or set up the platform for dialogue.

The set of techniques used in a contact programme must reach the requisite number of target publics and get the desired content across to them with enough impact so as to influence them in some way. And this must be done at a reasonable cost. So the public relations practitioner needs to select from a menu of activities of the kind shown in Figure 7.1.

FIGURE 7.1 Range of tactics available to practitioners

MEDIA RELATIONS	INTERNAL COMMUNICATION
Press conference	Videos
Press releases	Briefings
Articles and features	Newsletters
One-to-one briefings	Quality guides
Interviews	CD/DVD
Background briefings/materials	E-mail
Photography	Intranet
Letters to editors	Business TV
Story ideas	Meetings
Advertorials	One-to-ones
Guest editorials	Social media
Media directories	
Video news releases	
Website	
E-mail	
Digital and social media	
ADVERTISING	**CORPORATE IDENTITY**
Corporate and product	Logos
Magazines	Buildings
Newspapers	Product branding
Websites	Clothing
TV, cable, radio	Letterheads
Billboard posters	Publications
Signage	Website
Merchandise	Merchandise
Digital and social media	Vehicles
	Digital and social media
DIRECT MAIL	**SPONSORSHIP**
Annual report	Sport
Brochures/leaflets	Arts
Customer reports	Worthy causes
External newsletters	Education
General literature	Buildings/places
Merchandise	Charities
CD/DVD	NGOs
Letters	Co-branding

FIGURE 7.1 *continued*

EXHIBITIONS	LOBBYING
Trade and Public Literature Sampling Demonstrations Multi-platform media	One-to-one briefings Background material Literature Group briefings Hospitality CD and DVD Data sticks
CONFERENCES	RESEARCH
Multi-platform Literature Hospitality	Organizations Public relations programmes Issues monitoring Results monitoring
COMMUNITY RELATIONS	CRISIS MANAGEMENT
Direct involvement Gifts-in-kind Sponsorship Donations	Planning Implementation
SPECIAL EVENTS	LIAISON
AGMs SGMs Special occasions Fairs Carnivals Social events Fundraising	Internal (including counselling) External
CUSTOMER RELATIONS	FINANCIAL RELATIONS
Media relations Direct mail Advertising Digital Social networks Exhibitions Retail outlets Sponsorship Product literature Newsletters	Annual report Briefing materials One-to-one briefing Media relations Hospitality Online

Careful choices have to be made about the combination of techniques to be used and the balance between the various activities selected. Each technique (and channel) has its own strengths and weaknesses. The idea is to select a range of techniques that complement each other and which, when taken as a whole, provide a powerful raft of communication.

Some examples will illustrate the point. If a company wants to launch a new and highly visual product, such as a new range of expensive cosmetics, it is important that techniques are selected that allow the physical qualities of the product to be demonstrated and where there is some opportunity for some two-way communication. Techniques employed might be an interactive website, videos, exhibitions, sending product samples to journalists and specialist interest online sites and communities, brochures with high-quality photographs and a coupon response that can be followed up by sending samples, a campaign with specialist magazines with product samples attached for consumers, sampling opportunities at retail outlets, and demonstrations at fashion events.

In another situation, say where a company chairperson wants to give detailed financial information to some key investors, the visual and tactile aspects would not be so important, neither is the chairperson talking to a mass audience. In this instance it is important that the message is closely controlled, so an on- and offline mass media campaign would not be the best method. The methods chosen might be seminars, detailed briefing papers and one-to-one or small group meetings. In these instances, the opportunity for one-to-one interaction to check understanding and support would be critical.

Sometimes the type of campaign clearly dictates the selection of techniques. It would be a brave (or foolish) car manufacturer who did not take its new model to motor shows and allow journalists to test drive it.

Likewise, some techniques are more appropriate to certain types of campaigns. In the consumer area stunts and attention-grabbing, creative ideas that can be used with the media or online are often a part of the programme, but this is not usually the case in serious lobbying campaigns (although sometimes it is).

An effective way of deciding which techniques to use is to match them with the stakeholder mapping given in Chapter 6. The thinking behind the method is that those with most power and interest require most attention, and that communication should be personalized and designed to engage them. Those with least power and interest should have least attention devoted to them, the techniques should be less personal (mass) and engagement is not important. Figure 7.2 provides the strategy (headings in bold) with example tactics for the power interest matrix.

However, there is a danger with this approach as indicated in Chapter 6. Those people with low interest and low power may be exactly the kind of individuals with whom an organization wishes to engage; therefore by using more interactive and personal communication, attempts can be made to stimulate engagement with them.

FIGURE 7.2   Methodology for linking strategy and tactics[1]

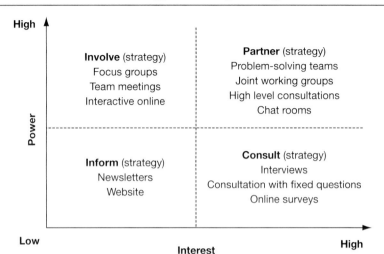

Clearly there is an enormous range or tactics available, so how is the final selection made? There are two tests to apply:

- *Appropriateness.* Will the technique actually reach the target publics being aimed for? Will they have the right amount of impact? Is this a credible and influential technique to carry the message the organization is waiting to relay? Will the message get through using this technique? Do the techniques suit the message (content, tone, creative treatment)? Is it compatible with other communication devices that the organization is using?

- *Deliverability.* Can these techniques be implemented successfully? Can they be done within the budget and to the required timescale? Is there access to the right people with the right expertise to implement the techniques?

Having made the decisions about which broad techniques to employ, consideration has to be given to the specific media to use. Thus, if it is decided that an exhibition is a most suitable technique, then the question becomes which exhibition needs to be attended? Here judgements have to be made on areas such as how many target publics attend the list of available exhibitions. There may be a particular sub-set that needs contacting. How does the cost compare between the different exhibitions and which is most cost-effective? What sort of fellow exhibitors will there be and are they likely to enhance or detract from the organization's reputation? How influential are those exhibitions? Can the organization afford not to be there? Who is of importance, for example the media, and will they be there? What are the logistical practicalities of attending one as opposed to another exhibition?

It is in the area of tactics that creativity can shine. A good creative idea adds sparkle and difference to a campaign, and it doesn't have to be entirely wacky either. A nice example is provided by a residential care community looking after adults with long-term mental health and physical disability problems. The members of the community are virtually self-sufficient and a key part of their working lives centres on a farm. To encourage support, the community mails out packs of postcards, showing, in high-quality photographs, the life and surroundings of community members and how they are doing all they can to help themselves. These photos also populate the website. It is a simple, relatively cheap and effective way for the community to encourage others to support their work.

Checking the tactics mix

Once having decided on the range of tactics it is essential to check whether the mix that has been chosen actually delivers on the range of criteria that the planner decides is critical for success and to the audiences that have been prioritized. A simple matrix approach will identify any gaps as Figure 7.3 demonstrates.

The analysis in Figure 7.3 shows a number of things: for example that Audience 1 will probably need more tactics aimed at it that deliver emotional impact and that only two of the tactics chosen are suitable for the content required. For Audience 2 only two of the tactics will have any relevance. For Audience 3 there is an issue with source credibility, but perhaps the content of the YouTube video can be adjusted, or perhaps a separate video made to remedy this issue.

Of course not all tactics have to be used for all audiences. The merchandise and brochure were not designed to be used with Audience 3.

There is also evidence[2] that audiences need to see content between 3 and 5 times (and probably from different sources) to begin to give it credence, so again this matrix will indicate what the 'hit' rate might be so that it can be determined whether audiences are being contacted often enough and from a requisite range of sources.

Different campaigns need different tactics

To illustrate different approaches using very different techniques, here are three detailed case studies. All the campaigns have been successful – they won CIPR Excellence Awards – but they were aimed at very different audiences and therefore required quite different treatments.

FIGURE 7.3   Plotting tactics against critical audience factors

Target Audience 1: Critical factors	Tactic: YouTube	Tactic: Hard copy magazine	Tactic: App	Tactic: Merchandise (calendars & mousemats)	Tactic: Brochure
Reach?	✓	✓	✓	✓	
Credibility?	✓	✓	✓		
Emotional impact?	✓		✓		
Suitability for message/content?			✓		✓
Target Audience 2: Critical factors					
Reach?	✓		✓	N/A	N/A
Timeliness?	✓		✓	N/A	N/A
Ability to deliver animation?	✓		✓	N/A	N/A
On-demand?	✓		✓	N/A	N/A
Target Audience 3: Critical factors					
Reach?	✓	✓	✓	✓	✓
Source authority?		✓			✓
Long-term availability?	✓	✓	✓	✓	✓

CASE STUDY   First World War Centenary commemorations: A low-cost integrated campaign by the Department of Culture, Media and Sport

The First World War Centenary commemorations are highly significant and symbolic. That war was the first truly global conflict fought not only in Europe, but on many continents and involving soldiers and civilians from around the world.

Among the many challenges for those charged with organizing the commemorations were: to strike the right tone, to make it inclusive and to sustain it for the four years that the war lasted. The programme as a whole is large, but this case study focuses on one part, the campaign around the commencement of the commemorations on 4 August 2014.

Background

In October 2012 the Prime Minister David Cameron set out the UK Government's vision for the First World War (FWW) Centenary:

Our ambition is for a truly national commemoration, worthy of this historic centenary that will provide the foundation on which to build an enduring educational and cultural legacy.

The Department for Culture, Media and Sport (DCMS) was tasked with leading the communications around the FWW Centenary working with other Whitehall departments and a range of partners who would deliver the activities and events.

Its communication approach focused on supporting the Prime Minister's vision by positioning Government as leading and facilitating the national commemorations and, just as importantly, promoting public engagement in the months running up to the official launch on 4 August 2014. This was a centenary that had to be 'owned' by the British people as a whole and by all those in the Commonwealth who had supported the war effort.

In October 2014 the thinktank British Future published a new survey showing that over two-thirds of the public believed Government and its delivery partners had set the right tone for the centenary and that nearly 60 per cent of the public were inspired to learn more about the First World War as a result. This case study sets out how DCMS achieved this result through a minimum cost integrated campaigning approach.

The communication challenges

Communications handling arrangements around the FWW Centenary programme on 4 August were immense, presenting issues and challenges that were unprecedented for a Government department.

Three Government-led events were to take place: a cathedral service in Glasgow in the morning, an event with significant cultural content in the Saint Symphorien military cemetery in Belgium as dusk fell and a vigil at Westminster Abbey concluding at 11pm.

Three discrete events in three different countries, each with very senior political and royal attendees and international media interest, a demand for live outside broadcast coverage at each stage and an extensive group of stakeholders:

- Westminster Abbey
- Royal Household
- No 10 (the Prime Minister's Office)
- Ministry of Defence
- Metropolitan Police
- Glasgow City Council
- Glasgow Cathedral
- Commonwealth War Graves Commission
- Mons City Council (Belgium)
- National and international broadcasters and media

Some of these were organizing their own complementary events. Add to this the fact that no one had ever marked the centenary of a war's *beginning*, and the scale and scope of what DCMS had to undertake can be sensed.

But one of the hardest challenges for the communications team to begin with, however, was not the many *practical* issues that had to be managed, but what exactly the messaging should be.

In setting out his vision for the FWW Centenary, the Prime Minister made clear that remembrance should be at the heart of the Government programme, with a particular emphasis upon young people. Subsequently communications activity was planned around three themes: understanding, remembrance and recognition. These ran through all the messaging and their reach and penetration were key evaluation metrics.

DCMS also had to remember the many other organizations were embarking on their own centenary-related activity. Government could not own all the communications around the FWW Centenary and neither should it try to. Government's role was to lead the national commemorations and provide the structure around which broadcasters and other organizations could operate across 2014–18.

There was also to be 14–18 NOW – a major cultural programme taking place across the UK inviting contemporary artists from home and overseas to explore the resonance of the First World War today. 14–18 NOW commissioned large-scale special projects which are selected to encourage people from every community to reflect on how the First World War has shaped today's world and our attitudes to conflict now. While the content of the cultural programme was not directly controlled by Government, the fit with the official events had to be clear and easy to understand by a public audience.

Planning

Communications planning began around 18 months in advance with regular meetings of communications professionals from each of the stakeholders including:

- Imperial War Museums
- Commonwealth War Graves Commission
- Arts Council
- English Heritage
- Heritage Lottery Fund
- National Archives
- MoD
- Foreign Office
- Department for Communities and Local Government
- Ministry of Justice

There was separate liaison with the broadcasters who wanted to organize live coverage. It was clear from the outset that an integrated and collaborative approach was essential. To that end all partners signed up to the DCMS communications strategy to ensure a joined-up approach and consistent use of key messages and narrative.

There were three clear and distinctive communications objectives:

1 position the Government as leading and facilitating the major national commemorations across the four years of the centenary;
2 promote the centenary programme, through announcements and delivery partners' activity;
3 drive public interest and engagement with the centenary through DCMS-led communication.

Fundamental to the DCMS overall campaign were:

- partner working and celebrity endorsement
- creative and innovative content
- regionalization
- digital engagement both in UK and internationally.

Implementation

DCMS took a low cost, fully integrated approach, using proactive communication.

Social media was central to activity and the DCMS digital team used a range of innovative ideas such as a First World War Tweetathon – a full day of FWW experiences – involving a range of partners including Tesco, Imperial War Museums, National Archives, English Heritage, who all put forward experts giving the public a chance to ask questions and learn more about the Great War. This shed a hugely positive response on social media achieving 242,000 impressions. A poppy vine, created in-house using simple illustration to promote the British Legion's campaign encouraging the public to grow poppies to mark the centenary, had over 25,000 views.

Classics Professor Mary Beard and actor Christopher Timothy were among those who joined the social media campaign to mark World Poetry Day. They were joined by Baroness Williams who read a poem by her mother, Vera Brittan, author of *Testament of Youth*. The hashtag #WorldPoetryDay had 17,000 mentions and over 8 million Twitter impressions.

A series of digital postcards covered themes such as: the role of women, technology, nutrition, sport and PR – this was the first war to capture footage for news consumption.

Added value was achieved by highlighting the work carried out by partners across Whitehall. So Department for Education's programme of school visits to battlefields, the Communities Department's work to mark the home towns of FWW Victoria Cross recipients with paving stone plaques and the Ministry of Justice's project to make servicemen's wills accessible to descendants online – to give three examples – helped set the consistent tone and messaging.

Delivery partners also played a central role providing stories and initiatives to capture the public imagination and help harness support. The Imperial War Museums, a DCMS-funded institution, managed a major new FWW gallery construction project for 2014, creating an enduring monument to the centenary.

English Heritage's project to list war memorials and its Home Front Legacy project inviting the public to trace the archaeological footprint of the FWW in their local communities as well as the Heritage Lottery Fund's grants programme – with the emphasis on supporting small, community-focused ideas – all helped take the message across the whole of the UK.

Strong local stories were key to securing local coverage so DCMS provided local authorities and organizations with a comprehensive FWW toolkit, packed with ideas and background data around national themes to provide context.

Content is available at **https://www.gov.uk/government/uploads/system/uploads/attachment_data/file/320244/First_World_War_centenary_programme_2014-2018.pdf**

Research had shown that people were particularly interested in the social impact of the war and those elements, what was happening on the home front, the role of women and the effects in local communities and individual families. These insights helped shape communication. The 'Back in Britain' tumblr provided a rolling procession of stories around the social changes taking place in Britain as the fighting raged over the Channel. Stories around the role of animals in the war, how, with so many young men being away, women took a leading role in sporting events, and an account of how Jack Cohen used his demob money from the war to buy surplus Naval, Army and Airforce Institutes (NAAFI) stock for his market stand that eventually became Tesco all proved popular.

The impact of the DCMS work was particularly well demonstrated by the phenomenon of trench cake. This was the fruit cake made by families back in Britain and sent out to their loved ones in the trenches. The Comms team originally sold it into the parenting magazine titles and websites, but it proved so popular that an online campaign was developed fronted by Frances Quinn, the 2013 winner of BBC TV's *Great British Bake-Off*. The idea – and the recipe – were featured in national and regional newspapers. Partners the England and Wales Cricket Board served it at the FWW Commemoration Test Match against India and it was featured on the BBC's *Test Match Special*.

All this activity helped set the context for the first landmark day of the FWW commemorations.

Three national commemorative events marked the First World War Centenary opening on 4 August 2014, the 100th anniversary of the date that war was declared. The events in Glasgow, Mons in Belgium, and London formed a key part of the UK Government's centenary programme and took place across the whole day.

DCMS managed the media handling at each of the three events which included:

10am – Glasgow Cathedral – Commonwealth-themed service and Cenotaph service in George Square

Organized in partnership with Glasgow City Council, the service reflected the Commonwealth contribution to the war. Followed by a wreath-laying service at the Cenotaph in George Square where a commemorative plaque was unveiled. HRH The Duke of Rothesay (as the Prince of Wales is known in Scotland) attended and the cathedral service was shown live in George Square, which was open for public access.

7.30pm (UK) – St Symphorien Military Cemetery in Mons, Belgium – Commemorative event

This commemorative event for around 500 guests was organized in partnership with the Commonwealth War Graves Commission and was based around music, poetry and readings which reflected the history of the site. HRH The Duke of Cambridge, accompanied by HRH The Duchess of Cambridge, attended with HRH Prince Henry of Wales. Mons City Council screened the event live in Mons Town Square for members of the public wishing to be involved with the event.

10pm – Westminster Abbey – Candlelit vigil

Westminster Abbey hosted a candlelit vigil and an evening of prayer and reflection. This included the gradual extinguishing of candles with the final candle being extinguished at 11pm. HRH The Duchess of Cornwall attended and the vigil ended with the cathedral in darkness except for a single light on the grave of the unknown warrior. Anglican churches around the UK also participated, along with other faith groups, to complement the event in London, including services at St Anne's Cathedral in Belfast and Llandaff Cathedral, Wales.

Evaluation

The task for the DCMS was to produce and execute a far-reaching and cost-effective campaign raising public awareness around the centenary, with a focus on the national events taking place on 4 August. In the event, evaluation shows that its impact on public awareness and understanding of the centenary exceeded everyone's expectations – coverage reached 84 per cent of the UK adult population. Message penetration around the themes of Recognition and Remembrance achieved 81 per cent and 82 per cent respectively across all UK adults. The St Symphorien event reached 1.5 million viewers and the Westminster Abbey candlelit vigil nearly 2.5 million. BBC2's viewing figures were 40 per cent above average for Monday evening. The social media toolkit sent to partners resulted in 90 tweets from Government departments achieving 28.5 million impressions.

The DCMS poetry readings accrued over 1,700 plays on Audioboos. #WorldPoetryDay had 17,000 mentions and over 8 million impressions on Twitter. DCMS ranked top 8 key influencers on Twitter, driving traffic to our FWW content.

Our #LightsOut Thunderclap (a crowd speaking platform that allows a single message to be mass-shared, flash mob-style, so it rises above the noise of social networks. By boosting the signal at the same time, Thunderclap promotes mass participation and action) encouraging the public to turn off all their lights save for a single light or candle massively exceeded its supporter goal by almost three times. This resulted in 119,000 tweets and 225 million potential impressions and @DCMS was the number one influencer on Twitter on the day for this collective moment of remembrance. This effectively conveyed a sense of hope for the future, an entirely appropriate note for a national commemoration of this nature.

The DCMS FWW Toolkit material sent to local authorities and organizations has been downloaded over 2,500 times, and regional reporting has been extensive as a consequence and continues.

Future events

4 August 2014 marked the official opening of commemorations, but the FWW Centenary spans four years to November 2018 with each year marked by major national commemorations covering:

Gallipoli – April 2015

Jutland – May 2016

The Somme – July 2016

Passchendaele – July 2017

Armistice Day – November 2018

Having reflected on the 4 August event, DCMS has taken forward some learning for these future events including:

- Focusing around an event leads to higher reach and penetration in a day than is usually obtained over a month – so secure the benefits of focusing activity around key events/bursts of activity.

- Innovative use of social media works; for example, using Thunderclap to issue a call to action for Lights Out performed well, exceeding targets.

- Traditional media can still reach larger audiences, but digital media allows for greater engagement, interaction and participation.

- Live monitoring of social media can alert to emerging issues so that swift action can be taken.

Websites of interest

Official FWW Centenary website
www.gov.uk/government/topical-events/first-world-war-centenary

DCMS Back in Britain Tumblr – looking at the social impact of the Great War on the home front **http://backinbritainww1.tumblr.com**

Points about this campaign

- There were multiple challenges around this campaign including striking the right stance, the range and significance of partners and interested parties involved, and the fact that war is a controversial topic. The evidence points to this being done successfully.

- The scale of the task did not mean that it entailed great expense. All the DCMS activity was undertaken in house by the existing team. The only additional cost was staging the three commemorative events.

- The opening commemorations were just part of an unfolding set of activities, but it was vital that it set the tone and expectations for the whole four-year period.

- Setting direction and an overall framework for the commemorations had to be balanced with allowing freedom for partners and the public to take ownership of the project in ways that were significant and meaningful for them.

CASE STUDY McArthur River Mining: An internal and community relations campaign by Creative Territory and the MRM community relations team

Internal and community relations campaigns have particular challenges. They involve 'knowing' communities – communities that know organizations from the inside or from very close up. These communities have a very personal stake in organizations and have communication needs and expectations that go beyond many other stakeholders. This case study illustrates how those specific requirements can be responded to in very practical ways. It also illustrates that sometimes goals and objectives come before research which then needs to be undertaken to establish the best way to address the challenges and opportunities presented.

Background

McArthur River Mine (MRM) is located in the remote Australian Gulf of Carpentaria, 1,000 km from the nearest major centre of Darwin.

The MRM community includes 700 employees and contractors who work on a fly-in fly-out basis as well as their families back home.

Engaging with such a diverse group of people offers a number of challenges:

- the geographic spread of the community;
- constantly changing personnel among the contractor workforce;
- the need to communicate with people both on and off site;
- the desire to include workforce families in communication.

Three events in 2013 underlined the need to find a new channel to communicate with the community. The first was a two-day telephone outage that left workers on site unable to contact their families back home. *How could those families be reached?*

The second was a major power outage on site affecting all fixed telephone and IT systems. Management was unable to get messages to the estimated 400 people on site at the time, some at work, but most in darkness in the accommodation village. *How could the workforce in the village be reached?*

The third was a cyclone warning that was of concern to people who had never experienced a cyclone before. *How could the community be reassured?*

Aims and objectives

Aim

To keep target audiences informed in times of critical need.

Objectives

- Target audience has access to timely, accurate and authoritative information in times of need.
- The business has the ability to deliver information when traditional communication systems fail.
- The workforce and their families feel a sense of belonging to the MRM community.

Target audiences

- staff and contractors at work on site;
- staff and contractors staying in the accommodation village;
- staff and contractors off site;
- families and loved ones of staff and contractors.

Research

Creative Territory explored a number of traditional communication options including:

- A mobile phone database to enable broadcast SMS: this method was discounted because of the difficulty in maintaining the database with a large turnover of short-term contractors. It would be even more difficult to maintain a database of family phone numbers.

- Internet/intranet: the workforce is diverse and includes truck drivers, environmental scientists, cleaners, engineers, geologists, electricians, cooks and administration staff. Not all have access to computers. In times of power outage, computers would not be available.

It became clear a new channel was needed that would overcome the issues associated with these traditional options.

A few hours on site quickly generates the understanding that smart phones are the media of choice for the predominantly young, male workforce. Research showed that more than 95 per cent of people on site had a personal mobile phone and more than 80 per cent of these had the capacity to download apps from either iTunes or Google Play.

Discussions with a range of people across site indicated they would be prepared to download and use an app on their private device to access information about their workplace.

Strategy and planning

The solution was to create MRM Community, an app that could be downloaded and used by anyone working or visiting the site as well as their families. While the app would meet a specific business need, it was also an opportunity to engage more broadly with the workforce and their families and create a sense of community among the MRM family.

The advantages of this solution include:

- Experience shows that the mobile telephone tower is most likely to continue operating long after other systems fail because of its battery backup.

- Access to the app is self-regulated by users. There is no need to establish and maintain a database of phone numbers that will quickly date.

- MRM have the ability to update the app and message users via mobile or even satellite devices. They do not need to rely on telephone, IT or power being operational.

- A broader opportunity to engage with the MRM community on a more personal level. Communication is two-way, not just one way.

- A portable information service for key information that can be used anywhere, anytime.

Initial scoping indicated a budget of A$7,000 would be required to deliver the app. This was considered to be value for money given the cost of alternative solutions.

View the app at http://app.bananamobileapps.com/html5/?appcode=MRMCommunity or search MRMCommunity in iTunes or Google Play for full functionality.

Implementation

Obtain buy-in from senior management: MRM's General Manager was an early supporter of the proposal and was crucial in bringing the team along with him. At all times, the business needs of the company drove the project.

Consult with the target audience: Creative Territory and the MRM Community team spoke with staff across the site to determine what content would be useful from their perspective, as well as managers to ensure the app was aligned with business drivers.

Scope the app and its content: it was decided to make the app open to anyone for two reasons – the app should be inclusive of all the target audiences and it should be easy to use and deploy. In turn, this guided the level of detail that would be included in the content.

Curate the content: all content was compiled and approved before the building of the app commenced.

Build and deploy the app: a specialist agency was engaged to build and deploy the app as well as provide training to internal staff to update content. This would ensure MRM could control information flow in times of urgent need.

Promote the app to staff and families: promotion occurred through a number of means including the quarterly magazine *Memorandum*, toolbox talks, posters and presentations to staff. A guide to using the app was used to help staff navigate it and QR codes made it easy for people to download it.

Keep it alive: the key to ongoing engagement is to keep the content alive so people have a reason to keep on coming back. Content is refreshed on an as-needs basis, but at least weekly.

The content of the app has grown since its launch in January 2014 as feedback from the community has come in. The following examples show how its content is shaped by the needs of the business and community:

- The power station shuts down at 4am, cutting power to the whole site. The mobile phone tower continues to be operational. Using a mobile phone, MRM direct messages all app users to give them instructions on what to do.
- The fibre optic cable that provides telephone services to the region is cut. Using a satellite internet connection, MRM can direct message app users that no phone connections are available. Families off site know why they have not heard from their loved ones.
- A contractor arrives on site for the first time. He opens the app on his phone, brings up a map of the village and zooms in to find his room.
- An employee spots a snake in the camp. She opens the app, snaps a photo of the snake and submits it. The phone automatically sends the GPS coordinates of where the photo is taken to one of the MRM trained snake handlers, who is able to identify the snake and its location before deciding if it should be removed.
- A contractor needs to clear some land and needs to understand MRM's policies around sacred sites. He doesn't have his manual with him, so he checks on the app.
- An employee wants to sign up for a free skin cancer check under the Healthy Living Program. She opens the app and signs up on the spot.
- An employee wants to report a broken light switch in his room. He fills in the maintenance request from within the app.

Evaluation

Against the original objectives, the solution has shown its value.

Objective	Results
Target audience has access to timely, accurate and authoritative information in times of need.	The app has been used to used to deliver messages in a number of times of need: • Cyclone warnings in the Gulf region and Darwin in January and March • Major power outages in March • Fixed phone outages in February.
The business has the ability to deliver information when traditional communication systems fail.	When fixed telephone systems failed on site in February, the business was able to inform its community via the app.
The workforce, families and friends feel a sense of belonging to the MRM community.	Anecdotal evidence from those using the app suggest this is the case, as outlined below.

If it is assumed that 80 per cent of the workforce has the capacity to download the app, and that each of them will encourage one family member to do the same, the app has a potential audience of around 1,120.

In the 12 months since its release in early 2014, the app was downloaded 1,020 times. This represents 97 per cent of the target audience. More than 200 maintenance requests have been lodged via the app, representing 63 per cent of all maintenance requests lodged during this period.

Importantly, evaluation has come from members of the community who have downloaded and experienced the app themselves.

The last time the phones went down, at least I knew what was going on because I got a message on the app. The time before that I couldn't contact my husband for days. Wife of MRM manager

I love the Maintenance Request Form. It allows me to conveniently fill out a Maintenance Request Form anytime without having to walk to the mess and submit in paper form. And I also get to read the latest Memorandum Magazine before it goes to print. Employee

My family lives interstate and have the app on their phones so they know what's happening, especially in cyclone weather. Supervisor

It's very easy to use. I downloaded it before I got on the plane. My girlfriend wanted to know if she could download it too because I was telling her all about it. New recruit

I'm in a different room every time I visit so I use the village map all the time. You can zoom right in and find your room, even in the dark. Contractor

It's handy to have contact lists and emergency contacts when I'm both on site and on R&R. Employee

Points about the campaign

- Although it is good practice to have SMART objectives, this is not always possible or sensible. However the objectives given here are tangible and measurable over time.
- The strategy here is 'tactic driven', in that it became apparent through research that an app was the solution. The lesson is to design strategies that solve the problem.
- The content and the channel has been driven by the needs of the users *and* the needs of the business. It is possible to satisfy both.

- The channel used, although singular is not self-limiting... it is possible to upload a range of content in a variety of formats.
- The solution chosen is cost-effective and efficient.

Sustaining long-term programmes

One of the key issues in longer-term public relations programmes is sustainability. How is a programme kept going year after year maintaining focus and interest? Running an event with a single, short-term objective that is achieved in a determined timescale, eg holding a Christmas party for employees and their families, is rather different from sustaining a long-running programme on financial advice.

Here is an example of a long-running programme that has 'rolled-out' over many years.

CASE STUDY   Lansons' campaign for unbiased.co.uk, the organization promoting the benefits of independent financial advice to consumers

Lansons has been working for unbiased.co.uk for over 20 years. Starting with a series of topic-based campaigns, the strategy has been to build confidence in and use of regulated Independent Financial Advisers (IFAs) by the public so that they obtain high quality, professional financial advice. Initial campaigns focused on topics around tax efficiencies, helping consumers to reduce any unnecessary tax payments. This kind of tax advice has nothing to do with the aggressive tax-avoidance schemes exposed by the media, but everything to do with ordinary people not knowing how to handle their everyday tax affairs.

As far back as 1993 Lansons launched a year-long campaign called *Tax Action* which focused on the amount paid by the general public on unnecessary tax. The work on that continues up to present and the Tax Action 2015 report shows that £4.9 billion pounds is wasted on such things as unclaimed tax-relief on pension contributions, poor use of tax-efficient savings schemes such as Individual Savings Accounts (ISAs) and over-payment of capital gains and inheritance tax.

Subsequent initiatives focused on, for example, *Britain's Undiscovered Billions* which identified 'dead money', ie money that was being left in accounts yielding little interest and 'buried treasure', ie money that can rightfully be claimed, such as legacies and state benefits, but is left unclaimed. As long ago as 1994 over £12 billion was found to be left undiscovered.

Tax Action has remained a backbone of Lansons' work and it has ensured a constant level of media interest over the years. However, having a long-term theme does not mean that the on-going programme is purely about updating. Lansons have to keep alert to the issues of the moment and those that might be predicted. So, for instance, in 2009 in the depths of the financial recession the research revealed that 72 per cent of adults expected taxes to rise as well as highlighting the nation's most resented taxes: council tax, TV licence and fuel duty.

Over the years the public relations strategy has shifted focus to keep in line with the evolving business strategy. In 2007 unbiased.co.uk moved entirely online and the current focus is on driving traffic to the unbiased.co.uk website to find an IFA. Now unbiased.co.uk claims to be the UK's Number 1 professional advice portal, offering consumers the largest online database of verified financial and legal advisers. The website – **https://www.unbiased.co.uk/about-unbiased** – states:

> Unbiased.co.uk is the UK's most comprehensive professional adviser search website, focused on empowering users with the resources they need to make better informed financial and legal decisions. We not only help consumers find the best adviser for their needs from over 24,000 IFAs, mortgage advisers, solicitors and accountants listed on our search but we also help them research the market by providing relevant information and tools.

The company solely relies on PR, search engine optimization and online partnerships to promote its database to consumers.

Background to current campaign

One of the issues that has bedevilled the IFA world over the years has been the system of commissions that advisers are paid by financial product providers. In turn advisers offered 'free' advice, but the suspicion was that the two were not unrelated. The retail distribution review, or RDR, was a new set of rules enforced in the UK from the beginning of 2013 to introduce more transparency and fairness in the investment industry. The most significant change was that financial advisers were no longer permitted to earn commission in return for selling or recommending investment products. Now investors have to agree fees with the adviser upfront. In addition, financial advisers have to offer either 'independent' or 'restricted' advice and explain the difference between the two – essentially making clear whether their recommendations are limited to certain products or providers.

It was this change that was the focus for Lansons in 2013/14. Their challenge was to highlight the benefits of professional financial advice against a backdrop of major criticism and doubt about the effectiveness of the regulatory changes. Furthermore, by highlighting for the first time ever the real cost of advice a major risk was posed to unbiased.co.uk's business model. However, it also created an opportunity for unbiased.co.uk to own a large-scale consumer education campaign, reinforcing its central mission which is to communicate the benefits of gold standard advice. In response unbiased.co.uk created positive talking points in the consumer media, demystifying industry jargon, tackling and explaining what matters the most to consumers – proving that there is value in paying for good quality financial advice.

In order to tackle these challenges, unbiased.co.uk set out on a proactive engagement strategy utilizing PR as its main tool.

Objectives

- Prove that advice is worth paying for.

- Increase its level of annual consumer searches.

- Defending its position as the largest adviser database.

- Be known as the number 1 source of insight on consumer and adviser behaviour pre and post RDR.

Research

The team analysed existing collateral on the RDR (based on research papers, media coverage and commentary).

The research highlighted that:

- Output in the run up to RDR (for the last 7 years) had focused on the upcoming changes to advisers and their businesses. Very little had been communicated to the most important audience – consumers – who for the first time were being shown explicitly that there was a cost attached to advice.

- The concept of paying for advice was alien to many consumers who would benefit from taking financial advice (and that there is a misconception that advice is 'free').

- The impact of RDR could disenfranchize a large proportion of consumers with the advice process.

Lansons' research showed the focus of any research to date had been on the cost of advice, rather than the value people are getting from the advice received, making it well worth paying for. Based on insight and research, the team decided to focus on an in-depth quantitative and qualitative report, looking to demonstrate the

'Value of Advice'. In order to define the best methodology and angles, unbiased.co.uk gathered a selection of advisers from across the UK at a workshop, to brainstorm different themes and to hear about consumer concerns and real-life client scenarios.

Strategy

In order to achieve its objectives and to emerge in 2013 with a strong and compelling proposition, unbiased.co.uk embarked on the following strategy:

- Launch a large-scale consumer education campaign, utilizing its website and media relationships to offer a consumer perspective on the 'Value of Advice' and to become the central information point on not just the upcoming RDR changes but more importantly on the importance and benefits of seeking professional advice.

- Relaunch and update its website and database to create a compelling consumer proposition.

- Launch an active engagement strategy to get buy in and support from its database of advisers, utilizing social media.

Implementation

Its consumer education campaign included the following elements:

- Value of Advice report: a detailed consumer and adviser research report, outlining the monetary benefits as well as the added knowledge and peace of mind seeking financial advice can bring. Key elements of the report included:
  - insight and data on consumer access to and demand for advice;
  - type of products and money held by consumers and the differences in financial circumstances, confidence and knowledge between advised and non-advised consumers;
  - the consumer advice journey;
  - upcoming changes and how to pay for advice;
  - the report also included adviser insight and consumer case studies to add real life examples.

- Media and industry launch: following a suite of senior media meetings for chief executive Karen Barrett to talk about the upcoming campaign, the report was launched at an industry roundtable in July 2012, including senior trade and consumer media, and a selection of unbiased.co.uk advisers debating the challenges consumers are facing.

- Website enhancements: unbiased.co.uk launched a downloadable consumer checklist on its website, as well as a suite of guides and adviser blogs to help consumers make sense of the upcoming changes and to gain knowledge on the advice process.

- Social media activity and database engagement: pre-briefed media advisers on the findings of the Value of Advice report as well as subsequent activity, asking them to share client success stories and top tips on social media. Ran a blog programme highlighting different advice areas on the unbiased.co.uk website.

Evaluation

Unbiased.co.uk is an online-only service and the following metrics have been put in place to assess the effectiveness of any campaign:

- number of searches on the find an adviser tool, unique visitors to website/ particular pages, number of downloads, advisers on the database, number of paid for profiles via server reporting;

- number of journalists/advisers signed up to use the unbiased.co.uk media database, calls to the media hotline, number of comment requests;

- number and tone of media coverage, editorial back-links and partnerships through Precise and Meltwater;

- number of social media followers, re-tweets, hashtag usage and opening rates and click-throughs on e-mail communication to advisers measured by analytics packages;

- meeting growth measured by sales reports.

Over the last 12 months and solely driven by PR, the campaign surpassed all targets:

Consumer engagement:

- Unbiased.co.uk entered 2013 with website traffic up by 15 per cent.

- The site had over a million unique users and dealt with over 450,000 searches for professional advice in 2012.

- The Value of Advice page received over 1,000 visits and the dedicated blog pages received more than 300 page views within launch month.

Media profile:

- Media coverage beat the target of 20 pieces of coverage by 400 per cent with over 100 in-depth pieces across all national PF pages and sites.

- The Value of Advice report was downloaded more than 100 times during launch month.

- Total reach of press coverage audience of over 17 million with over 95 per cent positivity (Precise).

Adviser–industry engagement:

- Unbiased.co.uk's Twitter profile now has more than 3,500 followers across advisers and industry, up 35 per cent over the campaign period.

- Over 300 tweets spread the word on its adviser facing social media channel using #ValueOfAdvice.

- Campaign specific e-mail newsletters to advisers had an opening rate of over 20 per cent, a massive improvement over industry standard of 11.4 per cent.

As a not-for-profit organization, unbiased.co.uk has access to a limited budget to support its wider marketing campaign, having to punch above its weight to compete with larger budget campaigns run by providers and other relevant parties.

As a result of the profile raising activity around the Value of Advice campaign, unbiased.co.uk has since achieved the following:

- 40 per cent increase in meetings with target providers from within the life, pensions, asset management industry to talk about sponsoring unbiased.co.uk to run similar campaigns.

- Industry meetings to talk about joint efforts and campaign link ups to support consumer access to advice.

- Over 400 new adviser listings on the search, providing more choice for consumers and more marketing revenue for unbiased.co.uk.

- The media has widely recognized unbiased.co.uk as THE source for insight and information on consumer access to and adviser provision of financial advice – 450 journalists are signed up to unbiased.co.uk's media database, requesting over 300 comments for advice related articles per month.

Points about the campaign

- There is a clear thread through this long-lived programme demonstrating a solid provenance and strong narrative which has developed via various campaigns, but which is enduring and consistent.

- There has been a consistent theme throughout, people's ongoing concern about tax, which has attracted ongoing interest, but the programme has developed to take on other concerns and issues as they arise, in this latest case concern about the RDR.
- Because people are interested in these issues, so are the media.
- Lansons have cleverly capitalized on what might have been regarded as a threat (the RDR legislation) by turning the lack of knowledge into a thought-leadership and educational opportunity thereby reinforcing the positioning of their client group, the IFAs.
- Focusing on the issues of the moment, and of tomorrow, keeps the IFAs front of mind, not just at the point at which tax forms are completed.
- The role of public relations here is to raise awareness and interest and drive traffic to the IFAs. It is not to sell financial products, which is a job that is left to the experts – the IFAs themselves. The role of public relations has been clearly delineated and stops at the appropriate point.
- Long-term programmes must evolve to sustain interest, have to take on board developments from the wider business environment and must change to accommodate different media consumption patterns.

Contingency and risk planning

All good public relations plans cater for the unexpected. There isn't room in this book to go into the whole area of crisis management. That subject, along with issues management, is dealt with in *Risk Issues and Crisis Management in Public Relations*, another book in this series.

Contingency planning

However, it is necessary to be prepared for the unexpected at both the strategic and tactical levels. Strategic-level threats are those that have the potential to fatally or very seriously damage the organization. At the strategic level a contingency plan is needed for a number of possibilities, for example:

- if the reputation of the organization is badly damaged;
- if its financial position is jeopardized;
- if its ability to function is interrupted;
- if its supporters desert it;
- if the public decides its operations are no longer legitimate.

These are major crises requiring a considered response that needs planning. Examples of activities that might precipitate such a crisis are new or proposed legislation, life-threatening competitor activity, product withdrawal, an acquisition or takeover, strikes, an act of terrorism, a factory closure or heavy redundancies, suspect trading activities or operating in a sector that is no longer seen to be acceptable.

In some of these situations tightening up on quality control, improving industrial relations or improving the quality of intelligence-gathering processes could help prevent problems becoming crises. It is the public relations professional's job to look out for the possible problem areas and to ensure that there are plans in place to deal with the communication implications. It is rare for issues to arise out of the blue, but there are many examples of organizations who have not recognized the warning signs. It will be necessary to liaise with other key people in the organization such as the chief executive, marketing function, sales/distribution, finance and quality areas, not to mention the lawyers and insurance advisers. It will also often be necessary to liaise with external bodies such as regulators, valued partners and trade associations in preparation for strategic threat management.

The public relations professional's tasks will probably include:

- planning for potential crises with others in the company and possibly external bodies;
- helping to put together a crisis management team, training them and ensuring there is clear communication between members;
- allocating responsibilities to crises team members;
- putting together the crisis plan;
- initiating 'trial-runs' of the plan;
- keeping the plan up to date;
- training key members of staff to handle the media and other key stakeholders;
- ensuring media enquiries are planned for and that there is suitable back-up;
- putting together key policy statements;
- acting as a part of the crisis management team if required;
- learning from the crises to improve contingency plans.

Of course, at the strategic level, each of the various scenarios will need to be considered in its own right and a separate plan of action developed. There will be common areas in each plan, such as the process for dealing with media, but tailor-made solutions are required for events of such importance.

At the tactical level contingency planning follows the same principles, but the degree to which these principles are applied will vary. For example, a crisis team may not be needed, but there will need to be an individual to take responsibility. This requires a careful examination of each tactic in the programme to find out what might go wrong. Thus, if an outdoor event is planned, what happens if the weather is bad? What if there are accidents or incidents at the event? What if some of the equipment fails? A balance has to be struck between the ideal and the realistic. If a fireworks show has been arranged another display cannot be ready just in case, but the performance record of the supplier will have been checked, and time will have been allowed to ensure the set-up can be thoroughly checked. Certainly the organizer will ensure that there are umbrellas available or a covered stand so that people are kept dry.

Risk

A topic related to contingency, but preceding it is risk. If risks are identified then contingencies must be put in place. Risks are those threats, sometimes hidden, but sometimes known about, that may place the organization in jeopardy in some way. Professional public relations planners always undertake a thorough risk assessment of their programme at all stages, but particularly with certain elements.

Key areas of risk always need careful assessment, such as the publics that are being worked with and the tactics that are employed. With publics there can be risk attached to who the programme is being targeted at: are they the right people, are there any unintended consequences that might occur? If so, how serious will the impact be?

There can be a risk associated with using certain individuals or organizations as partners. Celebrities can turn out to be liabilities, or behave in ways that do not promote the product. For example, a celebrity may be paid to promote a certain brand of clothing, but be seen to be frequently wearing another brand. Similarly, an organization that appeared to be the perfect partner, such as a campaigning group, may discover other aspects of the business with which they are unhappy and decide to withdraw co-operation, with all the attendant difficulties that will create.

Turning to tactics, there are some that are inherently more dangerous than others – for example stunts or events involving large crowds. Other tactics may seem less risky, but could be found to be otherwise. For example it could be that a new website has all kinds of innovative visual features but because of the type of imaging it uses, it may induce epilepsy.

Risk is not assessed necessarily to remove it, but to make the planner aware of its extent and likelihood. These two parameters are often used to plot risk, as Figure 7.3 shows.

Using this grid can help the planner decide whether the risk is acceptable. If the likelihood of a risk event happening is very high (nearer five on the likelihood scale) and its adverse impact on reputation or on a key relationship is also high (nearer five on the impact scale), then it could be that the planner will decide not to work with that organization or use that tactic. If the likelihood is high, but the impact is low, then that may be a risk worth taking. If the likelihood of a risk event happening is low, but the impact will be high, again a judgement will have to be made about whether to go ahead. Of course, if likelihood and impact are low, then risk is low.

FIGURE 7.3 A risk assessment tool

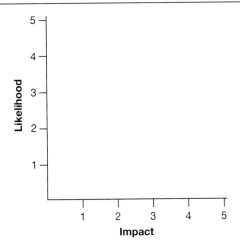

One other thing to note. The risk grid implies that impact is negative. Of course impact can be positive. In this case instead of it being a risk tool, the matrix can be turned into an opportunity tool to judge which tactics should be given the greatest priority.

Planning the strategy and tactics of a campaign is fun. It is challenging and demanding, both intellectually and creatively, but there is something uniquely rewarding about planning and then executing a programme that is well thought out and well judged. Good public relations plans are the result of much hard work and consideration. To come up with a strategy that works requires a great deal of research and incisive thinking. Tactics, too, should be chosen not just because they are imaginative, but because they are appropriate to the publics towards whom they are directed and because they are without doubt the correct medium to carry the message.

Planning with care puts the practitioner in control. It enhances the probability of success and it ensures that the right things are focused on.

Notes

1 For further information see Gregory, A (2007) Involving stakeholders in developing corporate brands: the communication dimension, *Journal of Marketing Management*, **23**, pp 59–73.

2 Edelman Trust Barometer (2013) See www.edelman.com/trust-downloads/global-results-2

3 Hon, L C and Grening, J E (1999) Guidelines for measuring relationships in public relations. Available from www.instituteforpr.org/wp-content/uploads/Guidelines_Measuring_Relationships.pdf

08
Timescales and resources

Timescales

Two things are certain in a public relations practitioner's life. The first is that there is never enough time to do everything that needs to be done – the tasks and possibilities for action are always far greater than the time available. The second is that because public relations tasks often involve other people and the coordination of several elements, it always takes longer than you thought to get the job done.

There are two interlinked key factors that must be observed when considering timescales. The first is that deadlines must be agreed so that the tasks associated with a project can be completed on time. The second is that the right resources need to be allocated so that the tasks in hand can be completed. Timescales can be brought forward if more resources are brought in to complete the task.

Deadlines can be internally or externally imposed. Examples of internally imposed deadlines might be company keynote events such as the announcement of the chief executive's retirement; the announcement of an acquisition; the diaries of senior people who might be involved in the public relations campaign.

Externally imposed deadlines might be involvement in fixed events such as major shows and occasions like the Boat Show or the Summer Paralympic Games. There might be calendar dates that have to be worked to such as Chinese New Year or Valentine's Day. Then there may be what would be regarded as most appropriate dates. Ideally new garden products would be launched in the spring when most people start to work in their gardens, but technically they could be launched at any time.

So how does the planner ensure that deadlines are met? The key thing is to identify all the individual tasks that have to be done in order for a project to be completed. Below is a list of the main elements of a straightforward press conference:

- Create invitation list.
- Investigate and organize venue.
- Book catering.
- Issue invitations.
- Book multimedia equipment.
- Write speeches.
- Prepare presentation materials.
- Prepare media packs.
- Follow up invitations.
- Prepare final attendance list.
- Rehearsals.
- Attend conference.
- Follow up.

Each of these elements then needs breaking down further into their component parts. Thus, for example, a fairly simple press pack might have in it a press release, some background briefing material, a data stick containing photographs, some product literature or a brochure and a specially designed press folder. To put the pack together will include briefing and monitoring designers, printers and photographers, writing the press material, liaising with the marketing department to get the product literature, liaising with senior management to get approval for the material, reproducing the press release and background briefing, collating the press packs and organizing delivery to the conference.

Task planning techniques

There are a number of ways that the information can be organized visually to help planning.

Gantt Charts

Gantt Charts list each element of the project and then assign a time to it. These are then organized on the chart to show overlapping tasks. Using the chart also identifies when there are times when too many tasks are required to be undertaken at once. It could be that by completing one self-contained task early or later, time can be freed up in busy periods. If this is not possible, additional resources may be needed to help.

A Gantt Chart for the press conference might look something like Figure 8.1.

FIGURE 8.1   Gantt Chart for press conference

	November														December		
	4	6	8	10	12	14	16	18	20	22	24	26	28	30	2	4	6
Create invitation list	X	X															
Investigate and book venue	X	X	X	X													
Book catering				X													
Send out invites				X													
Book multimedia equipment					X												
Write speeches						X	X	X	X	X	X	X	X				
Prepare presentations								X	X	X	X	X					
Prepare media packs							X	X	X	X	X	X	X	X			
Follow up invites													X	X			
Prepare final attendance list														X			
Rehearsals														X			
Attend conference															X		
Follow up																X	X

This particular chart involves some tasks that will need breaking down into smaller component parts. For example, the writing speeches task will involve a preliminary draft, initial approval and suggestions for alterations by the person delivering it, possibly CEO approval, redrafting, final approval, preparation of cue cards or auto cue, etc. This would be built into the Master chart. Similarly the press pack will have several elements too. A good practice is to allocate the names of the responsible people for each activity. Investigating and booking a venue may be outsourced to a specialist events agency and once they are briefed they should be able to get on with the task with minimal supervision. The media packs, as indicated earlier, will involve several individuals and possibly several companies and that requires greater project management and someone to coordinate. Responsibility lines must be very clear.

Critical Path Analysis

An alternative method for time-lining projects is Critical Path Analysis (CPA). Having split the project into its individual components, CPA requires the planner to identify those elements of a programme that involve the greatest amount of time. It is these elements that dictate when a project can be completed. CPA also recognizes that more than one task can be undertaken at a time and therefore enables participants to work as efficiently as possible. A critical path for our press packs is shown in Figure 8.2.

FIGURE 8.2 Critical path for putting together a press pack

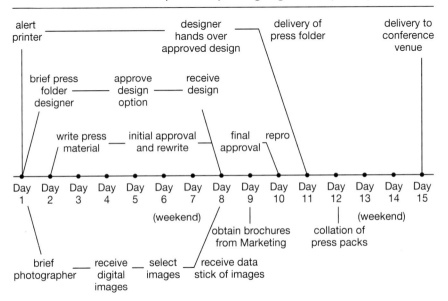

This represents a very tight timetable, and assumes that designers, printers and photographers are all available. Sometimes, of course, they are not. In practice most professionals will have a number of suppliers they can call on, and most projects do not begin from a standing start as shown in the example. However, the principle holds. Several things have to be done to put together a simple press pack, and they need to be carefully coordinated and timed with, preferably, a little contingency at the end (notice a whole day for collation and another one for delivery, with an intervening weekend) in case of emergencies. It is also good practice to get as much done as early as possible to give time at the end for any unforeseen problems. It would have been possible to brief the photographer on Day 4 and still have the data stick of images back in time to collate the packs, but it would have been putting unnecessary pressure on the project.

Obviously, if pushed for time and there is a need to complete tasks earlier, ways must be sought to shorten some of the critical path activities. It may be, for example, that existing company folders are used to put press material in. Or it may be by allocating additional resources and paying the designer to work over the weekend, a folder can be produced in a shortened timescale. If by shortening the crucial path as much as possible a fixed deadline cannot be met, the activity itself must be questioned and an alternative communication technique selected.

Having once broken down the putting together of the press packs into its own critical path, this can then be put into the larger critical path for the press conference as a whole.

The final programme might look something like that shown in Figure 8.3.

FIGURE 8.3   Critical path for press conference

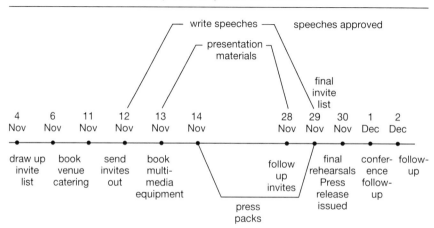

There are several project planning software packages on the market that will produce automatic schedules and diary prompts, but the basic groundwork of deciding how long a task will take and who is involved will still have to be done, so understanding the principles behind techniques such as Gantt Charts and CPA is important.

It is vital that public relations practitioners manage their time effectively and work as efficiently as possible by having in place practices and procedures that regularize standard tasks, and by planning ahead. It is a mark of the professional manager. It is good practice to maintain and use a range of checklists for typical public relations tasks such as event planning and specifications for suppliers. Checklists are the practitioner's friend and should be used to ensure that everything is covered and in the correct order.

Longer-term plans

Putting together plans for individual projects is essential, but if care is not taken the big picture is lost. It is absolutely critical that multi-stranded programmes and the whole of the public relations department's activities are planned in as much detail as appropriate and an overall timetable for action is constructed. Many practitioners work to long-term objectives and may have outline plans for a number of years ahead. Getting those plans documented and approved is important because it helps maintain a focus beyond the immediate here and now. It is very easy to become so embroiled in day-to-day matters that the strategic vision becomes obscured and larger objectives become lost as the urgent takes over from the important.

Certainly, working to at least an annual plan is important. It helps to ensure that things happen when they are supposed to and it gives a level of control. If other activities arise, a judgement can be made as to whether they or the planned activity should be pursued or if a case needs to be made for additional resources.

Overleaf is an example of an annual media campaign for a garden centre chain – see Figure 8.4 on page 172. It is immediately apparent where the peaks of activity are. February, May and August are going to be heavy months, and it might be that extra resources are needed in the form of consultancy or freelance help.

Obviously, a large department or a consultancy carrying out comprehensive programmes will have several activity plans like this covering the whole gamut of public relations work. For example, they could well have an internal communications plan, a community relations plan, a business-to-business plan and several specific issues-based campaigns which will all need to be collated into a prioritized master plan. It is then that decisions on resources can be made. Either the plan will be accepted and resourced accordingly or, as is often the case, resources will be limited and therefore activities will have to be cut from the bottom of the priority list upwards. When making decisions on which areas are to be cut, great care has to be taken to ensure that the overall integrity of the campaigns or overall programmes of work are maintained and that what remains is a well-integrated campaign and overall programme that provides a good complementary raft of activities. What is crucial is that the agreed activity will achieve the desired objectives and address the needs of all the essential publics.

FIGURE 8.4 Annual planner for garden centre media campaign

Activity	Jan	Feb	Mar	Apr	May	Jun	Jul	Aug	Sep	Oct	Nov	Dec
Editor briefings (one-to-one)	Trade press x 2 briefings	Consumer press x 2 briefings	Trade press x 2 briefings	Consumer press x 2 briefings	Trade press x 2 briefings							
Advertorials with key journals (to be negotiated)		*House & Garden*		*Horticultural Journa*	*Garden Answers*			*Horticultura Week*		*Amateur Gardener*		*Royal Horticultural Society Journal*
News stories (including new products)	News story – garden pests app	Launch of lawncare advice service	New Centre opening	Launch of tree surgeon service	News story – junior gardener game	New Centre opening	Barbecue promotion	News story – 50th anniversary	New centre opening	Launch of new power tool range	Christmas plants promotion	New centre opening
Seasonal themes (for regional press)	Tools		Spring is here		Care of fruit trees and bushes		Pest control		Care of borders		Winter lawncare	
Competitions with local press		Power tools promotion			Garden furniture promotion			Water features promotion			Indoor garden promotion	
Exhibitions with press reception					Chelsea Flower Show	Gardeners' World		Royal Horticultural Society				
Virtual press office	Website relaunch	Celebrity gardener video	Spring products	Gardening and youngsters	Celebrity gardener video	Summer planting	Water-saving tips	Celebrity gardener video	Gardening and the elderly	Late planting	Celebrity gardener video	Indoor decorations

CASE STUDY The *Grand Départ*: Tour de France in Yorkshire by Welcome to Yorkshire

An example of meticulous planning while capitalizing on the opportunities that are a part of a major occasion is the work done by *Welcome to Yorkshire* who won the bid and then hosted the Tour de France, the world's largest annual sporting event. This case focuses mainly on the media relations elements of the event and shows how timing and logistical considerations are vital to success.

Welcome to Yorkshire is the tourism agency for the biggest county in the UK. A small team based in the city of Leeds promotes Yorkshire to a local, regional, national and international audience. The communication department at *Welcome to Yorkshire* is an experienced team working across local, regional, national and international media who aim to deliver a minimum of £1 million of value a month.

In 2011, chief executive Gary Verity had an idea: to bid to host a major sporting event. With the London 2012 Olympic and Paralympic Games not far away, Gary's aim was to broaden the international spotlight on another part of the UK – and incidentally, to a county who would have come 12th on its own in the Olympic medal table by bringing the Tour de France to Yorkshire. Approximately every second year the race starts outside France, and the Yorkshire experience was going to be special.

As soon as an interest was officially registered with race owners Amaury Sport Organisation (ASO), *Welcome to Yorkshire* immediately launched the 'Back le Bid' campaign to generate support from the public. Back le Bid received over 100,000 signatures and demonstrated the immense support from all corners of Yorkshire to host this iconic race: support from the public, from the county's MPs, current and ex-athletes, as well as thousands of businesses.

Much of the media work during this time focused on Yorkshire's cycling pedigree, demonstrating the history and heritage of racing in the region and highlighting the beauty of the Yorkshire landscape.

Event objectives

By hosting the world's biggest free-to-spectate sporting event in the UK, *Welcome to Yorkshire* aimed to bring Yorkshire to the attention of a massive global audience. The iconic race is one of the most instantly recognized sporting brands in the world, being broadcast in more than 100 countries and hosting the Grand Départ (the name given to the first two days of the race) is a hard fought-over honour.

The Grand Départ is the start of a gruelling three week test of skill and strength and covering over 2,000 km, and the Tour de France is one of the toughest professional bike races in the racing calendar. The Grand Départ stages would need to test the riders, but also fit into the rest of the route, creating an exciting and ambitious event for organizers and the teams taking part.

Welcome to Yorkshire knew that the Tour already attracted media of all types, from local press to global, including the official broadcasters, ITV and Eurosport. The Yorkshire version needed to take advantage of all the existing coverage, and take it up a notch – not just as a sporting event but make it *the* spectator event of the year, the chance to show off the huge variety of landscapes and the welcome only Yorkshire could offer the race.

Working with the media

There were an enormous range of stakeholders. In the bid phase, use of the media was carefully managed, not just in terms of proactive work but also not reacting to some of the national media negativity and cynicism, or to comments from competing host nations.

Once the bid was won and during the run up to the race, the team had to engage a large number of non-cycling journalists and editors who had a notion, but little experience, of what was about to happen. It was known that the cycling media would engage with the biggest cycling event in the world, so the strategy was to make sure they were positive and remained so throughout.

A concerted effort was also made to engage not just with other sports journalists and publications, but to broadened the appeal to all media with a key message that the event would be a once in a lifetime experience. The communication department proactively targeted family media and non-cycling titles and also made use of businesses along the route for case studies of how local businesses were preparing.

Welcome to Yorkshire assisted the international cycling teams when they brought riders over for reconnaissance trips. This further stimulated media interest and raised the profile of riders and international sponsors . They worked with the farming, caravan, heritage and environment press to get across the message about how to prepare for delays and how spectators could enjoy the day, but leave no trace and maintain the historic (and legally protected) landscapes the race travelled through.

Working with the ASO, the communication team, also arranged a number of trips from international media who were fascinated by Yorkshire's history and heritage; dozens of crews visited in the weeks before the race, and used their footage during the event itself. Regional television news crews were supportive from the start and the team ensured that each had a steady stream of stories in the run up to the race.

As a well-established sporting event, it's fair to say even the ASO didn't anticipate the massive amount of coverage achieved in the build up to the race and on race weekend itself. Media stakeholders were many and varied, and throughout the campaign the communication team worked with every title from the BBC to Al Jazeera, the *Financial Times* to *Harrogate Advertiser*, international media visits were organized to show off the famous and the lesser known parts of Yorkshire; over 10,000 Tour Maker volunteers were recruited, with many telling their stories on Twitter and Facebook, charting their training and then race-day roles. International TV crews were helped with requests to fly drones over historic landmarks; local and central government were engaged with directly and through media work; in short, every aspect of the race was utilized, for the benefit of Yorkshire and the race itself, in a way that the Tour de France had never witnessed before.

What very quickly emerged was an immense sense of pride in the prospect of the race coming to Yorkshire. Local people and businesses completely embraced the event and every single media request, proactive or reactive (in some cases with very little notice) was met with 'Of course we can do that.' Independent bike shops lent journalists bikes to ride the stages; Tour Makers took time out of holidays to get to interviews; professional racers took time out of their schedules to film supportive films to engage fans; the yellow bikes which were seen across walls, rooftops and pavements swept across the region. The yellow bikes came in all shapes and sizes, from cardboard cut-outs to real bikes, all painted in bright yellow (the colour of the race leader's jersey after each stage) and the phrase 'Tour de Yorkshire' was to be heard everywhere.

Fundamental to engagement with the public was the website, **www.letouryorkshire.com** which received unprecedented traffic and the social media campaign. Most bike races in the UK fall down on engagement with non-cycling fans, so the communication team created a site where people who had never been to a race before could learn, understand and appreciate what was about to land. The site's spectator guide helped tourists and residents plan their day with the message from the start being 'plan ahead and get there early'. With the road closures needed for a race of this size and calibre, spectators needed to know they had to be in position early in the morning and be prepared to stay there for some time. On average spectators travel 130 km to see a stage of the Tour and then spend over 6 hours at the roadside: 30 per cent of spectators are women.

One way to alleviate the potential pinch points on the race was the network of spectator hubs, places were many thousands of people could watch the race on big screens and enjoy the party atmosphere. All of this needed communicating and with a strong message which started many months ahead of the race.

Implementation on the day of the event

Race week began on 1 July 2014 as dozens of trucks and vehicles rolled off the ferry in Hull. The ASO brought their entire race entourage, including all commentary and media positions; as with any stage of the race, it is packed with military precision and rolled out early each morning.

3 July saw a spectacular team presentation ceremony with Thursday and Friday being days for team press conferences and the annual media scrum over the most famous riders like Mark Cavendish. It is estimated that 2,000 journalists representing 35 nationalities attend the Tour every year, with 121 TV channels showing the race. Over 5,000 hotel rooms are needed each night just for the teams, tour personnel and the media.

Very early on Saturday morning, race day for Stage 1, the roads were closed in preparation for the race. Areas needing barriers were prepared; outside broadcast trucks began to park in Leeds and Harrogate; space for the team buses were marked out and reserved; and the Village became a hive of VIP activity.

The cyclists and their teams were given detailed briefings of timings (see Figure 8.5) and the terrain they would cover, along with route maps and information on the towns and villages they would pass through.

FIGURE 8.5   Detailed timings for those involved in the race

KILOMÉTRES					HORAIRES			
A parcourir	Parcourus		Étape 1		Caravane	44 km/h	42 km/h	40 km/h
			GRANDE-BRETAGNE					
			WEST YORKSHIRE					
			LEEDS (VC-A61-A659)	DÉPART FICTIF	09:10	11:10	11:10	11:10
			The Harewood House					
190.5	0	A659	LEEDS	DÉPART RÉEL	10:00	12:00	12:00	12:00
188.5	2		Arthington		10:03	12:03	12:03	12:03
186	4.5		Pool (A659-A658-A659)		10:07	12:06	12:06	12:07
182	8.5		OTLEY (A659-A660)		10:13	12:12	12:12	12:13
176.5	14	A660	Carrefour A660-A65		10:20	12:19	12:20	12:20
173	17.5	A65	ILKLEY		10:26	12:24	12:25	12:26
166.5	24		Addingham (A65-VC-A65)		10:36	12:33	12:34	12:36
			NORTH YORKSHIRE					
160.5	30		Draughton		10:45	12:41	12:43	12:45
158	32.5		Carrefour A65-A6069		10:48	12:44	12:46	12:48
156	34.5	A6069	SKIPTON (A6069-A6131-VC)		10:51	12:46	12:49	12:51
147.5	43	VC	Rylstone		11:04	12:58	13:01	13:04
146	44.5		Cracoe		11:07	13:00	13:03	13:07
141.5	49		Threshfield		11:13	13:06	13:09	13:13
137	53.5		Kilnsey		11:20	13:13	13:16	13:20
132	58.5		Kettlewell		11:27	13:19	13:23	13:27
129	61.5		Starbotton		11:32	13:24	13:28	13:32
126	64.5		Buckden		11:36	13:27	13:31	13:36
123.5	67		Cray		11:40	13:31	13:35	13:40
122.5	68		Côte de Cray		11:42	13:33	13:37	13:42
113.5	77		Newbiggin		11:55	13:44	13:49	13:55
111.5	79		West Burton		11:58	13:47	13:52	13:58
109	81.5		Carrefour VC-A684		12:02	13:51	13:56	14:02
108	82.5	A684	Aysgarth		12:03	13:52	13:58	14:03

Several hundred journalists were in Leeds as the race rolled out towards Harrogate and the Harewood House where the royal party, Prince Harry, Prince William and the Duchess of Cambridge awaited them, with a Royal Air Force acrobatics team flypast.

Over the two stages of the Grand Départ for the Tour de France, 4 million spectators viewed the race from the roadside as 198 riders and 22 top international teams from 34 nationalities covered 391.5 km of Yorkshire's roads.

Results

The results of the traditional and digital media campaign speak for themselves:

- 3.5 billion global TV viewers for the Tour de France
- 188 global territories broadcast the race live
- 2,000 accredited journalists attended the event
- 230 million Twitter reach
- Trended worldwide on Twitter
- 7.7 million page views on **letouryorkshire.com** during race week
- 201 countries and territories visited the website
- 5.8 million Facebook reach

While not an approved evaluation measure, it was estimated that it would have cost £330 million to purchase the media coverage obtained for the Yorkshire Grand Départ.

Points about this case

- An event including such a range of international, specialist and non-specialist media adds significant complexity, including the need for translation, time zone considerations and, of course, accommodation.
- The scale of the event required considerable cooperation from a range of partners and a host of stakeholders, all requiring different information. Coordination and regular information flow is a key theme.
- Building an ecosystem of helpers and advocates such as the Tour Maker volunteers and the local business community, expanded the in-house communication team resource while offering significant payback to those involved.
- The integration of all the channels and platforms used meant that there was an efficient and effective media resource.
- Meticulous planning meant that the event went off safely, without one reported major incident and great fun was had by all.

Resources

Resourcing public relations adequately but effectively is of course necessary for organizational efficiency.

Resourcing of public relations programmes comes under three principal headings. The first is human resources, the second is operating or materials costs and the third is equipment.

Human resources

Whether working in-house or in consultancy the time and skills of individuals have to be paid for. The more experienced and skilled the individual, the more expensive he or she is. Clearly the level of human resourcing depends on two things: the size of the programme that is to be undertaken and the nature of the programme.

There are tasks that most competent public relations practitioners would be expected to perform. For example, most would be expected to be able to run a media relations programme and populate a website to a good standard. However, highly complex lobbying or social networking programmes demand rarer skills and for a premium will have to be paid.

A public relations professional with adequate administrative and equipment support can run a reasonably broad-based programme of limited depth. Alternatively he or she can handle a highly focused in-depth programme. The more comprehensive and multi-layered the programme, the more human resources will be required to run it, and the greater the levels of skill and experience needed.

In an ideal world an optimum programme of work is devised and justified, and the human resources required allocated. More realistically there is a trade-off between the ideal and the human resource overhead that an organization is prepared to carry.

However, a real problem comes when human resources are cut. Public relations is a relationship-driven activity and relationships are created by and between people. By cutting human resources the ability of public relations to do its job is severely threatened. When times are tight, every other avenue for cost cutting must be explored before cutting people. This is a battle that is sometimes hard to win because it is usually the human resource costs that are the greatest in a public relations department. A simple comparison with advertising illustrates the point. An advertising department may have a staff bill of £100,000, but spend £1,000,000 on media. If cuts come their way, it could be possible to cut the media bills by, say, £100,000 without causing irreparable harm. The public relations department may also have a staff bill of £100,000, but its operating costs could be very low because the programme focuses on media relations, online activities and a face-to-face-based internal communications programme. Costs might be £50,000 or less.

Costs might be saved by trimming the operating budget by the same percentage as the advertising/media cost budget, but 10 per cent of £50,000 is just £5,000. The obvious 'solution' is to cut the human resources where substantial savings can be made. This could spell disaster. Journalists' reasonable expectations might not be met, online communities may be ignored and the internal communications programme may be reduced. Overall the reputation of the organization will suffer, relationships will be damaged and it may take years to recover.

Human resource costs are linked to the number of people on the programme and the time they spend on it. This is a reasonably simple calculation for in-house departments, but is rather more complicated for consultancy human resources – see later in this chapter. Human resource costs are usually given in terms of hours for the tasks or in person days. So, for an in-house person their total employment costs are taken, the number of days worked per year are calculated (minus weekends and, in some organizations, holidays) and the salary is divided by the number of working days to give a day rate. Hence the cost of an individual day rate may be:

	£
Salary	50,000
Other employment costs (pensions etc)	10,000
	60,000
Days in the year	365
Minus weekends	104
Minus holidays	25
Minus statutory holidays	8
Working days	228

Day rate = 60,000 ÷ 228 = £263

Operating or materials costs

These kinds of costs are those items that are associated with delivering the programme, for example, media pack, banners, merchandise, cost of room hire, incentives for filling in questionnaires, cost of advertising space on a website, etc.

When costing out public relations activities two key things need to be borne in mind: effectiveness and efficiency.

The right techniques need to be selected in order for a programme to be effective. When the techniques have been chosen it is then incumbent on the public relations professional to be as efficient as possible. So, for example, it might be decided that an effective way to communicate with important customers is via a magazine. Then choices have to be made on such things as format, number of pages, weight of paper and colour content. There is no need to produce a full-colour magazine just because it looks good. If the content and the right tone can be set by producing a two-colour magazine, then that should be the choice. Against that position, it might be argued that competitors send out colour material and that the organization can't afford to look cheap by comparison. Similarly, if the publication is to be mailed out, the size and weight of the paper will be critical since that, combined with the number of pages, will determine postage costs. Efficient use of resources is important not only from a management point of view, but it may also enable the planner to undertake additional activities within the same overall budget.

The above examples are fairly straightforward. There are other types of decisions that are less easy and are part of the effectiveness debate. Take, for example, a media relations campaign. Virtual press rooms are relatively cheap, but they are of variable impact. Face-to-face interviews can be extremely effective, but are very costly in terms of time and a limited number of people can be reached. Somewhere in between there are highly targeted communications, tailor-made to discrete sectors of the press. The same questions of effectiveness and efficiency have to be asked, and the answer will vary depending on the importance of the message and the public being addressed.

Two vital questions need to be asked when looking at effectiveness and efficiency.

Can what is wanted be achieved by spending less money?

By thinking laterally it may be possible to achieve exactly the same objective for a fraction of the cost. Examples of this are use of piggy-back mailings. For instance, some building societies and banks still post out statements to customers, an ideal opportunity to include additional material.

How about partnerships with complementary organizations or products? The washing machine and washing powder link-ups are very familiar. It may be possible to sponsor an activity that will give opportunities to raise name awareness or undertake corporate hospitality at a fraction of the cost of putting on alternative activities that are totally funded by the organization.

At the other end of the spectrum is the other question on effectiveness.

Will spending a little more add a great deal of value?

Effectiveness does not mean looking to spend the least amount of money all the time; it means getting the most value from the money available. Sometimes, by spending a little more, a great deal of value can be added. Take a customer brochure. It could also be mailed out to selected press, to shareholders, to the company pensioners, just for the cost of a run-on of the print plus postage. The effect could be worth many times the extra cost.

It could be that holding an investor briefing on site and getting them all there might be costly, but it could be very effective in visually demonstrating the worth of a new business asset and its potential.

Equipment

It goes without saying that a programme or campaign cannot run effectively unless there is the right sort of equipment to support it. Public relations professionals do not require vast amounts of equipment, but it is important that it is up to date. Communication professionals need access to, and use of, technology appropriate to their needs. Video conferencing, mobile technology, access to printers, etc are necessary to do the job.

A note of caution should be sounded. When working on or with international programmes it is easy to assume that every country has ready access to the latest technologies. This is not the case. It is important therefore not to become wholly dependent on the very latest technology. A fax machine may seem dated, but it might be vital.

In summary, when drawing together a budget these three factors must be borne in mind. An example of the main budget headings for a public relations campaign is given below.

Budget headings

Human	Operating and materials costs	Equipment

Staff salaries
Employment costs
  (eg pensions, benefits)
	Print and production
	Photography
	Media relations
	Conferences, Seminars
	  Sponsorship, etc
	Operating expenses
	  (eg telephone
	  contracts, stationery,
	  post, travel,
	  subsistence)
	Overheads and
	  expenses (eg heat,
	  light, office space)
		Office furniture
		Computer equipment
		  and consumables
		Telephones, cameras
		  special software etc

Working with consultancies

The costs given above are essentially the same whether working in-house or in a consultancy. However, when employing consultancies the fees element is obviously different. Fees are payable for the work agreed upon.

These fees can be negotiated in several ways.

Retainer fee

This covers an agreed level of consultancy advice, attending meetings, preparing reports, etc. This is usually based on a fixed amount of time per month and the cost will depend on the seniority of the consultant involved. Consultancies like retainers because it guarantees a level of monthly income. Clients like retainers because they have access to expertise on an ongoing basis and often the fee can be negotiated down from a standard hourly rate. Over recent years retainer-style contracts have been diminishing in favour of project-based fee structures.

Project fee

This covers the amount of executive time required to deliver an agreed programme of work. The rate for the project is fixed before it is undertaken and therefore the client can budget precisely what the costs will be. However, if the client brief is not complete, the consultancy will bill for additional items, so skill is required in procuring project work.

Hourly fees plus costs

This covers the actual amount of time spent on the project with time being charged at a pre-agreed rate. The hourly rate will vary depending on the level of expertise needed. The consultancy will also add the costs of materials and expenses and sometimes they add a mark-up on bought-in items (see later). Hourly fees can be an effective way of using consultancies if the task is well scoped. However, if it isn't, large bills can be forthcoming: crisis management assistance is often charged on an hourly rate given that it is difficult to scope this kind of work.

Payment by results

This is an increasingly popular way of billing consultancies. They will be paid on the basis of achieving the results that have been agreed. Often these results are *outputs*, such as number of press stories placed, number of people attending an event and so on. It is a brave consultancy that will be tied to specific *outcomes*, such as X per cent will change their behaviour, since there are so many unknown variables at play.

A number of organizations use a mixture of these ways to procure consultancy advice depending on the nature of advice and support they need.

Consultancy charging structures

Consultancies will sometimes charge a 'mark-up' on bought-in services such as photography and print where the consultancy has a legal and financial responsibility for client work (the UK Public Relations Consultants Association[1] reports that this has been historically 17.65 per cent but is less prevelant as a practice now). It is worth checking. Media buying usually still attracts a mark-up). Procurers will usually have to pay value added tax (VAT) unless the consultancy is very small and not registered.

A typical monthly invoice (note: mark-up is not usually shown separately) from a consultancy might look as follows:

Invoice Headings	£
Executive time (35 hours at £100 per hour)	3,500.00
Video (for website)	5,200.00
Photography (for school event)	875.00
Design and print for event literature	3,050.00
Design and print for schools pack	5,750.00
Operating expenses (phone, stationery, post)	350.00
Travel (day return to London and subsistence)	114.50
	18,839.50
VAT at 20%	3,768.00
	22,607.50

Overall budgets will be the subject of negotiation. There are, however, a number of approaches to budgeting. The first is to adopt a formula approach that applies company-wide so as to determine the proportion of resources allocated to each function. Typical formulae that are applied are: a percentage of the organization's profits or sales turnover, the same as last year or a fixed increase on the previous year's budget, or a sum comparable to that of the closest competitor. The main problem with these approaches is that they take no real account of the actual job of work that is required from public relations. The year ahead may involve a great deal of public relations input, for example if the organization is to mount a major rebranding campaign. The range of publics to be contacted varies from organization to organization, from year to year and from campaign to campaign. For some organizations, public relations as opposed to other forms of marketing communication may be the largest or even the only means of communicative activity.

An alternative approach is to start with the objectives that public relations needs to achieve, cost the tactics required to deliver them, and negotiate the budget on the basis of what is required. This does not give carte blanche to the public relations professional, since it is likely that each activity will be carefully scrutinized and will need to be justified. Wherever possible a cost:benefit analysis should be provided to support public relations expenditure. This entails listing the costs of an activity on one side against the benefits obtained on the other. If a monetary value can be put against these benefits and they outweigh the costs, so much the better. If the benefits include or are largely non-monetary, then the case for funding must be argued on the basis of reputational or relational benefits or the costs associated with these elements not being undertaken. It is also worth doing a reverse analysis and listing the negative costs of not undertaking the activity.

In most instances a mix of formula and costed approaches is taken. Generally speaking an initial indication of the overall budget available will be given, the practitioner will then put together a detailed plan with costings attached, and the final budget will be negotiated. Inevitably compromises will have to be made; however, carefully detailed plans will demonstrate the consequences or risks to which the organization will be exposed if programmes are cut or indicate a list of essential core activities, as well as itemizing the benefits of the full programme.

Note

1   The Public Relations Consultants Associations guidance on mark-up rates and fees can be downloaded from www.prca.org.uk/assets

09
Knowing what has been achieved: evaluation and review

Measuring success

Public relations is no different from any other business function in that it has to demonstrate that it adds value to the organization. Practitioners need to know how effective they've been in meeting their objectives and if they've not been as effective as they thought they should have been, they need to discover why. They also need to be able to demonstrate an appropriate return for the investment that has been made, although it's a mistake to believe this can always be quantified in financial terms. Albert Einstein said: 'Not everything that can be counted counts, and not everything that counts can be counted.'

First, defining terms. **Evaluation** is an ongoing process when talking about longer-term campaigns or programmes. Thus, there will be regular evaluation of the performance of the website by making a monthly critical analysis of activity. As a result of this there may more focused effort on particular sections of the website, or its navigability features. This ongoing evaluation is often called monitoring.

Similarly, at the end of a specific campaign, there will be an evaluation of the results. So if the objective was to prevent the closure of a factory, there will be a clear-cut indication of the result at the end. The organization has either succeeded or failed. If the objective was to raise awareness by a fixed percentage, then awareness will need to be researched to come to conclusions about levels of success.

Review is a regular management practice. It is extremely sensible to take a good, hard look at the campaign or programme each year. Review involves looking at what the evaluation over the year has shown, revisiting the programme objectives and scrutinizing the strategy. The circumstances surrounding the project will also be looked at. Have there been changes that now render it irrelevant, even though evaluation shows it is very successful in itself? It could well be that the project proceeds as before, but it may be that a complete reorientation is needed. More on this later.

In a nutshell, evaluation is both monitoring as the project proceeds and an analysis of the end results of a campaign or programme, while review is a periodic step back to identify any more strategic changes that need to take place.

The benefits of evaluation

If undertaken properly, evaluation both helps spot danger signs before real problems develop and it helps prove a campaign's worth. Here are a few reasons why evaluation should be built into campaigns and programmes:

- *It focuses effort.* If is is known that the campaign is going to be measured on a number of agreed objectives, it will be focused on the important and keep the urgent in perspective.

- *It demonstrates effectiveness.* There is no success like success! If the practitioners achieve what they have aimed to achieve, they are able to demonstrate their contribution to the organization.

- *It ensures cost efficiency.* Because the things that should take priority are being concentrated on, the budget and time (which is also money) will be spent on the things that count and achieve the big results.

- *It encourages good management.* Management by objectives, having clear goals, brings sharpness to the whole public relations operation. The irrelevant will be quickly identified and rejected.

- *It facilitates accountability.* Not only the practitioners' accountability to produce results, which is perfectly in order, but it also makes other people accountable in their dealings. The public relations professional can quite legitimately say, 'If I spend time doing this unscheduled project, it means that I cannot complete this important, planned activity. Which is it to be?' Then clear choices can be made about what may be new and pressing priorities. If the planned activity is also essential, then extra help may be needed – so the practitioner is in a powerful position to ask for more people or extra budget. Good managers not only accept accountability for themselves, but they are in a strong position to challenge others to be accountable and to gain access to valued resources.

Why practitioners don't evaluate

In their book on evaluation for this series, Watson and Noble[1] conclude that many practitioners lack confidence in promoting evaluation methods to clients and employees.

When questioned about their motives for undertaking evaluation, 'prove value of campaign/budget' came out a very clear leader, followed by 'help campaign targeting and planning' and 'need to judge campaign effects'. Another reason, 'help get more resources/fees', came a distant fourth.

Watson's own research showed that practitioners were defensive about their activities. They used evaluation techniques to present data on which they could be judged rather than using evaluation to improve programmes.

The most used technique was providing an output measure for media relations (eg the range of publications in which coverage was obtained) rather than measuring the impact of the media relations campaign itself. Generally speaking, output measurement was seen to be more relevant than gauging impact or gaining intelligence so that programmes could be improved.

Watson also pinpointed the main reasons why programmes were not formally evaluated. These were, first, lack of knowledge (possibly disinclination to learn about evaluation techniques), second, 'cost', followed by 'lack of time' and 'lack of budget'. When added together, 'cost' and 'lack of budget' became the dominant reasons.

There are other reasons why evaluation is seen to be problematic.

- *Understanding what it is that has to be evaluated.* The levels at which evaluation takes place will be discussed later in this chapter, but at this stage suffice to say that often what is measured is output not outcome. There is still an emphasis on media relations and the size of the clippings file. There may be some more sophisticated forms of media analysis like trying to measure the worth of a clipping depending on its position on the page, its size, the number of key messages it contains, whether it is routine or negative and so on. There are several companies that provide such a service. Some will provide a more detailed analysis, for example, a breakdown of how many times specific publications or journalists used press stories and the types of treatment the story received.

   However, in the long run it doesn't matter how big the clippings file is; what matters is what those clippings achieved (the outcome). For instance, was there a 20 per cent increase in attendance at the AGM and did they vote in favour of the motion? Has the attitude of key publics altered?

- *Understanding what can be achieved.* Public relations practitioners need to make sober assessments on this. It is just not possible to get the chief executive on the front page of the *Financial Times* every month unless he or she or the organization is exceptional in some way (or notorious!). What is required is an honest appraisal of what can be achieved. That knowledge comes with good research and the benefit of experience of similar situations. Managing expectations is a key practitioner task.

Unrealistic expectations on what can be achieved belies a lack of knowledge of the psychological art of the possible. As detailed in Chapter 5 it is very difficult, or at least will require a very determined and skilful campaign, to convert people who have a fixed view to take on a different view. It is a less onerous task if the target public has no view at all, or it is reasonably well disposed because the organizational message confirms or aligns with its own desires or beliefs. Again research will identify attitudes and therefore the size of the public relations task.

- *Aggregation.* Sometimes it is difficult to identify precisely what the public relations' contribution was if there were other forms of communication activity, such as special promotions or favourable comment in a social network.

- *Range of evaluation techniques required.* Public relations is unlike some other forms of marketing communication, such as selling through a website, where the evaluation is relatively simple: the number of returns and the business transacted. Public relations addresses many audiences in many different ways and different types of evaluation technique are needed. So practitioners need to be aware of the different research techniques available and to have the knowledge and resources necessary to undertake them.

  More recently there have been a number of positive developments that have moved the evaluation agenda along and there are useful guides and books on the subject, such as the CIPR[2] evaluation policy document, the German Public Relations Association[3] online resource on evaluation and, for Government, the publication by the UK Government Communication Service (GCS).[4] The GCS helpfully also provides a list of free-to-use evaluation tools and resources.[5] The most comprehensive set of evaluation materials are freely available from the American Institute for Public Relations[6]. The book by Prof Tom Watson and Paul Noble in this series provides a comprehensive and practical overview of evaluation. These contributions have helped to take some of the mystique and fear out of the subject.

  It is impossible in this book to give an evaluation blueprint for every type of public relations activity. For some activities evaluation will be relatively easy. If a practitioner is running an exhibition stand it is a simple, quantitative exercise to count the number of product enquiries, take contact addresses and then trace back subsequent product orders.

  Other things like the effects of a long-term sponsorship programme are much more difficult to evaluate.

Principles of evaluation

There are a number of principles of evaluation that help to set the context and make the task easier.

- *Objectives* are critical. Public relations campaigns can be seen to be effective when they achieve their objectives in a well-managed way. So objectives need to be achievable and measurable and, to ensure that they are, they need research and pre-testing wherever possible. 'Raising awareness' is not a good objective unless qualified by how much (1 per cent or 99 per cent?) and with whom (define the public). Research will help to show you what is possible. There is also likely to be a timeframe over which to work. A long-term campaign to change the general attitude towards the decriminalization of drugs is likely to have patchy, incremental results over a long period. However, even in this situation it is possible to lay down clear benchmarks. For example, a legitimate objective would be to persuade the majority of police chiefs to support the campaign by the year 2020, or give up the campaign.

  The achievement of objectives is the clearest way to evaluate any programme or campaign. Hence, it is also imperative that these and the measurement criteria that will be used to assess them are agreed with those who will judge success.

- *Evaluation* needs to be considered at the beginning of the process. It's too late to ask the question 'How did we do?' at the end if the mechanisms for measurement were not built in at the beginning.

- *Evaluation* is ongoing. Programmes should be monitored as they progress and initial findings scrutinized to judge both whether the indicators point to success, and to fine-tune the programme where adjustments need to be made.

- *Evaluation* is at all stages of the communication process. The decisions that have to be taken all along the communication chain affect the communication outcome. Practitioners have to decide on the content, the tone, the medium, the level of exposure, whether the target is receiving and interpreting the communication correctly. If one element is wrong, the desired outcome will be in jeopardy. Unfortunately, the converse is not true. Just because each element is right doesn't mean automatic success, but getting any of the elements wrong diminishes the chances of success.

- *Evaluation* must be as objective and scientific as possible. This means that public relations practitioners need to be proficient themselves or need to enlist the services of specialists who know about social scientific research and evaluation methods. Sometimes less rigorous research gives an indicator and in all that is possible to do, but even here evaluation must be valid and demonstrably reliable if it is to be taken seriously.

- *Evaluating* programmes and processes. Public relations programmes and campaigns require evaluating for the results of the communication activity, and also for their management. It is useful to separate out and list the achievements of programme objectives (eg sponsorship achieved objective of 20 per cent awareness in target group) and the fact that the campaign was managed well (eg 10 per cent under budget).

Evaluation terminology

There are a number of terms that are often used in evaluation that merit explanation. For each programme or campaign there will be:

- *Input.* This is what the public relations professional 'puts in' to their communication 'products'. For example, they might write, design and produce an in-house journal. When evaluating inputs, elements such as the quality of the background research, writing, effectiveness of design, choice of font and size, paper and colour can all be evaluated.

- *Output.* This is how effectively 'products' are distributed to and used by the target publics, either by the target public directly (eg how many employees received and read the journal) or by a third party who is a channel or opinion former to the target public (eg how many bloggers used the key messages?). So evaluation of outputs often involves counting and analysing things, for example, readership and circulation, reach of websites and content analysis.

- *Out-take.* This is the intermediate position between an output and an outcome, and describes what an individual might extract from a communications programme, but it may or may not lead to further action that can be measured as a result. If a message in the house magazine is about discounted membership of the local cinema club, how many employees actually remember that message can be measured, ie have extracted the relevant information from the article, but there is likely to be a difference between the number who demonstrate an out-take from the magazine and those who go on to sign up for membership.

- *Outcome.* This involves measuring the end effect of the communication. How many employees who read the magazine took up the opportunity to join the local cinema club at a reduced rate?
  Outcomes are measured at the three levels at which objectives are set (see Chapter 5):
  - changes at the thinking or awareness level (cognitive);
  - changes in the attitude or opinion level (affective);
  - changes in behaviour (conative).

To measure these outcomes sometimes requires sophisticated research, including attitude surveys, focus groups, tracking web or social networking traffic and content and individual interviews. For some campaigns, however, measurement can be relatively easy, for example as sales at the launch of a product.

However, what is clear is that if changes in opinion are wanted as the result of the campaign, this will be the objective, and to evaluate the programme opinions will need to be measured. It is not good enough to provide newspaper cuttings that contain the message practitioners wish to get across in order to change opinions. Media relations is a route by which the end may be achieved, and success in this area is worth noting, but it is not the end result. Success in the media is an output, not an outcome.

Measuring success at the output level and claiming that by implication an outcome has been achieved is called 'level substitution' and is invalid. Of course it is perfectly legitimate to measure outputs as an indicator along the way, but that is how they must be described. Figure 9.1 shows how the

FIGURE 9.1 How the UK Government uses evaluation terms

Inputs
• The website, social media or other digital space and related content created to meet communication objectives • The cost
Outputs
These will include: • The number of the end audience visiting the site or digital space at least once during the evaluation period (unique users) • The source of visitor referrals.
Out-takes
• What people think, feel or recall about the webspace. You may also be able to infer attitudes and understanding from comments that people leave on your website or social media space.
Intermediate outcomes
These will include: • Average length of time spent on site • Bounce rate • The number watching any videos or embedded content on your site (starting to watch and watching whole clip) • The number of pages visited. Also consider including metrics that look at actions carried out on social media websites, such as: • Number of 'likes' on Facebook • Number of retweets on Twitter. Always ensure that you tie these standard metrics back to your website or digital space's objectives and consider what you are trying to get people to do (register, read a particular piece of content, retweet content etc). This will enable you to interpret the data appropriately.
Final outcomes
• Final outcome measures should assess whether your website or digital space met its overall communication objective, and its effect on the overall policy objective that you are working to and the effect that this has had. Choose performance metrics that enable you to measure the activity's impact on both.

Used with permission of the Government Communication Service (GCS).
Correct as of going to print: March 2015

UK Government uses these terms when evaluating websites and social media communications.

Outflow

'Outflow' is not a common term used in the literature, but it is helpful. It is the long-term cumulative effects of public relations in terms of individual programmes, or the aggregated effect of several campaigns and programmes. Hence, this may be, for example, improvement of the reputation of the organization as a result of numerous campaigns over time; or it might be a long-term change in one particular behaviour as a result of several campaigns, or one long campaign that comprises several stages each with their own outcomes, but whose cumulative effect is more than the aggregate of those campaigns. For example, smoking is decreasing in the Western World, but that is the result of many different campaigns over several years. The outflow of this programme is not only a cut in *smoking* with the attendant health benefits, which was the original outcome aimed for, smoking has become less socially acceptable and individuals are making routine choices not to invest in tobacco companies.

Levels of evaluation

Chapter 1 described the contribution of public relations at four levels: societal, corporate, stakeholder/value chain and functional levels. In a similar vein, evaluation can be undertaken at these various levels. At the societal level, apart from the societal contribution that organizations can make, public relations can have a role to play in bringing to the public agenda things that are significant for the whole of society, such as, for example, explaining and convincing people of the need for action over climate change. It can also bring to public notice the concerns of minority groups who might otherwise lack the power to claim attention. Hence, the plight of elderly people who find difficulty in paying their fuel bills can be highlighted by activist groups who use public relations very effectively. Public relations can be involved in bringing together groups who are in conflict, as in Northern Ireland, with profound positive social effect.

As Chapter 1 explains, for organizations, public relations at the societal level can be used, for example to promote social responsibility and be the eyes and ears of the organization, helping it to adapt to changes in the environment.

Evaluation of the impact of public relations activity at the societal level requires tools that will measure things such as public opinion: hence public opinion polling by the interested organization, whether that be government or a corporate body, or by one of the larger opinion survey organizations, such as Ipsos MORI, will provide feedback. Other tools such as quantitative and qualitative surveys and detailed dialogue with a range of societal stakeholders are also relevant here. At this level, as for the other three levels, awareness, attitude and opinion and behaviour towards the organization will need to be evaluated.

At the corporate level, public relations will make a contribution to the overall reputation of the organization by ensuring management decisions are informed. It may also contribute directly to profits. As Chapter 1 indicated, intangible assets now account for 80 per cent of organizational value. Being the guardian of the organization's reputation and safeguarding the quality of key relationships with stakeholders will be invaluable. Profit is a tangible asset that can be added to the balance sheet, but reputation and the quality of relationships form part of the intangible assets of the organization and are not immediately amenable to a financial measure. However, when the organization comes to be sold, these intangible assets begin to realize their true value. Organizations that are taken over are often paid more for the value of their brand (that is, their reputation and the relationship people have with the brand) than for the tangible assets (buildings, money, equipment, etc). Hence, organizations now often use the balanced scorecard approach to assess their worth. Balanced scorecards attempt to evaluate both the tangible and intangible assets of an organization and therefore provide a fuller picture of its value than a summation of its financial worth alone. Figure 9.2 gives an example of how such a scorecard can be adapted to evaluate public relations' contribution at the corporate level, along with two example questions that might be asked under each heading.

FIGURE 9.2 A balanced scorecard approach to evaluating corporate-level public relations performance

Financial	**Reputational**
• Did our financial PR efforts increase share value? • Did PR contribute to product sales?	• Is the organization held in higher esteem than it was 5 years ago? • Has the level of negativity about our corporate decisions decreased in the last 5 years?
Relational	**Cultural**
• Do we have the right relationships in place and are they strong enough for us to gain support for our business decisions? • Do our key partnerships last longer than they did 5 years ago?	• Is there closer alignment between what we say and do internally and externally than there was 5 years ago? • Can we assure ourselves that decisions are value-based rather than primarily profits-based?

To evaluate at this level there will have to be in-depth qualitative and quantitative research using techniques such as: focus groups, one-to-one interviews, opinion surveys, online discussion groups, online opinion sampling and organizational profiling, in-house questionnaires and surveys, analysis of sales returns and so on.

At the value chain level much more detailed work needs to be done on producing solid evaluations. At this level every stakeholder group connected with the organization will need to be analysed to judge the status and quality of the relationship that exists and its trajectory: is it improving or deteriorating? Is this a relationship that needs fostering or maybe it is time to move on because a common agenda no longer exists. Stakeholder relationships fall into several categories as the analysis in Chapters 6 and 7 demonstrated. Those stakeholders who are regarded as Key Players and who need to be partnered will need a close and well-looked-after relationship which will need to be carefully monitored and regularly reviewed to ensure it is being maintained and enhanced.

Those with much Interest but little power can be very demanding of time and that relationship will need oversight to ensure they are informed, but not over-serviced. It is likely that these stakeholders will always want more communication than can be sustained within the resources available, so it has to be accepted that there could well be a level of dissatisfaction. As long as it is carefully monitored to ensure it is within a band of tolerance, the organization can be kept safe. However, issues management with this group is crucial.

Those with power, but less interest will expect their needs to be satisfied, but may well wish to be left alone until there is something that prompts or merits their interest. Again, monitoring the status of the relationship with this group is essential.

All these nuances need to be taken into account when making judgements about the quality of relationships with stakeholders. Relationships can last for a long or a short time. Sometimes groups come together for a particular purpose and then dissolve. Sometimes relationships are long lasting and it is important not to take them for granted. It is enlightening and helpful to monitor their quality from time to time.

The best way to gain a judgement about the quality of relationships is to ask those involved This can be done quite simply, but a comprehensive survey instrument to do this has been written by Linda Hon and James Grunig[8] and it readily available. It's advisable to 'temperature check' the quality of enduring relationships every 12 months or so. It is also helpful to track the progress of long-lasting relationships over time. Aggregating the results of the annual temperature check over a number of years can be very revealing. A tracker such as the one shown in Figure 9.3 shows graphically the direction of travel of these crucial relationships. The upward arrow shows a more positive response to the quality questionnaire to the previous year, the downward arrow a more negative response and a horizontal arrow means no difference year on year. The RAG rating (Red, Amber, Green)

FIGURE 9.3   Relationship tracker

	Year 1 Direction of relationship	Year 2 Direction of relationship	Year 3 Direction of relationship	Year 4 Direction of relationship	Year 5 Direction of relationship	Risk rating
Stakeholder 1	↑	↔	↑	↑	↑	G
Stakeholder 2	↔	↓	↔	↑	↔	A
Stakeholder 3	↔	↑	↔	↑	↑	G
Stakeholder 4	↑	↑	↔	↓	↓	R
Stakeholder 5	↓	↔	↔	↔	↑	A

shows the level of risk that is attributed to the relationships and shows immediately where action needs to be taken. Looking back over the history of the quality of the relationship indicates where relationships are stable and progressing, but also where they are unstable and/or fragile and where care and work needs to be judiciously applied.

At the functional level, as Chapter 1 indicated, the public relations function advises other departments and determines for itself which public relations activities have to be undertaken to help the organization meet its objectives. Again this requires public relations to monitor and evaluate the relationships it has with these other departments (and senior management) and the kind of survey mentioned above, along with good customer care, formally measured through satisfaction surveys can help keep track of that.

The other major task here is to monitor and evaluate the public relations programmes and campaigns that public relations undertakes and the next section covers this in detail.

A campaign evaluation model and some other measures

It is possible to come up with a generic model that can be applied to most programmes, but there is no set blueprint for evaluation – individual programmes and campaigns need tailor-made evaluations.

However, a useful device widely used today is the macro model of evaluation devised by Jim Macnamara[7] (see Figure 9.4). The model forms a pyramid.

FIGURE 9.4 Macnamara's macro model of evaluation adapted by Gregory

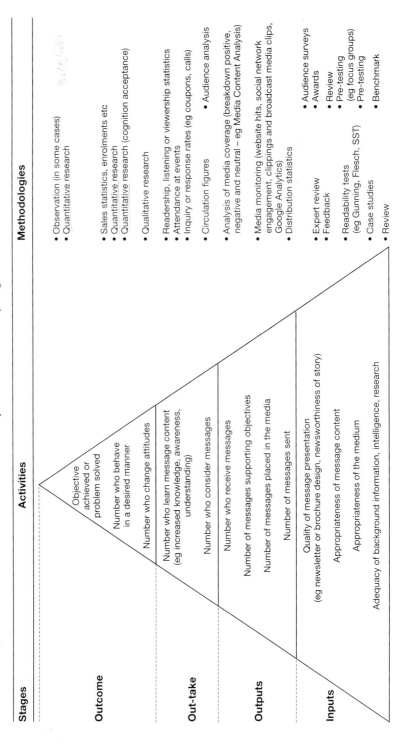

Evaluation of public relations programme

Stages	Activities	Methodologies
Outcome	Objective achieved or problem solved	• Observation (in some cases) • Quantitative research
	Number who behave in a desired manner	• Sales statistics, enrolments etc • Quantitative research • Quantitative research (cognition acceptance)
	Number who change attitudes	• Qualitative research
	Number who learn message content (eg increased knowledge, awareness, understanding)	• Readership, listening or viewership statistics • Attendance at events • Inquiry or response rates (eg coupons, calls)
Out-take	Number who consider messages	• Circulation figures • Audience analysis
	Number who receive messages	• Analysis of media coverage (breakdown positive, negative and neutral – eg Media Content Analysis)
	Number of messages supporting objectives	
	Number of messages placed in the media	• Media monitoring (website hits, social network engagement, clippings and broadcast media clips, Google Analytics)
Outputs	Number of messages sent	• Distribution statistics
	Quality of message presentation (eg newsletter or brochure design, newsworthiness of story)	• Expert review • Feedback
	Appropriateness of message content	
	Appropriateness of the medium	• Readability tests (eg Gunning, Flesch, SST)
Inputs	Adequacy of background information, intelligence, research	• Case studies • Review
		• Audience surveys • Awards • Review • Pre-testing (eg focus groups) • Pre-testing • Benchmark

At the base are inputs, basically information and planning, and at the peak, objectives achieved. Each activity is split down into the various steps of the communication process. At the input stage the model asks the user to make a judgement on the quality of information, the choice of medium and the content of the communication. It then considers outputs, that is the communication produced, for example, the newsletter, the press release, the brochure, the website. It goes on to look at out-take, that is, what receivers have paid attention to and retained, and then it considers the results or outcomes – what the communication actually achieved. Alongside the steps is a list of evaluation methods that might be used for a media campaign, a newsletter, a website and so on.

The model needs to be customized for each project, but the principles remain the same. Its strength is that it recognizes a range of evaluation methods and allows flexibility.

The more advanced evaluation methods further up the pyramid measure outcomes. They are more sophisticated and of course more expensive. The ones lower down the pyramid are more basic and can be seen as tests that things are being done right, more akin to quality control. However, these basic checks are not to be missed. There can be more confidence of success higher up the pyramid if the basics are right.

In practical terms how does this translate into reality? Here is a resume checklist of critical factors to consider when planning evaluation into a campaign or programme:

- set measurable and realistic objectives;
- build in evaluation and quality checks from the start;
- agree measurement criteria with whoever will be judging the success of your work;
- establish monitoring procedures that are open and transparent, for example, monthly reviews of progress;
- demonstrate results.

As mentioned earlier in this book (Chapter 5) communication is not only about rational engagement; emotions also play a significant role. While the author would always recommend evaluation to be scientifically evaluated, it is true that subjective as well as objective measures are made.

Objective evaluation measures

Typical objective measures that might be employed are:

- changes in behaviour (if an activity is given public relations support, behaviour can be tracked);
- responses (return of coupons, website comments, social media traffic, salesforce quotes, etc);

- changes in attitude, opinion and awareness – especially important for opinion-former work (can be measured through telephone research, questionnaires, one-to-one interviews, online surveys);
- achievements (80 per cent of retailers came to promotional conference);
- media coverage, content, distribution, readership, share of voice (content analysis, readership data);
- budget control and value for money (a process measure).

It is sometimes relatively easy to put in checks when measuring the effectiveness of editorial when working on a product promotion programme, if working in conjunction with other marketing colleagues. For example, when the author worked in-house for a large financial institution, she was able to place editorial material next to a financial product advert that had been running for a few weeks in the *Sunday Times*. The number of policies that came from the two adverts previous to the editorial were 27 and 21 respectively. The advert with adjacent editorial resulted in 94 policies being sold tracked with a unique advertising code.

Similarly, for another financial product it was found that adjacent editorial doubled the returns from a series of adverts in the *Sunday Telegraph*.

Subjective evaluation measures

Apart from quantitative objective measures, subjective measures of performance are also inevitably employed. Public relations is a human business and human judgements will be used. These factors may be especially important in the client/consultancy relationship, but are also highly prized in the relationships that in-house departments build with other departments within their organization. In fact what often wins business for consultancies (all things being equal) and ready cooperation from other departments are these subjective yardsticks:

- enthusiasm;
- efficiency and professionalism;
- creativity;
- initiative;
- an instinct for what is right in a given situation (based on judgement gained through experience);
- people chemistry.

Evaluating the process

A critical part of evaluation is to monitor how the campaign is managed: the process. Part of this is the effective deployment of both staff and budgets. Regular, rigorous monitoring of both is required.

Staff need to be continuously developed to cope with and exploit the rapidly changing communication environment. It is also essential that public relations staff are well motivated and well directed. They are, after all, the handlers and managers of the organization's reputation in a most overt sense. If they do not believe in what they are doing, how can they do their job proficiently and professionally?

Likewise, the management and effective use of budgets is a duty laid on every manager, including the public relations professional. With so many options open on how to spend what is often quite a limited budget, he or she must have a keen regard to the careful stewardship of resources. Every pound should count. Chapter 8 gives a more detailed exposition on how budgeting can be done effectively.

Evaluation remains an issue for the public relations industry. Research by the PR Academy[8] in 2015 among its students who are all practising communicators found that 35 per cent of still do not evaluate. Until this issue is firmly addressed the profession will continue to struggle demonstrating its contribution.

CASE STUDY   Evaluating the impact of AkzoNobel's corporate reputation

This case study demonstrates how research and evaluation is crucial to demonstrating the value of effective communication. It illustrates how benchmarking research sets the baseline for effective evaluation and how building in evaluation metrics from the start can build an evidence base for important business decisions.

Is having a famous product brand enough?

Is having the world's most famous paint brand enough, or does the reputation of the corporate organization behind the brand actually matter?

For most people around the world, the Dulux dog comes to mind. For others, it's the speciality coating in Formula One. Others praise its anti-malaria paint, saving lives across India. Few think AkzoNobel synonymous with these well-known and well-regarded products. The exam question posed to the executive team by the AkzoNobel board was: does this actually matter? Is there real material advantage to be gained by building corporate reputation?

AkzoNobel is one of the world's largest paint and coatings companies and is a leading producer of speciality chemicals. The organization has a long and distinguished history dating back hundreds of years, with the last two decades seeing the merger of Akzo and Nobel as well as the acquisition of two high-profile companies, Courtaulds and ICI. Today, with operations in more than 80 countries and about 47,000 employees, AkzoNobel has transformed from a diversified conglomerate into a focused chemicals and coatings company.

Despite owning Dulux, the world's best-loved paint brand, and being responsible for ground-breaking innovations from fire-retardant coatings for the Apollo space missions to high performance finishes for McLaren Formula One cars, AkzoNobel as a corporate entity is little known outside of its home market of the Netherlands. It was with this in mind that AkzoNobel partnered with Mindful Reputation to conduct the most comprehensive audit of corporate brand awareness and reputation ever undertaken by the company.

For AkzoNobel's Corporate Communications Director the starting point was: 'If we are going to have our future licence to exist as mega corporations, society will increasingly say I know I can buy your product but what do you stand for? Do I like you?'

The reputation research brief aimed to measure corporate brand awareness by market, stakeholder audience, segment and product brands; understand drivers of trust and behaviour; and assess the relationship between the corporate brand and the product brands. The programme had to:

- provide a baseline to track progress over time, benchmarked against a host of international competitors,

- develop an integrated Reputation Scorecard for the Board, and

- deliver actionable, evidence-based insights for the leadership and communications teams.

Priority markets were identified as the traditional home markets of the Netherlands and UK, and also fast-growing and hugely important emerging markets such as Brazil, India and China.

Research approach

The team sought to determine the alignment or otherwise between how AkzoNobel sees itself, how the outside world experiences it and expects it to be, and how the owned, earned and paid-for communication positions the group from Brazil to China. Given the scope of what was needed, the research was both quantitative to provide key KPIs and drive insights for the business, and also qualitative to get behind the 'why' and 'why not' questions.

As part of the planning stage, the AkzoNobel leadership from a variety of functions in each of the target markets explained how they saw the organization.

This was used to frame the questionnaire for the external phase as well as providing a snapshot of AkzoNobel's identity.

AkzoNobel is a highly complex business with both a B2B and B2C focus. The research included external audiences consisting of three main groups:

- consumers;

- business customers – the research used set sample quotas across each business segment from automotive to industrial;

- opinion formers – media, the financial community, government, NGOs and industry experts.

The research method and materials were adapted to each of these three groups – an online survey was recommended for consumers while business customers and opinion formers respond best to a semi-structured telephone interview. Importantly, each of the business leaders were involved in the targeting and research process which proved essential on sharing the findings and ensuring that they were actioned.

Finally, as most organizations only have some 30–50 publications that actually drive their brand and reputation, the team worked with the countries and businesses to focus on only the top-tier print, online and social media to benchmark AkzoNobel's profile and relationships against chosen competitors across each market.

Results

The findings provided statistically robust evidence that AkzoNobel, as a corporate entity, is little known by consumers outside its home market of the Netherlands. However, AkzoNobel enjoys an excellent reputation among those consumers, business customers and opinion formers who know them.

The corporate brand endorsement strategy was validated by findings that consumers and business customers (who know AkzoNobel) are more likely to purchase a product if AkzoNobel is known as the manufacturer. A direct result of this was CEO approval of proposals by the corporate brand team for more consistent and prominent corporate logo placement across the entire product portfolio, and broader corporate brand stories focusing on innovation and excellence to generate greater recognition of AkzoNobel's strong reputation.

Findings on AkzoNobel's 'employer attractiveness' among sub-groups of potential employees and students of chemistry, engineering and business were used by AkzoNobel's global recruitment HR team to feed into their strategy for developing the employer brand.

AkzoNobel's corporate communications and media relations teams took on the research insights, including a renewed focus on storytelling and messaging around innovation and sustainability and an enhanced corporate social media presence. AkzoNobel has since restructured its corporate communications team to facilitate this.

The storytelling and messaging is also being driven by the company's global Human Cities initiative, which was launched in June 2014. It builds on the fact that a significant percentage of AkzoNobel's business comes from products and services that are linked to the urban environment. Designed to help cities become more inspiring, energizing and vibrant, it is focused on six main pillars: colour, heritage, transport, education, sport and leisure, and sustainability. The initiative also involves partnering with major organizations such as The Rockefeller Foundation. A key reputation driver, Human Cities plays a vital role as it links the company to an important global issue – the challenge posed by rapid population growth in urban areas – and is an ideal platform for AkzoNobel to explain why its products are so relevant to today's world. AkzoNobel has since restructured its corporate communications team to facilitate both the research findings and the new focus on Human Cities.

Results

The results of the benchmarking research and the ongoing media tracking can be seen in the charts shown in Figure 9.5.

Ongoing media analysis already shows an improvement in AkzoNobel's proactively generated media profile. More broadly, the research has worked hard for multiple internal stakeholders at a country and global level and has set a baseline for tracking progress over time.

Not least, presentations to AkzoNobel's CEO and Executive Committee and the AkzoNobel Board focused on the evidence of materiality and where 'money was being left' on the table as the research demonstrated the impact of corporate brand awareness (or otherwise) on likelihood to purchase product. This has put AkzoNobel's corporate reputation and communications engagements at the centre of the group's growth strategy.

Points about this case

- Setting research-based benchmarks is the key to rigorous evaluation.
- Ongoing monitoring and evaluation provides key insights on how existing activities should be adjusted and fine-tuned.

FIGURE 9.5 AkzoNobel's benchmark research and ongoing media tracking dashboard

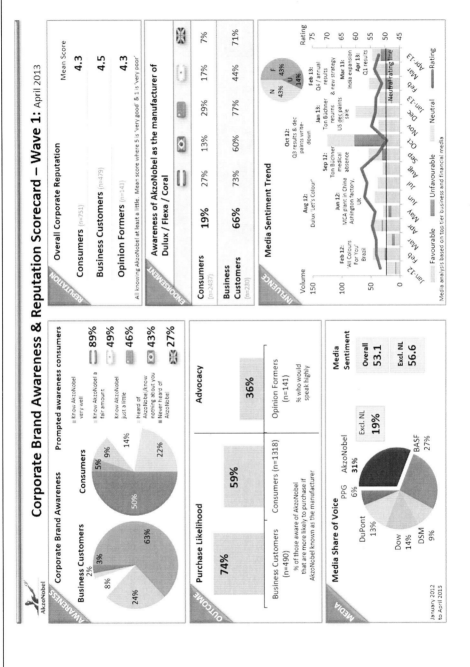

- In this case ongoing monitoring and evaluation provided evidence of new and unexploited opportunities.
- Providing evidence has allowed communication to position itself as a strategic asset for AkzoNobel and secured ongoing resources for its activities.
- Through the persuasive evidence of research and evaluation the communications department has placed itself at the heart of AkzoNobel's business strategy.
- Rigorous research generating an evidence base is taken seriously by senior management and Boards.

Reviewing the situation

While monitoring and evaluation takes place on an ongoing basis, a thorough review takes place less often. As explained earlier (Chapter 4), a major review including extensive research may well be triggered by a significant event such as a takeover or a new Chief Executive arriving. That will entail a close examination and analysis of both the external and internal environments, and probably a repositioning of the organization, as well as all the aspects of constructing a viable plan outlined in this book.

While it is essential to tweak tactics as a plan unfolds, especially in the light of information that ongoing evaluation brings, the plan itself should remain as the route-map, with some flexibility to accommodate opportunities and problems as they arise. This approach is sound as long as the objectives remain the same and the strategy holds good. However, it is essential to bear in mind that public relations is conducted within a dynamic environment and there must be the capability to respond as soon as possible, either in a proactive way to lead or forestall events, or in a reactive way to deal with an emergency situation. A review is required if the overall objectives need to be changed or if the strategy is seen not to be working.

It is also good practice to undertake a regular review of campaigns irrespective of whether there are major changes that demand such a response. A look every 3 or 6 months and a longer look every 12 months ensures that everything is on track, and that any new situations are taken into account.

The annual review will need to be tough and may involve examining new or ongoing research. A day or couple of days away from the office with colleagues who are working on the campaign is time well spent to ensure that all is in order. It is done in addition to the full evaluation at the end of a campaign.

The strategy's not working

If the underlying strategy for a campaign turns out to be wrong, this is a very serious business. To get the strategy wrong indicates fundamental flaws in research or the interpretation of research. An example will illustrate. Suppose a company wants to launch a high-quality new product and the public relations strategy is to mount a traditional and social media relations campaign including a press launch with product demonstrations, merchandising packs for the regional and consumer press, on- and offline competitions, consumer offers, Twitter and Facebook activities and a couple of stunts designed to attract the attention of traditional and online media.

Suppose after all this, the product doesn't sell at all well. There are a number of explanations and here are just a few:

- The product is sub-standard. As soon as the public relations professional becomes aware of this the company must be advised accordingly. If the company insists on going ahead, at least it was told. The public relations professional may resign over such an issue. The damage to long-term reputation could be severe.

- The product is a 'me too' and has no distinguishing features. No amount of good public relations will persuade people to buy this type of product rather than their current favourite, unless of course there are brand strengths. Public relations should not over-promise.

- The product and the contents of the campaign are aimed at the wrong target markets. There is a major flaw in research.

- The content is not being accepted. It could be that the wrong things are being said, or in the wrong way, or that the medium or the timing is wrong. There is lack of research or misinterpretation of information.

- The product needs to be sampled by consumers for them to really appreciate it. Then why choose media relations as the main communication vehicle?

- The press aren't interested. The right media hook has not been identified: they are not being approached in the right way. It could be lack of research. Maybe another big consumer story is breaking at the same time as the launch. Sometimes all the market intelligence and research in the world can't protect from this nightmare. In this case the strategy may even be right, but either that or tactics will have to be changed quickly to get back on the front foot again. Creativity counts.

If the strategy is not working two questions need to be asked:

- *Are the objectives right and realizable?* If the answer to that is 'no' then no matter how brilliant it is the strategy will not work. If the answer is 'yes' then the second question is necessary.

- *What's wrong with the strategy?* What basic points have been overlooked or misinterpreted? This means a return to the research, and a careful analysis. Were the right questions asked in the first place? Were they all asked? What do the unanswered questions really indicate? Is there a clear understanding of publics and what can be achieved? Do the messages have credibility and can they be delivered via the tactics selected? Is the campaign too ambitious or perhaps not sufficiently ambitious? Is the campaign adequately resourced? The killer question is whether a media relation campaign was the right strategy at all.

It is embarrassing to say the least to get the strategy wrong but, if careful research has been done and there can be confidence in the interpretation, it is likely that the tactics, not the strategy, needs correcting. However, as with all things, it is better to admit when something is wrong and correct it, rather than limp along wasting time and resources, and damaging professional reputations.

External and internal review drivers

Through the regular evaluation and review process, adjustments will be made to campaigns or programmes. Objectives might be refocused or given a different priority and tactics may be altered. This is part of being effective and in tune with changing requirements. Minor ongoing changes can be expected. However, all the best-laid plans are subject to major review or even reversal if fundamental changes in the external or internal environment call for it. Thankfully these 'drivers' occur relatively infrequently, but it is wise to have contingency plans ready to deal with them if or when they do arise, because they usually require fast-footed action. Careful risk analysis should help in preparing for these eventualities along with an issue management programme (see Chapter 7 for more on risk assessment and management).

The list below gives a flavour of the sort of external drivers that could force a review:

- legislative change that either threatens or gives expanded opportunities to the organization;
- competitor activity, which threatens or gives opportunity;
- takeover or acquisition (note, if a company is taken over through a hostile bid it then has to switch its public relations endeavour from actively campaigning against the acquirers to working for them);
- major product recall or damage to corporate reputation;
- action by a well-organized, powerful, opposing pressure group.

Internal drivers can also make a review essential. The kinds of scenarios that would force this are:

- restructure with new priorities, which may entail the splitting up or restructuring of the public relations function;
- changes in key personnel such as the chief executive (or the director of public relations);
- budget changes, meaning that public relations activity is significantly cut or expanded;

- future needs: a programme or campaign may end or run out of steam; a fresh look is then required to reactivate and refocus the public relations work.

Once having decided on a review, the planning process then begins its cycle again. Figure 3.3 on page 46 outlines the process. Again the basic questions have to be addressed:

- What am I trying to achieve?
- Who do I want to reach?
- What do I want to say?
- What are the most effective ways of getting the message across?
- How can success be measured?

By systematically working through these questions, all the essentials of planning and managing a successful public relations programme will be covered.

And finally

This book has given the basic framework for putting together a well-founded public relations campaign. Careful, systematic planning will make life much easier. Add one more vital ingredient – flair, the ability to think creatively and not be bound by history or current working conventions, and work in public relations will be immensely rewarding. There is nothing more exciting than seeing a communication campaign work and take on a life that can only come from the sort of skills the public relations professional can provide. Communication is about making contact, developing relationships, building trust and achieving results which add to the success of the organization because key stakeholders are supportive. Careful planning and management lies at the heart of that.

Notes

1 Watson, T and Noble, P (2014) *Evaluating Public Relations*, Kogan Page, London
2 CIPR (2011). Research planning and measurement toolkit. Available to CIPR members at www.cipr.co.uk
3 DPRG (2011). Available at www.globalalliancepr.org
4 GCS (2014) https://gcn.civilservice.gov.uk/wp-content/uploads/2014/08/GCN-Evaluation-Book_v6.pdf
5 GCS (2014) https://gen.civilservice.gov.uk/wp-content/uploads/2014/09/Free-to-use-evaluation-tools.pdf
6 Available at www.Instituteforpr.org/research/measurement_and_evaluation
7 Macnamara, J R (1992) Evaluation of public relations: the Achilles' heel of the PR profession, *International Public Relations Review*, **15**, November
8 PR Academy (2015) Trends Survey. Available at www.pracademy.co.uk/wp-content

INDEX

Page numbers in *italics* denote figures.

accountability   15–19, 184
    corporate   22–23, 191
    functional   23
    societal   3, 22, *51*, 190
    value-chain   23, 192
achievements   36, 44, 109, 188, 196
active
    publics   99, 115, 117, 120–21
    support   27, 28, 119
activist groups   9, 11, 17, 97, 99, 119, 123, 190
activity plans   169–70
advance feature stories   87, 88
advertising (adverts)   13, *14*, 72, 79, 81, *132*, *135*, 176–77, 196
    Audi   128
    companies   67
    product recalls   130
    radio   80
advertorials   81, *132*, *170*
affective objectives   104
aggregation   186
AGMs   50, 103–04, 185
AIDA model   100–02
aims   102–04, 106, 107–09, 149
    see also objectives
AkzoNobel   197–202
all-issue publics   115
American Institute for Public Relations   186
analogies   125
analysis   45, 47, 48, 55–66, 73, 85
    content   9, 35, 188, 196
    cost:benefit   181
    critical path   167–68
    media   185
    network models   97–98
    PEST   57–60
    situation   46, *51*, *54*
    see also data collection; intelligence building; research
Andrex   126
annual
    plans   169–70
    relationship temperature checks   192–93
    reports   22, 91, 130
    reviews   202
anti-social behaviour   97–98

apathetic publics   115
Apple   31
Appleby Horse Fair   97–98
appropriateness, tactics   138
apps   150, 151, 152, 153
Argyle Communications   84–89
Armani   126
Asda   8
assessment, organizational   46, 62
assets   6–7, 16, 108, 191
attitudes   45, 90–92, 104, 105, 117, 121, 196
    attitude domino   *100*, 101
Audi   128
audiences   27, 108, 111, 139–40, 199
    mass   95–98, 137
    target   76, 79, 85, 105
    McArthur River Mining   149, 151, *152*, 153
    see also consumers
audits   64, 72–73
Authentic Enterprise, The (Arthur W Page Society)   1
aware publics   99, 114
awareness   46, 67, 69, 90–91, 104, 105, 106, 124, 127
    see also aware publics; brand awareness & reputation scorecard

'Back in Britain'   145
balanced scorecards   191–92
Beard, Professor Mary   144
Beckham, David   126
behaviour   16, 17, 28, 90, 105, 107, 114, 121
    anti-social   97–98
    change   117, 119–20, 130, 180, 188, 190, 195
        see also emotional content; persuasion campaigns; policy
    domino   *100*
beliefs   62, *75*, 91, 92, 94, 101
benchmarking   91, 106, 109, 187, 200
    see also AkzoNobel; Love Food, Hate Waste campaign
big picture issues   57, 60, 169
blogs (blogging)   7, 9, 12, 38, 96, 125, 158, 188

boundary-spanning   8–9, 15, 63, 97, 98
BP   34
brainstorming   133, 157
brand   3, 4, 134, 191, 197–98, 199, 203
    awareness & reputation scorecard   201
    see also branded coverage; employees;
        rebranding; reputation
branded coverage   88
bridge individuals   97
Britain's Undiscovered Billions   154–55
brochures   11, 30, 137, 140, 165, 178, 195
budgets   44, 107, 108, 179, 181–82, 185,
        196, 197
building societies   67, 69, 178
bus adverts   81
business strategy   14, 40, 155, 202
'buy one, get one free' offers   76

campaigns   25, 26, 55, 56, 123–24
    development   78, 83, 87
    dialogue-based   123–24, 127
    differentiation   85
    evaluation model   193–97
    FWW Centenary commemorations
        140–48
    garden centre   170
    Love Food, Hate Waste   74–84
    McArthur Riving Mining   148–54
    persuasion   123
    social marketing   119, 123
    unbiased.co.uk   154–60
    see also programmes
case studies   30, 125, 172
catalysts   23, 121
CATI   70
celebrities   8, 23, 77, 78, 109, 125, 143,
        162, 170
central beliefs   92, 101
champions   77, 80, 83
change, behaviour   117, 119–20, 130, 180,
        188, 190, 195
    see also emotional content; persuasion
        campaigns; policies
channel noise   93, 96
charging structures, consultancies   180–82
charities   29, 30, 56–57, 62, 83, 119, 126,
        128, 135
chief executives   8, 11, 93, 161
CIPR evaluation policy   186
clarification   56
co-orientation model   94–95
coaching   3, 17, 18
cognitive objectives   104
Cohen, Jack   145
commercial publics   112

commonly held beliefs   92
communication   10–12, 90–110
    audits   64, 72–73
    chain   92–100
    channels   7, 18, 32, 33, 113, 129, 130
    facilitators   21
    FWW Centenary commemorations
        141–43
    internal   80, 81, 135
    and liaison role   21, 22
    managers   21–22
    mass audience   137
    process model   93
    technicians   21–22, 23
    see also language
community
    engagement   80–82, 144–45
    objectives   107
    online communities   29, 35, 97, 117
    publics   122
    relations   136
    scientific communities   134
companies
    advertising   67
    research   67, 68
comparisons   125
competitors   3, 14, 33, 55, 63, 72, 161, 178,
        181, 204
Computer Aided Telephone Interview   70
computer packages   70
    see also software packages
conative objectives   105
conditioning   92, 94
conferences   30, 32, 107, 136, 165–66,
        168, 196
confidentiality   49
conflict resolution   44
conflicting opinions   114
conjecture   124
connectedness   7, 96, 118
constraints   107–08, 116
consultancies   62, 66, 179–82
    see also external researchers
consulting role   138
consumers   107, 137, 156, 158
content   45, 47, 48, 124–28, 151, 153,
        203
    analysis   9, 35, 188, 196
context   25–37, 49, 50–52, 60, 129
    challenges   1
    see also environment
contextual intelligence   8, 55–56
    see also research
contingency planning   44, 160–62
continuous research   67

control   130
convergence model   94, 96
cooking clubs (classes)   81, 83
core messages   79, 127
corporate
    accountability   15–17, 22–23, 191
    brand awareness & reputation
        scorecard   201
    character   2
    hospitality   178
    identity   66, 129, 134, 135
    objectives   107
    publics   121
cosmetics launches   137
cost:benefit analysis   181
costs
    human resources   176–77, 179
    operating   177–78, 179
CPA   167–68
Creative Territory   148–54
creativity   139, 203, 205
credibility   127, 129, 132–33
crisis management   32, 34, 136, 180
critical path analysis (CPA)   167–68
cultural
    programmes   142–43
    understanding   102
culture   2, 59, 108
    organizational   16, 17, 62, 191
Cumbria County Council   97–98
current affairs   35
customer
    publics   122
    relations   136

dashboards, media tracking   201
data
    analysis   73
    collection   119–20
    see also analysis; intelligence building;
        research
DCMS   140–48
deadlines   163
    see also timescales
decision-making   108
deliberative engagement   124
deliverability, tactics   138
demonstrations   30, 125, 137, 203
Demos   60
Department for
    Culture, Media and Sport   140–48
    Education   144
desk research   68
development, campaign   78, 83, 87
dialogue-based campaigns   123–24, 127

differentiation, campaign   85
digital adverts   79
direct
    communication   100
    mail   135
diversity   96
Domino Theory   100–01

economic factors, PEST analysis   58
editorial effectiveness   107, 196
effectiveness   44, 107, 178, 184, 196
efficiency   178, 184
emotional content   126–27
employees 3, 7, 9, 32, 107, 122
    employee relations   22, 32, 34, 47, 133
    see also staff
endorsements   85, 89, 125, 132–33, 143,
        199
engagement   2–3, 10, 124, 157, 158, 159
    community   80–82, 144–45
English Heritage   143, 144
entertainment   102
environment   9–10, 56, 57–62, 65–66, 116
    see also context
EPISTLE analysis   58–59
equipment   70, 166, 168, 179
European Week of Waste Reduction   81
evaluation   46, 48, 49, 51, 54, 55, 103–04,
        127, 183–202
    FWW Centenary commemorations
        146–47
    Love Food, Hate Waste campaign
        78, 82
    McArthur River Mining   152–53
    unbiased.co.uk   158–59
events   19, 80, 83, 136, 145–46, 147, 166
    see also launches
EWWR   81
examples   125
exhibitions   19, 30, 125, 138, 186
expectation management   186
expert
    prescribers   21
    spokespeople   87
external
    constraints   108
    deadlines   163
        see also timescales
    environment   56, 57–62, 65–66, 116
        see also context
    issues   34
    researchers   67
        see also consultancies
    review drivers   204
    timescales   36

Facebook 71, 79, 173, 175, 203
facilitators 21, 60
facts 92, 124
farming methods planning 61
fashion sector 23, 30, 137
fear appeals 126–27
feasibility testing 133
feature stories 87, 88
feedback 47, 84, 93, 94, 96, 190
fees 179–82
financial
    advice campaigns 154–60
    measures 191
    publics 112
    relations 136, 137
Financial Times 36, 173, 185
First World War Centenary commemorations 140–48
first-hand
    beliefs 92
    knowledge 91
five planning questions 45–50
fixed assets 7
flexibility 5, 20, 50, 60, 134, 195, 202
focus 43–44
    groups 70
food
    retailing sector 30
    waste reduction campaign 74–84
format, messages 129
formative research 54
formulation, strategy 46
frames 102
Friends of the Earth 28
functional
    accountability 18–19, 23
    organizational structures 19, 20
future events, FWW Centenary programme 147
futures research 60

gaming 59, 69, 124, 132
Gantt Charts 165–66
garden centre media campaign 170
general messages 128, 130
genetically modified foods 28, 35
German Public Relations Association 186
GlaxoSmithKline Healthcare 84–89
goals 15, 86, 88, 148, 184
Goody, Jade 109
Google 4, 72, 79, 132, 150, 194
Government Communication Service (GCS) 186
government departments 30, 47, 68, 112, 189

Grand Départ, The 171–75
Grayling see Trimedia
groups 27, 29, 35, 94–98
    activist 9, 11, 17, 97, 99, 119, 123, 190
    focus 70
growth, organizational 31
guilt appeals 127

Harley Davidson (Owners' Group) 16–17
hi-tech industries 30
higher education 59–60
    see also universities
hot issues 109
    hot-issue publics 115, 120
hourly fees plus costs (fee structure) 180
human resources 41, 176–77
humour appeals 126

identity
    corporate 66, 129, 134, 135
    personal 101
Imperial War Museums 144
implementation 45, 46, 51, 54
    FWW Centenary commemorations 144–46
    Grand Départ, The 173–75
    Love Food, Hate Waste campaign 76–77, 79–82
    McArthur River Mining 151–52
    Sleep Pod Hotel Media Tour 87
    unbiased.co.uk 157–58
implementers 23
in-house researchers 66, 67
inactive stakeholders 27
incompatible beliefs 101
incremental intelligence 12
independent financial advice campaigns 154–60
influence 3–4, 11, 23, 28–29, 45, 90
informal research 72
information 45, 58–59, 99, 101, 138
    campaigns 123
    flow 10
    sensitive 40–41
    technology 57
    tracking 67
Innocent 5
inputs 188, 194, 195
insight 119–20
integration 23, 96, 102, 175
intelligence building 8–10, 12, 16–17, 35
    contextual 55–56
    see also analysis; data collection; research

internal
  communications   80, 81, *135*
  constraints   108
  consultancy   19–20
  deadlines   163
  issues   34, 65–66
  publics (stakeholders)   112
    see also employees; staff
  review drivers   204–05
  timescales   36
internet   59, 68, 70–71, 98, 150
interrelationships, drivers   59
interviews   41, 69–70, 178
intranet   150
investor briefings   178
invoices, consultancy   181
involvement   116, *138*
Ipsos MORI   60, 68, 190
Iraq war   132
isolates   97
issues   *25*, 34–35, 65–66, 85, 109
  analysis services   60
  big picture   57, 60, 169
  conflicting   76
  issues-based campaigns   55
  management   60–62, 99

Johnson & Johnson   32
journalists   *43*, 158, 174, 175

kitchen skills programmes   83
knowledge   *75*, 91
  domino   *100*

Lamarche, Sophie   87
language   11, 16, 93, 129
Lanson   154–60
latent publics   114
launches   77, 141, 157, 203
leadership   *2*
legal environment, EPISTLE analysis   59
level
  of involvement   116
  substitution   189
leverage points   101
liaison   21, 22, *136*
libraries   68
linear communication models   92–93
linking issues   65–66, 85
liquid assets   7
listening, organizational   11–12
lobbying   *136*
local advertising   80, 81
London Underground   79
long-term issues   62
longer-term plans   169–70

L'Oreal   16, 17
love appeals   126
Love Food, Hate Waste campaign   74–84

McArthur River Mining   148–54
Macnamara's macro model of evaluation
      193–97
macro environment   57
magazines   36, 68, 77, 81, 137, *140*, 145,
      151, 177–78, 188
management   184
  crisis   32, 34, *136*, 180
  expectations   186
  issues   60–62, 99
  strategic   45–46
managers   21–22
  see also senior advisors
manufacturing sector   30
marketing
  and public relations   13–14, 32
  social marketing campaigns   119, 123
markets, priority   198
marking up   180
mass audience communication   95–98, 137
materials costs   177–78, *179*
matrix organizational structure   20
media   87, 88, 95–98, 114, 120, 130,
      158–59, 196
  analysis   9, 185
  guidelines   *39–43*
  hooks   203
  launches   157
  offline/online   36, 91
  relations   21, 22, 86, *135*, 172–73, 179,
      185, 189
  research   72
  specialist calls   *41*
  tracking dashboard   *201*
    see also news consumption
mentoring   17
messages   79, 127–30
  FWW Centenary commemorations
      142
  message domino   *100*
Metro advertising   79
Ministry of Justice   144
Mintel   68
mission, organizational   33
mobile phones   150, 151, 152
models
  AIDA   100–02
  campaign evaluation   193–97
  co-orientation   94–95
  communication process   93
  convergence   94, 96
  linear communication   92–93

McNamara's macro evaluation model
193–97
network 96–98, 111
planning 45–46, 47, 48, 49, 51
process 93
two-step communication 95–98
momentum, maintaining 77
monitoring 47, 48, 57–62, 116, 200
research 54–55
Monsanto 35
motor sector 30–31
multi-faceted public relations programmes 49
mystery shoppers 71

name recognition, organizational 134
national media guidelines 41
navigators 22–23
negative emotional content 126–27
network models 96–98, 111
new
departments 56
media see social media
news consumption 113
Nike 5
Nokia 31
non-participant observation 71
non-publics 114

OASIS 47
objective evaluation measures 195–96
objectives 45, 47, 48, 50, 90, 102–09, 132,
133, 181, 203
evaluation 187
FWW Centenary commemorations 143
Grand Départ, The 171–72
Love Food, Hate Waste campaign 76, 79
McArthur River Mining 149, 152
McNamara's macro model of
evaluation 194, 195
public relations policy 40
Sleep Pod Hotel Media Tour 86, 88
SMART 153
unbiased.co.uk 156
see also aims
observation 71–72
offline media 36, 91
Omnibus surveys 67, 69
one-off surveys 68
one-to-one depth interviews 69–70
online
advertising 81
communities 29, 35, 97, 117
content analysis 35
media 36, 91
research 70–71
sector 30

openness, network 97
operating costs 177–78, 179
opinions 100, 104, 196
opinion leaders 95–96
public 9, 12, 25, 28, 35–36, 61, 112–14,
190–91
organizational
aims and objectives 106, 109
analysis (assessment) 46, 56, 62–64
characteristics 1–2, 25, 33–34
connection 29
culture 16, 17, 62, 191
decline 32–33
development 25, 30–33
influence 3–4, 28–29
issues 34–35
listening 11–12
location 28
maturity 31–32
mission 33
name recognition 134
nature 34
opportunities 63
power 28–29
purpose 4
range 28
reputation 5, 6, 34
resources 25, 31, 37, 47, 48, 49,
176–82
size 28, 33
start-up 31
strategy 8, 9, 10–11, 12, 14–19, 63
strengths 62–63
structure 7–8, 19, 20, 33, 40
threats 63
tradition 34
visibility 64
weaknesses 62–63
orienters 22
out-takes 188, 194, 195
outcome aims 103
outcomes 102, 106, 180, 185, 188–89, 194
outdoor adverts 81
outflows 190
outputs 180, 185, 188, 194, 195
over-promising 109
overseas publics 112
Oxfam 30

participant observation 71
partnering 138, 178
payment by results (fees) 180
people assets 7, 108
see also bridge individuals; employees;
staff
perception shifts 128

peripheral beliefs 92, 101
personability 129
personal identity 101
perspective 9–10, 44
persuasion 123, 128
PEST analysis 57–60
phones, mobile 150, 151, 152
physical environment, EPISTLE analysis 59
piggy-back mailings 178
planning 4–5, 43–45, 50, 53, 60
  contingency 44, 160–62
  FWW Centenary commemorations
    143–44
  Love Food, Hate Waste campaign 76
  McArthur River Mining 150–51
  models 45–46, 47, 48, 49, 51
  questions 45–50
  Sleep Pod Hotel Media Tour 86–87
  task 165–68
  12 stages of 47–50
plans 169–70
policy 39–43, 125
political
  context 60
  factors, PEST analysis 58
positive emotional content 126
posters 81
potential issues 35
power 28–29
  power/interest matrix 118–19,
    137–38, 192
pre-launch planning 76–77
presentation, messages 129–30
presentations 125
press
  adverts 81
  conferences 165, 166, 168
  packs 165, 166, 167–68
  releases 80, 82
  virtual press rooms 178
pressures 38, 65, 109
primary research 68–72
prioritizing
  issues 65–66
  markets 198
  objectives 107
  publics 121–23
private sector 30
proactivity 13, 42, 44
problem recognition 115–16
problem-solving process facilitators 21
process
  aims 103
  evaluation 196–97
  model 93

product
  benefits analysis 85
  calls 41
  flaws 203
  recalls 130
programmes 25, 26, 37, 49, 54, 56, 83, 188
  cultural 142–43
  see also campaigns
project fees 180
promotion techniques 14
propositions 124–25
public
  opinion 9, 12, 25, 28, 35–36, 61,
    112–14, 190–91
  relations 1–2, 4–23, 38–43, 64, 90, 106
  role 8–9, 15, 32, 63, 97, 98, 100, 138
  see also strategic public relations; tactical
    public relations
  sector 119, 124
publics 12, 13, 26–29, 47, 48, 57, 99, 106,
    108, 111–24
  see also employees; staff; stakeholders
Pulse of the Nation research (Asda) 8

qualitative research 67, 69, 70, 198
quantitative
  evaluation 195–96
  research 67, 69, 70, 198
questionnaires 69

radical transparency 8
radio advertising 79, 80
RAG ratings 192–93
rational content 124–25, 126
reactive public relations 12–13, 42
rebranding 181
receivers 27, 92–94, 95, 100–02
Reception Theory 102
regional PR 41–42
relationships 29, 191, 192–93
  building 8–10, 12, 15–16, 28
  stakeholder 1, 2–3, 192–93
repetition, message 129
reports, annual 22, 91, 130
reputation 5, 6, 109, 191, 197–202
  organizational 13, 15, 16, 34, 36, 64
  reputational history 34
research 45, 53–55, 60, 66–89, 106, 136,
    197–202
  McArthur River Mining 150
  unbiased.co.uk 156–57
  see also analysis; data collection;
    intelligence building
researchers 66–67
  see also consultancies

residential care community   139
resources   25, 31, 37, 47, *48*, 49, 176–82
responses   195
responsibilities, practitioner   38
results
   AkzoNobel   199–200
   Grand Départ, The   175
   McArthur Riving Mining   *152*
   Sleep Pod Hotel Media tour   88
retainer fees   180
reviews   47, *48*, *49*, 183–84, 202–05
Rhone-Poulenc Agriculture   61
risk   35
   assessment tool   162–63
roadshows   82
Royal Mail   128
Royal Society of Arts   60

SAAB   30–31
satisfaction surveys   67
scenario planning   60
scientific communities   134
scorecards   191–92, 198, *201*
seat belt use   119–20
second-hand knowledge   91
secondary research   68
sectoral considerations   25, 29–30, 33
   see also private sector; public sector;
      service sector; third sector
segmentation   67, 111–12, 114–20
self-completion questionnaires   69
senders   92–94
senior advisors   22, 23
service sector   30
sex appeal   126
share price sensitive information   *40–41*
shareholders   26, 27, 28, 29, 118–19
single-issue publics   115
situation analysis   46, *51*, *54*, 56
skills   1–2
Sleep Pod Hotel Media Tour   84–89
SMART
   objectives   107, 153
   phones   150
smoking campaigns   190
social
   audits   64–65
   environment   9–10
   factors, PEST analysis   58
   interaction   102
   marketing campaigns   119, 123
   media   1, 2, 79, 81, 144, 146, 147, 158,
      159
      see also Facebook; Thunderclap;
         Twitter

societal
   accountability   3, 15, 17, 19, 22, *51*, 190
   pressures   65, 109
software packages   168
   see also computer packages
source credibility   127
special events   *136*
specialist
   agencies   *42*
   media calls   *41*
specialization   23
spectator hubs   173
spokespeople   85, 87, 88, 129
sponsorship   *135*, 186
staff   197
   see also employees
stakeholders   10, *14*, 16–17, 18, 22–23, 25,
      26–29, 90–92
   analysis of   64–66
   identifying   45, 47, *48*, 57, 137
   relationships   1, 2–3, 192–93
   tracking information   67
   see also employees; publics
start-up, organizational   31
statistics   125
stockmarket floatations   32
strategic
   contingency planning   160–61
   inflection   1
   management   45–46
   public relations   4–5, 9
strategy   45, 46, 47, *48*, *51*, *54*, 131–34,
      138, 202–04
   business   *14*, 40, 155, 202
   McArthur River Mining   150–51
   organizational   8, 9, 10–11, 12, 14–19,
      63
   unbiased.co.uk   157
structural issues   34
sub-messages   128
subjective evaluation   196
Sunday Telegraph   196
Sunday Times   196
suppliers   *122*
support   27–28, 32, 77, 108, 119
   see also celebrities; champions;
      endorsements
surveys   67–68, 69, 71
SWOT analysis   62–64
syndicated studies   69

tactical
   contingency planning   161–62
   public relations   4, 11
tactics   47, *48*, *132*, 133–60, 162

target
    audiences   76, 79, 85, 105
    McArthur River Mining   149, 151, *152*, 153
    groups   27
task-orientated organizational structures   19, 20
task planning   165–68
Tax Action   154, 155
team structures   20, *40*
technicians   21–22, 23
technological factors, PEST analysis   58
technology   30, 57, 59–60, 99, 179
    see also apps; internet; intranet; mobile phones; software packages
Technorati   72
telephone interviews   70
temperature checks   192–93
Testament of Youth, (Brittan)   144
testimonials   125
think tanks   9, 35, 60
third sector   119
    see also charities
thought to action continuum   99
Thunderclap   146, 147
timescales   25, 36, 47, *48*, 49, 107, 108, 163–65
timing
    Grand Départ, The   174
    messages   129
Timothy, Christopher   144
tone, message   129
Tour Makers, The *Grand Départ*   173
tracking research   67
trade objectives   107
training support   32
transparency   8, 99
trench cake   145
Trimedia   75

trust   1, 3
12 stages of planning   47–50
Twitter   70–71, 79, 144, 146
two-step communication model   95–98

unbiased.co.uk   154–160
uniform public opinion   113–14
universities   29, 35, 60, 68
US Army   26
USA   113
Uses and Gratification Theory   101–02

value   179
    propositions   125
value-chain accountability   17, 23, 192
Value of Advice report   157, 158
values   1–2, 15, 17
VAT   180
vehicle livery   81
Verity, Gary   171
Virgin Industries   32, 59
virtual press rooms   178
virtue appeals   126
virtuous circles   5
visibility, organizational   64
visual evidence   125
Vodafone   8
volunteers   175
    see also Tour Makers

waste reduction campaign   74–84
websites   79, 80, 81, 98, 157, 158, 173
Welcome to Yorkshire   171–75
Williams, Baroness   144
Work Foundation, The   60
WRAP (Waste and Resources Action Programme)   74–84
Wylde, Bryce   85, 87